SAFE

THE RESPONSIBLE AMERICAN'S GUIDE TO HOME AND FAMILY SECURITY

WAYNE LAPIERRE

WND Books

SAFE
WND Books

Published by WorldNetDaily
Washington D.C.

Jacket design by Mike Fitzgerald
Interior design by Neuwirth & Associates, Inc.

WND Books are distributed to the trade by:
Midpoint Trade Books
27 West 20th Street, Suite 1102
New York, NY 10011

WND Books are available at special discounts for bulk purchases. WND Books, Inc. also publishes books in electronic formats. For more information call (541-474-1776) or visit www.wndbooks.com.

First Edition

ISBN: 978-1-935071-89-1

Library of Congress information available

Printed in the United States of America

10 9 8 7 6 5 4 3 2 1

CONTENTS

APPENDICES

INTRODUCTION

For nineteen years, I have served as Executive Vice President of the National Rifle Association of America. During those years, I've traveled to all fifty states and met face-to-face with thousands of NRA members from all walks of life. I've had countless discussions about firearms safety and the personal responsibility that comes with the freedom to own a gun. But I've also been asked numerous questions about crime and safety that have nothing to do with gun ownership, particularly when I've visited communities coping with natural disasters. Sometimes I've referred our members to various publications and experts in safety and crime-fighting fields. In many cases, I've reached out to these experts myself in order to become more knowledgeable in areas that were of interest to our members. Over time, it became apparent to me that there was no single reference that Americans could turn to for answers to their wide-ranging questions about crime and personal safety.

In the end, my discussions with our NRA members led to this book, which is an essential part of our NRA message of freedom and personal responsibility. The simple fact is that *safety, freedom, and responsibility can't be separated*— they all go hand-in-hand. If we enjoy freedom, we must also accept responsibility—not just with our firearms but also in our daily lives. In our free society, it is the duty of each and every citizen to accept the ultimate responsibility for his or her own well-being and for the safety of his or her home and family, and not to be overly dependent on the government or anyone else.

There are times when the government simply can't protect us. Hurricane Katrina is an example. September 11, 2001 is another. And while we don't know when or where disaster will strike again, the lessons of history make it clear that we will face additional catastrophic events in the future and that those who prepare in advance will have an advantage over those who don't.

Preparing for major disasters—including natural disasters such as hurricanes and floods or manmade disasters like terrorist attacks and civil unrest—is really only a small part of this story. Every single day, Americans find themselves in situations that may not make national news but that require preparedness, planning, and a cool head. If more Americans would take some simple, common-sense precautions around the home, thousands of deaths and injuries could be prevented each year. Thousands of burglaries, home invasions, and other crimes could be prevented. Simple precautions with our computers could prevent countless crimes from identity thefts to child abductions. Basic preparations and knowledge can help vastly increase our safety in the outdoors. This book can help you assess the threats that you face every day and take steps to avoid them. This book is about protecting your family from harm, no more and no less.

At the end of the book, you'll find an appendix that includes a variety of checklists to help you better prepare for emergencies. You're welcome to make copies of these checklists for your personal use. You'll find an additional appendix that lists various national emergency numbers, with additional space to add the numbers for your physician, hospital, veterinarian, and so forth.

Of course, no one can be perfectly safe, and not all of the ideas in this book will be appropriate for every individual or family. But there is a great satisfaction in knowing that, regardless of whether the police, the government, or even your neighbors can come to your aid in a moment of crisis, *you can meet your family's needs and take care of yourself.*

That's the reason many Americans own firearms. That's why forty states now recognize the right to carry concealed firearms for self-protection. That's why twenty-four states—and counting—have enacted "Castle Doctrine" laws that give citizens the ironclad right to defend themselves against violent criminals.

Of course, the NRA strongly supports these laws, but our mission extends far beyond defending gun owners' rights. More than any other organization in the world, the NRA is devoted to promoting firearms safety and the personal responsibility that comes with owning a gun.

Over the past fifteen years, NRA has spent more than $150 million teaching gun safety to our fellow citizens. Our Eddie Eagle GunSafe® program has reached more than twenty-one million schoolchildren in all fifty states, with a simple message for children who see a gun: "Stop. Don't touch. Leave the area. Tell an adult." Our hunting and shooting programs stress gun safety first and foremost. In fact, working in cooperation with the state of New York in 1949, we developed hunter safety training as it is known today. Special NRA programs tailored for law enforcement officials help America's police to use their firearms more effectively while staying out of harm's way. And our "Refuse to Be a Victim" seminars present time-tested crime-fighting strategies to Americans from all walks of life.

These efforts have paid off, not just for our NRA members but for all Americans. While the number of privately-owned firearms in America has reached all-time highs over the past generation, the number of accidental firearm deaths and injuries has fallen to all-time lows, especially among children.

Our NRA members have also made our association one of the leading crime-fighting organizations in America. We have been at the forefront of efforts to enact Three Strikes and You're Out legislation—mandating life sentences for three-time violent offenders. We've fought for Project Exile and similar initiatives to mandate that violent criminals *must* serve jail time and cannot plea-bargain their way into a slap on the wrist.

In short, our NRA cause extends far beyond the Second Amendment. And whether or not you choose to own a firearm, this book has something for you.

Regardless of whether you own a gun, *preparation is better than fear*. Regardless of whether you own a gun, *self-reliance is better than total dependence* on government authorities to protect you in a crisis. Regardless of whether you own a gun, *the lessons in this book can help you live up to your responsibility as a free citizen to make your family safer.*

In fact, by incorporating some of the ideas of this book into your own life, you will realize a great benefit regardless of whether disaster ever strikes. Simply by accepting a greater responsibility for the safety and security of your family and your home, you will enjoy greater peace of mind and become more truly free.

Wayne LaPierre
Fairfax, Virginia
August 2010

AUTHOR'S NOTE

No one can be an expert in all areas of personal and home safety. In presenting this book, I have relied on a number of authorities in their various fields, and I deeply appreciate their contributions to this volume.

I would also like to express my special thanks to the four million members of the NRA.

Over many years and indeed decades, our members have fought tirelessly, in Congress and in the state legislatures, to enact legislation to punish violent criminals while protecting the rights of law-abiding citizens to defend themselves. Our NRA members have made America a better and stronger nation, and I am very grateful.

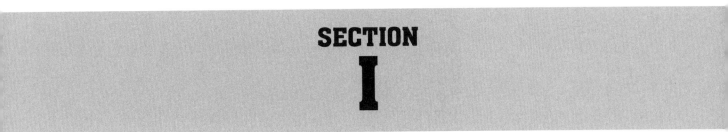

SECTION
I

SAFE IN A CRISIS

Few of us have ever been truly "on our own" for any length of time. In our technologically advanced society, we depend on others for our basic needs more than ever before in human history. Our food shows up at the grocery store, and we choose what we want. Our thermostats control our environment within a degree or two. Electricity and other utilities are delivered to us around the clock, as long as we pay our bills. We turn the tap for hot or cold water. We go to the doctor when we're sick or hurt, and we call a repairman when something in our home malfunctions.

America hasn't always been this way. Our earliest settlers arrived in ships with little hope of reprovisioning for months or even years. Our storied pioneers crossed the prairies with what they could carry in a horse-drawn wagon and nothing more. Settlers often lived miles from their nearest neighbors. Throughout our nation's history, millions of Americans have been genuinely on their own.

It doesn't happen often these days, but once in a while the systems we depend on go down in a big way—and Americans just like you and me find themselves on their own once again. Hurricane Katrina is probably the best example in recent memory, when hundreds of thousands were left without power, without running water, without a ready supply of food, or any other needed assistance. But each and every year, on a lesser scale, thousands of Americans experience similar challenges. Power outages, paralyzing snowstorms, and natural disasters occur with regularity in the United States, temporarily wiping out decades of technological advances and forcing us once again to rely on ourselves and our immediate neighbors for our basic day-to-day needs.

By taking a few simple precautions in advance and by taking time now to think about the key issues you might face, *you can be ready to keep your family safe in a crisis.*

1

General Disaster Preparedness

Every disaster scenario has its own character. No one can predict every contingency that might arise during the various kinds of crises that Americans might one day face. But at some level, many types of disasters share the same characteristics in that they all require similar planning and action to *understand your risks*, *develop a family disaster action plan*, and *prepare the emergency supplies you might need* for days or even weeks without outside help. By following the steps outlined in this chapter, you can better equip your family in the event of a disaster, as well as lessen the financial and psychological tolls that disasters can have on families.

In its "Red Cross Ready" checklist, the American Red Cross recommends these initial basic steps toward ensuring that your family is as well prepared as possible for any type of disaster:

Step 1. Know what emergencies or disasters are most likely to occur in your community.

Step 2. Develop a family disaster plan and practice it.

Step 3. Assemble an emergency preparedness kit.

Step 4. Ensure that at least one family member is trained in basic First Aid and CPR/AED (cardiopulmonary resuscitation and use of an automatic external defibrillator).

STEP 1: Know Your Risks

The Federal Emergency Management Agency (FEMA) and the American Red Cross are two of the nation's most recognized organizations that help citizens prepare for disasters of all types. In their jointly-issued brochure, *Your Family Disaster Plan*, they suggest that the first step toward ensuring your family's safety in a disaster is to assess the various risks you may confront. The easiest and most efficient way to assess your own risk is to contact your local emergency management offices or your local American Red Cross chapter and ask them the following:

- What types of disasters are most likely to occur in my community? Ask your emergency management office or the Red Cross to provide information on how to prepare for each type of disaster.
- Are there specific warning signals in place to alert my family in an emergency? What do these signals sound like, and what should I do when I hear them? If there are audible signals in place near your home, find out when they are going to be tested in order to determine whether they can be heard from your location.
- Are there special programs in place for disabled or elderly persons in the event of a disaster, and how can I help disabled or elderly persons in my neighborhood?
- What are the policies for animal care during and after a disaster? Due to health regulations, some shelters do not allow pets.

Keep in mind also that you may not be home at the moment a disaster strikes. Be sure to ask about disaster plans where you work and at your children's school or day-care center.

STEP 2: Develop a Family Disaster Plan

The next step that FEMA and the Red Cross recommend is to develop a Family Disaster Plan. Instead of alarming youngsters by presenting a plan that you've created on your own, make this an activity to be shared by the entire family.

Explain the potential dangers that might have to be faced, and ensure that your Family Disaster Plan includes the following:

- Discuss the potential emergencies that you might have to face.
- Choose two sites for the family to meet if a disaster strikes. One should be right outside your home (beside the mailbox, for example) in the case of sudden emergency such as a fire. The other site should be outside your neighborhood in case a disaster prevents you from returning to your home. Make sure that all family members have memorized the address and phone number of this second location.
- Designate an out-of-state family member or friend to be your "family contact" in case of an emergency. If local phone service is disrupted, it may still be possible to place a long-distance call. In the event of an emergency, all family members should call your "family contact" and let that person know where they are. Again, make sure that all family members have memorized this phone number.
- Discuss with your family the steps you would take if an evacuation were necessary. Talk about what to do before, during, and after an evacuation, including the steps you would take to ensure proper care for your family pets.

FEMA and the Red Cross also recommend these steps to ensure that all family members are prepared for various emergencies:

- Post emergency numbers by all phones. You may also wish to add these numbers to your cell phone address book. In addition, you'll find several important phone numbers in the back of this book, with room to add your own local emergency numbers as well.
- Teach your children how to call 9-1-1.
- Make sure all family members know the proper way to shut off water, gas, and electricity at the main switches, and when these steps might be necessary.
- Check your insurance coverage once each year.
- Show all family members the locations of your fire extinguishers, and make sure they know how to use them.

- If they are not already installed, add smoke detectors to each level of your home, especially near bedrooms.
- Determine the best escape routes from your home in case of fire or other emergency. Ideally, there should be two escape routes from each room.
- Find the safest locations in your home for each type of disaster.

STEP 3: Prepare an Emergency Supply Kit

As we've said, disaster preparedness means being able to take care of yourself and your family for a period of days or even weeks, without relying on outside help. In a sudden and widespread disaster, food, water, sanitary items, and virtually all other supplies could become completely unavailable almost in an instant. The only way to be sure that your family will have the resources you need is to assemble these items in advance, and make sure that all family members know the location of the kit.

Numerous government and nonprofit organizations have published lists of items to be included in family emergency supply kits. The following items are recommended by FEMA as a starting point for developing your family's emergency supply kit. Of course, you may wish to include other items to meet your family's unique needs, keeping in mind that you may need to transport your kit if evacuation is required.

- Three-day supply of nonperishable food. Store in a cool, dry location and replace food items as necessary.
- Three-day supply of water—one gallon of water per person, per day. Store in a cool, dry place and replace water every six months.
- Portable, battery-powered radio or television and extra batteries (Crank-type radios requiring no batteries are also available.)
- Flashlight and extra batteries
- First Aid kit and manual
- Sanitation and hygiene items, including moist towelettes and toilet paper
- Matches and waterproof container
- Whistle
- Change of clothing for each family member

- Kitchen accessories and cooking utensils, including a can opener
- Photocopies of credit and identification cards
- Cash and coins (in case ATMs do not work)
- Special needs items, such as prescription medications, eye glasses, contact lens solution, and hearing aid batteries
- Items for infants, such as formula, diapers, bottles, and pacifiers

Your emergency supply kit should not be stored in various locations all over your home. Instead, pack these items in a waterproof container so that they can be quickly packed in your vehicle and transported with you in case you need to evacuate. Remember that if evacuation becomes necessary for your family, tens of thousands of others may be evacuating alongside you. Many will be unprepared for the situation and will be looking for supplies in their new location. This may create widespread shortages that extend well beyond the area affected by the emergency. Be sure that all family members know the location of your emergency kit in case some family members are forced to evacuate from separate locations.

Keeping in mind that you may have to transport these items quickly, you may still wish to add additional items to your kit. Or you may want to place these items in a separate container for use only if you're required to "shelter at home" during an emergency (more on this later).

Items suggested by FEMA and other organizations that you may want to add to your basic kit include:

- Paper cups, plates, and plastic utensils
- Household liquid bleach to treat drinking water (do not use scented bleach)
- Sugar, salt, pepper
- Aluminum foil and plastic wrap
- Small cooking stove and fuel
- Duct tape
- Scissors
- Games, cards, toys, and books
- "Comfort" items for children including a stuffed animal, toys, and non-perishable candy
- Paper, pens, and pencils
- Work gloves

- Instant coffee or tea bags
- Inventory of valuable household goods
- Heavy-duty "contractor" garbage bags
- Extra car keys
- Blankets or sleeping bags, especially if you live in a cold climate

Keep in mind that infants and the elderly may have special needs. If your family includes individuals who may require extra supplies, here are some items you may want to add to your emergency preparedness kit.

For infants:
>Formula
>Powdered milk
>Bottles
>Diapers and wipes
>Medications
>Lotion and diaper rash ointment
>Baby food and juice

For the elderly:
>Medications
>Denture items
>Extra eyeglasses
>Hearing aid batteries

Finally, make sure that you have some basic supplies in your vehicle. Many people would be unable to return to their homes in a fast-developing, widespread emergency. By having at least a minimal emergency supply kit in your car or truck, you'll ensure that you can meet your basic needs for at least a few days. If your family enjoys traveling in backcountry areas—and I hope you do—there are some additional items that I'll talk about later in the book to help you prepare for contingencies in the great outdoors.

Vehicle Emergency Supply Kit:

- Battery-operated radio and flashlight (with extra batteries)
- Blanket
- Jumper cables
- Five-pound ABC fire extinguisher
- Bottled water and nonperishable, high-energy food (granola, peanut butter, raisins, etc.)
- Maps
- Shovel
- Flares
- Tire repair kit
- First Aid kit and manual
- Change of clothes
- Climate-appropriate gear including hat, gloves, hand warmers, waterproof poncho

STEP 4: Ensure That at Least One Family Member Is Trained in Basic First Aid and CPR/AED

A solid background in First Aid is invaluable for any family member who might one day be responsible for the immediate care of others. Not only will a First Aid course provide you with the skills you need in a medical emergency, but knowledge will help ensure that you can maintain a cool head if a family member is hurt or suddenly becomes ill.

The American Red Cross offers a variety of nationally-recognized First Aid courses for adults and young people, taught by certified instructors. The organization's Standard First Aid course curriculum includes how to check for life-threatening and non-life-threatening conditions, treatment for shock, fractures, sudden illnesses, heat and cold emergencies, bleeding, and much more. In addition, the Red Cross is a leading provider of CPR/AED training—cardiopulmonary resuscitation and the use of automatic external defibrillators, which are now common in airports, shopping malls, and other public places. For outdoor enthusiasts, the Red Cross also offers Wilderness First Aid training that builds on basic skills, focusing on emergency care in wilderness settings, caring for injured persons over extended periods of time, and simple evacuation techniques. To find course schedules in your area, visit www.redcross.org and find the link to your local chapter.

Every emergency supply kit you assemble should include a First Aid kit. The easiest and probably most cost-effective way to obtain the supplies you need is to purchase a preassembled kit. By purchasing a preassembled kit, you will avoid paying for larger boxes of individual supplies that you may never need. A wide range of kits are available and can be purchased online from outfitters like www.cabelas.com or www.bassproshops.com. If you choose to assemble your own kit, here are the items that are recommended by FEMA and other emergency-response organizations.

- Adhesive bandages, various sizes
- 5" x 9" sterile dressings
- Conforming roller gauze bandage
- Triangular bandages
- 3" x 3" sterile gauze pads
- 4" x 4" sterile gauze pads
- Rolled 3" cohesive bandage
- Germicidal hand wipes or waterless, alcohol-based sanitizer
- Antiseptic wipes
- Several pairs of large, medical-grade, non-latex gloves
- Tongue depressor blades
- Adhesive tape, 2" width
- Antibacterial ointment
- Instant hot and cold packs
- Small scissors
- Tweezers
- Needle
- Safety pins in assorted sizes
- Cotton balls
- Thermometer
- Tube of petroleum jelly or other lubricant
- Sunscreen
- CPR breathing barrier, such as a face shield
- First Aid manual

- Aspirin and non-aspirin pain reliever
- Anti-diarrhea medication
- Antacid for stomach upset
- Laxative
- Syrup of Ipecac
- Activated charcoal
- Hydrogen peroxide
- Antihistamine
- Rubbing alcohol
- Cold and cough medicine

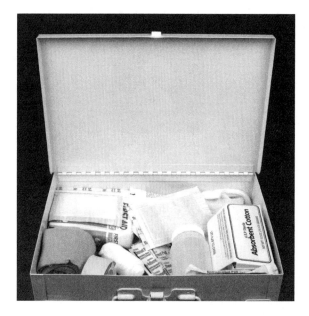

2

Meeting Your Immediate and Long-term Needs

So far, we've talked about general disaster preparedness. By following the guidelines we've already outlined, you and your family should be able to cope with most disaster situations for a few days without extreme hardship. But what if you find yourself on your own for a longer period of time? In this chapter, we'll take a more in-depth look at your family's needs, including steps you might take to be self-reliant for a period of weeks or even months if necessary. We'll consider four key areas: *water*, *food*, the *special needs of family members*, and the *special needs of your pets*.

Water

Fresh water is the first thing that becomes scarce during a disaster. Public water supplies can not only become disrupted but can also become contaminated, potentially causing gastrointestinal problems, as well as hepatitis, cholera, amoebic dysentery, viral infections, and typhoid fever.

As we discussed in the previous chapter, you should always have a three-day supply of clean water on hand for each family member. But in facing a longer-term crisis, you'll need to find the means to continually replenish your water supply.

As long as public water supplies remain uncontaminated, you can not only use this water as you need it, but you can stockpile it in your home. Filling bathtubs is a common practice during emergencies, and water from municipal systems contains enough chlorine to keep it safe for some time.

However, if you know or suspect that the public drinking water system has been compromised or contaminated, you must immediately shut off the flow of water coming into your home so the contamination won't reach you. Obviously, once you take this step, you are limited to the stockpiles that are already in your home, including your emergency supply kit. However, there are other sources in your home right now that may provide additional stockpiles of safe, clean drinking water, including your hot-water tank, your toilet tanks, and your pipes.

To access the water in your hot-water tank, be sure the electricity or gas is off, and then open the drain at the bottom of the tank. Turn off the tank intake valve, and turn on any hot water faucet to let air into the plumbing and enable the water to flow freely from your tank. Note that if you turn off your gas supply, only a professional can turn it back on.

Water dipped from the tank of a toilet (not the bowl) can be used for drinking, and the water in the bowl can be used for pets. *Do not* use water that has been chemically treated or "blue" water. To use the water in your pipes, identify and turn on the highest faucet in your home to allow flow. You can then get water from the lowest faucet. Melted ice cubes may provide some additional water, as can the liquid from canned fruits and vegetables and other canned goods. Water from swimming pools and spas can be used for personal hygiene and cleaning but not for drinking. Nor should you use water from radiators, waterbeds, or home heating systems (hot-water boilers) for drinking purposes.

Storing Water from a Clean Source

To store water, the Centers for Disease Control (CDC) make the following recommendations:

- Water should be stored in sturdy plastic bottles with tight-fitting lids. Thoroughly rinsed chlorine bleach bottles work well for water storage. FEMA also recommends the use of two-liter plastic soft drink bottles, sanitized with a solution of one teaspoon of non-scented bleach in a quart of water. Make sure that the sanitizing solution touches all surfaces of the bottle, and thoroughly rinse the bottle with clean water. Plastic containers for juice and milk do not work as well because they tend to crack and leak more readily and cannot be adequately sanitized. All containers should be labeled to include the date they were filled.
- Stored water should be changed every six months.
- Avoid placing water containers in areas where toxic substances, such as gasoline and pesticides, are present. Vapors may penetrate the plastic over time.
- Do not store water containers in direct sunlight. Select a place with a fairly constant, cool temperature.

Purifying Water in an Emergency

Campers, backpackers, and hunters who venture into remote areas for more than a few days have always needed to replenish their water supplies from local sources. Water is heavy, and we simply can't carry more than a few days' supply on our backs. America's outdoor enthusiasts have come up with a number of ways to make water safe for drinking, and the techniques that they've developed are perfectly suitable for use in a disaster. In general, these techniques involve boiling, filtering, adding small amounts of certain chemicals to water, or combinations of these techniques. In effect, these are the same techniques that are used by your municipal water supplier right now.

The safest method to purify water is to bring it to a rolling boil for one minute. Boiling water will kill most harmful bacteria and parasites.

If boiling your water is not possible, the CDC advises treating the water with chlorine or iodine tablets, or unscented household chlorine bleach (5.25% sodium hypochlorite). If you use tablets, follow the directions on the package. If you use household bleach, add 1/8th of a teaspoon of bleach per gallon of water if the water is clear, or twice that amount for cloudy water. Before using the water, allow it to stand for thirty minutes. Keep in mind that boiling is still your best option, and some parasitic organisms may not be killed by chlorine tablets, iodine tablets, or liquid bleach.

In addition, you might want to consider a filtration/purification system such as those that are popular with campers, backpackers, and scientific researchers who work in remote areas. These systems can provide you with clean drinking water from a variety of sources.

These purifiers can remove bacteria, cysts, viruses, chemicals such as pesticides and herbicides, and dirt that can give even safe water an unpleasant taste. The output capability of these units varies, but even a smaller unit can provide enough drinking water for a large family. Look for a unit that is certified to EPA Guide Standards for microbiological purifiers (this will be indicated on the product packaging), and note the capacity of the filtration canister. This is the maximum amount of water that can be purified before the disposable canister must be replaced. You may wish to purchase additional canisters along with the unit itself.

Food

After water, food will be your next major concern in a disaster lasting for a considerable length of time. Unlike water, where we use a variety of sources and purification techniques, your food supply may be considerably more difficult to replenish.

FEMA recommends some common-sense measures for making your food supply last in an emergency: use perishable foods first, then items from your freezer (which should last at least two days, as long as you minimize the number of times you open the freezer door), and nonperishable items last.

In determining the amount of food you'll require in a crisis, you must consider your own values and your own personal feelings about how long you might have to survive without outside help, and the costs and benefits of maintaining a long-term food supply.

Do you want to prepare for a natural disaster where you might have to sustain yourself for a few days but where outside help will probably be on the way within a reasonable amount of time? If so, the food in your emergency supply kit, along with whatever else might be in your home when a disaster strikes, will probably be sufficient. Do you want to be prepared for an epidemic or pandemic of a new influenza strain—and have enough food on hand so that your family could remain isolated from disease for a period of weeks or even months? Or do you want to be prepared for a "worst case scenario"—a total breakdown of the American economy and civil authority—and have food on hand to sustain your loved ones and pets for as long as a year? These are questions that only you and your family together can answer. But let's put all the options on the table—and look at all the potential situations you might face—so that you can make a more informed decision about what's right for you and your family.

Whatever length of time you prepare for, choose foods that your family *likes to eat*. Many food products can be stored for long periods of time, but in the end you will want to rotate your emergency provisions—avoiding waste by eating items before they reach their expiration date, and replacing them with fresher products. Clearly mark the items you purchase so that they can be used prior to their expiration dates. Whatever foods you choose, store them in a cool, dry, and preferably dark place.

If you've prepared an emergency supply kit for your family, you already have three days' worth of food on hand. If you wish to stockpile foods to sustain your family for a longer period of time, consider these shelf-life guidelines published by FEMA.

These foods may be stored for up to six months:
- Boxed powdered milk
- Dried fruit
- Dry crackers
- Potatoes

These foods may be stored for up to one year:
- Canned condensed meat and vegetable soups
- Canned fruits, fruit juices, and vegetables
- Ready-to-eat cereals and uncooked instant cereals
- Peanut butter
- Jelly
- Hard candy and canned nuts
- Vitamins

These foods may be stored indefinitely, in proper containers and conditions:
- Wheat
- Vegetable oils

- Dried corn
- Baking powder
- Soybeans
- Instant coffee, tea, and cocoa
- Salt
- Non-carbonated soft drinks
- White rice
- Bouillon products
- Dry pasta
- Powdered milk (in nitrogen-packed cans)

Also, remember to plan for your pets if you elect to stockpile food, in the same way that you would provide for their needs in your three-day emergency supply kit.

Preparing for the Special Needs of Family Members

During a disaster, those with specific medical needs or conditions may require extra assistance, and additional items may be required in your emergency supply kit. Whether you choose to evacuate a disaster area or to stay where you are and "shelter in place" (more about these options later in the book), your family's emergency planning, as well as your emergency supply kit, will need to be tailored to these special needs.

Special Medical Needs

Emergency supply kits for those with particular medical needs should contain at least a three-day supply of all medication, in their original containers, a detailed list of all medications including the name of the medication, dosage, frequency, and prescribing physician, a minimum three-day supply of any frequently-used supplies such as syringes, and vital medical records like insurance cards and powers of attorney.

If a member of your family uses any type of breathing equipment or oxygen, keep a reserve supply of tanks, tubes, solutions, and so on. If a family member uses an IV or feeding tube, make sure that the equipment has a backup battery, and discuss manual infusion techniques with your home health-care provider in order to be prepared for a power outage. In addition, attach written usage instructions to the equipment.

Those who rely on medical equipment powered by electricity need to be especially careful in making a backup plan in case of electrical outages. Again, ask your home health-care provider for information about battery backup power sources, or consider a generator, as we'll discuss in the next chapter.

Visual Impairments

For persons with visual impairments, consider the extra preparation and supplies that you might need that are appropriate to the impairment. Some of these suggestions may be appropriate for your family member:

- Include a cane for the blind in your emergency supply kit.
- Label supplies in large print, or in Braille.
- Use security lights in each room to keep pathways well lit.
- Add eyeglasses to your emergency supply kit.
- Keep high-powered flashlights with wide beams and extra batteries on hand.
- If you have service animals, make sure they are properly harnessed, leashed, or confined; and remember that stress may change an animal's behavior in a disaster.

Hearing Impairments

Likewise, for the hearing impaired, consider the special considerations you may face, including these suggestions:

- Include extra hearing aid batteries in your emergency supply kit.
- Keep and maintain an extra supply of TTY and phone light batteries.
- Keep pens and paper in your emergency supply kit.
- Develop a plan for hearing-impaired individuals to communicate with emergency personnel when no interpreter or hearing aids are accessible. Consider keeping prewritten cards with messages such as "I speak ASL,"*

---

* American Sign Language

"I do not write or read English," or "If you make announcements, I will need to have them written or signed" in your emergency supply kit.

- Install battery-operated smoke alarms that include visual as well as audible alerts.
- Predetermine which news broadcasts will be captioned or signed in the event of an emergency.

Mobility Issues

Consider these ideas in your emergency planning:

- Maintain a spare battery for motorized wheelchairs, and set aside a lightweight manual wheelchair if appropriate.
- Ensure that your emergency supply kit can be accessed by those with mobility concerns.
- Add heavy gloves to your emergency supply kit in case wheelchair occupants must maneuver over heavy debris.
- Check with your wheelchair or scooter vendor to find out whether you can charge the battery using the cigarette lighter in your car (a converter will probably be necessary).
- Keep a patch kit or seal-in-air product and extra inner tubes in your emergency supply kit if your wheelchair does not have puncture-proof tires.
- If you live above the first floor of a building, coordinate an advance evacuation plan with others in the building, and discuss with them the proper ways your family member can be lifted and transported.

If You Have Special Needs

Most communities offer special assistance to those with special needs in the event of an emergency. Contact your local office of emergency services or local fire department to register for assistance. Develop a support group consisting of neighbors, relatives, friends, and coworkers to help you in an emergency, and keep a list of their names and contact information. Teach members in the group how to operate any necessary equipment, and let them know of any special concerns you may have. Make sure to discuss your situation with your employer as well.

If You Are a Caregiver

Be sure to establish a communications plan with your loved one or client(s) in case you are separated during a disaster.

Offering Assistance to Others

If you do not have special needs yourself, please consider offering your help, in advance, to friends and neighbors who might need extra assistance in an emergency.

Preparing for the Special Needs of Pets

Like our children, pets rely on us for their every need. Rarely can pets survive a disaster when left on their own. In fact, our leaving a disaster area for just a "short time" is dangerous for our pets since that period of time can increase despite our best intentions. In the event of an evacuation, you must take your pets with you to ensure their survival. As I mentioned in the previous chapter, pets will require their own provisions in your emergency supply kit. In addition to the food, bowls, and leashes included in your basic supply kit checklist, you may want to consider the following additional items.

- Medicines and medical records stored in a waterproof container
- Veterinary First Aid kit (check with your veterinarian)
- Harnesses and carriers
- Recent photos in case your pet gets lost
- Litter pan, if needed
- Can opener, if not already included in your basic kit
- Written information on feeding schedules, medical conditions, behavioral issues, and the name and number of your veterinarian
- Bedding and toys
- Carriers for pets, as needed, including carriers for birds, small mammals, and reptiles
- A written list of locations where your pets might be able to stay if you cannot care for them during an emergency

You'll also want to do some advance planning to make sure your pet will be cared for in an evacuation situation even if you cannot do so. Some shelters, including Red Cross shelters, cannot accept pets. If you are a pet owner, you may wish to research some locations in advance where both your family and your pets will be welcome.

Contact hotels and motels outside your immediate area to determine which ones will accept pets, and find out any restrictions on the number, size, and species of animals they allow. If they have a "no-pet" policy, ask them if they make exceptions in emergencies.

Likewise, contact veterinarians, pet boarding facilities, and animal shelters outside your immediate area. However, use animal shelters only as a last resort, since shelters tend to overflow with animals during a disaster.

Before an Impending Disaster

Before an impending disaster, all pets should be brought inside. Animals may behave erratically if they are frightened, so bring them inside to ensure they will not run away. Make sure that emergency supplies for your pet are on hand, as well as your list of alternative sources for pet care. Dogs and cats should have collars on that are securely fastened with current identification.

During a Disaster

During a disaster, keep a supply of newspapers to use for sanitary purposes. You can also conserve water by feeding your pets moist or canned food so they will need less water to drink. Consider separating cats and dogs. Animals that normally get along may behave differently toward each other during an emergency.

After a Disaster

After a disaster, keep your pets leashed for the first few days, since the normal visual and scent cues that they are accustomed to may be significantly altered.

3

Coping with a Long-term Power Outage

The average American family loses power once every nine months for reasons other than hurricanes and strong storms, and the average power customer goes without power for 214 minutes—about 3 1/2 hours—each year.

Usually, this is nothing more than an inconvenience—a few hours without T.V. or computers, a stubbed toe looking for flashlight batteries, and cold sandwiches instead of a hot dinner cooked on the stove.

But when power goes out for a longer period of time—days, weeks, or sometimes even months—the game changes, and the situation can become far more unpleasant and even serious. Food spoils. It becomes more difficult for you and your family to stay comfortably warm or cool. Pipes freeze. Chores such as cooking and maintaining basic sanitation become more difficult, as does maintaining a fresh water supply.

In this chapter, we'll address these issues and more—how to prepare for a long-term electrical outage and, hopefully, maintain a reasonable level of comfort for all members of the family should the power go out for an extended period of time.

Advance Preparation

- If you've assembled an emergency supply kit for your family, then you've already assembled most of the items you'll need immediately during a power outage, including flashlights, extra batteries, and a battery-powered or hand-crank radio. Due to the risk of fire, avoid using candles during a power blackout.
- For medications that require refrigeration, check with your physician to see how long these medications can be kept.
- If you have reason to believe that you're likely to lose power, consider filling plastic containers with water and placing them in your refrigerator or freezer (leave room in the containers for ice to expand). The chilled and frozen water can help keep food cold if the power goes out.
- Likewise, before a severe winter storm, hurricane, or other event where power is likely to go out, keep at least a half tank of fuel in your car since gas stations also rely on power to keep their pumps running.
- Back up computer data regularly, and use a high-quality surge protector for your computer and other expensive electronic equipment.
- If you have an electric garage door opener, learn how to release the power opener and raise the door manually.
- Keep in mind that your cordless phone will not work without power. Plan to rely on your cell phone, and keep it charged (although even cell phones will not work if the local towers have no power).
- If you have any life-sustaining medical equipment in your home, make sure it is registered with your utility company, and have an emergency power supply available.
- Learn what plans and provisions are in place to deal with a power outage at your child's school or day-care center, and how they will communicate with parents.
- Keep some extra cash on hand. An extended power outage may prevent you from withdrawing money from ATMs and banks, and it may prevent merchants from processing credit card transactions.
- Know how to shut off your electricity and other utilities.

- Talk to your neighbors before an emergency happens. Find out who has a generator, a snow blower or tractor, a 4-wheel drive vehicle, a well-equipped tool shop, medical knowledge, or any other equipment or skills that might be helpful. At the same time, find out if there are elderly or disabled individuals in your neighborhood who might benefit from your help during a power outage, disaster, or other emergency.

"Shelter in Place"

Before or during a widespread emergency, management officials may recommend that you either evacuate a disaster area or stay where you are and "shelter in place." We'll talk more about evacuations in Chapter 5 of this book. We'll also talk about specific precautions and steps that you might need to take in particular types of disasters or emergencies. In the meantime, here is a list of general ideas to keep your family, home, and property safer if you're stuck at home without power for days or even weeks.

- Turn off any electrical equipment that was in use when the power went out.
- Turn off all lights except one central light that will alert you when power comes back on.
- Turn off all utilities if there is damage to your home or if instructed to do so by emergency management personnel. Remember that if you turn off the gas, only a professional can turn it back on.
- When power is restored, wait a few minutes before turning on major appliances to help eliminate further problems caused by a sharp increase in demand.
- During a power outage, don't use 9-1-1 for basic information. Use the battery-powered or hand-crank radio in your emergency supply kit.
- Check on neighbors who may need your help, particularly the elderly and those with special needs.
- You can cook meals in your fireplace or on a campfire outside. If you use a camp stove or charcoal grill, you must cook out-of-doors to avoid carbon monoxide poisoning.

- Likewise, never use gas ovens, ranges, barbeques, or portable or propane heaters to heat indoors.
- Virtually any water supply, including stream and pond water, can be used for flushing toilets. Pour the water from a bucket directly into the bowl to avoid contaminating the clean water in your toilet tank. When enough water is poured into the bowl, your toilet should flush.

Protecting Your Home from Damage

If you leave home for an extended time during a power outage, include these steps in your planning:

- Turn off and unplug appliances.
- Open cupboard doors to allow available heat to reach pipes.
- Shut off the water to minimize potential damage from an indoor flood.
- Button up the house. Make sure windows and doors are sealed as tightly as possible.
- Do not turn off your heat; set the thermostat at a minimum of 55°F.
- If a neighbor is remaining behind, ask him or her to check your house daily for any signs of major water leaks or other damage.
- Take a contact list with you, including your local phone book, so that you can begin arranging service calls, if necessary, even before you arrive back home.

Food and Water Safety

We've already discussed the food and water issues that you'll need to consider in assembling your emergency supply kit, as well as the additional hurdles you might face if you need to sustain your family for an extended period of time. Here are a few more suggestions that might be helpful in the event your electrical power is out for longer than a day or two:

- Eat quick-to-spoil foods first.

- Plan your refrigerator and freezer openings. Grab what you need as quickly as possible then close the door.
- In cold weather, use a cooler placed outside, or even buried under snow, to keep food cold. Put the cooler on the shady side of your house.
- Most canned food can be eaten straight from the can without heating.
- Heat and cold can damage food supplies. If a food can shows signs of damage, swelling, or corrosion, throw it out.
- Food that has thawed and is still "refrigerator cold" can be eaten. Foods that still contain ice crystals can be eaten or refrozen.
- Never ration food for children, pregnant women, or those with medical conditions.

Dealing with Heat and Cold Extremes

One of the most uncomfortable aspects of losing power for a long period of time is losing the ability to run your heating and air conditioning. In meeting your responsibility to ensure your family's safety, you need to know the signs and symptoms of common heat and cold emergencies which require immediate medical attention, including heat exhaustion, heat stroke, hypothermia, and frostbite.

These potential life-threatening emergencies will be discussed in Chapter 19, when we talk about First Aid considerations in outdoor and backcountry situations. In the meantime, here are a few ideas for preventing these heat and cold emergencies, as well as maintaining comfort and morale among your family members in the event that your heating and air conditioning systems no longer function.

Heat

Here are a few recommendations from the CDC and FEMA, as well as some knowledgeable outdoorsmen:

- Avoid hot foods and heavy meals that can add heat to your body.
- Drink plenty of fluids, but limit alcoholic beverages.
- Dress in loose-fitting, lightweight, light-colored clothing. Wear a light, wide-brimmed hat in the outdoors. Dress infants and children using these same guidelines.

- Limit sun exposure during midday hours. If you have outside chores to accomplish as part of dealing with a disaster, do these late in the day or, preferably, in the early morning hours.
- Never leave infants, children, or pets in a parked car.
- Provide plenty of fresh water for your pets, and leave the water in a shady area.
- Stay on the lowest floor out of the sunshine if air conditioning is not available. Plan on sleeping on the lowest floor of your home as well.
- Check regularly on elderly neighbors and those who may have special needs or medical conditions.
- Open the highest windows in your house to let the warmest air out.
- Take advantage of pools, clean streams, or any other water source to cool your body. Even water that feels almost bathtub warm can have a cooling effect. Or simply wipe your body with a wet towel and let the evaporation cool you.
- A wet towel placed on the inside of your wrist or on your neck will begin immediately to help you feel more comfortable.

Cold

Once again, we can learn a great deal from those who hunt, ski, or camp in cold weather. Here are some suggestions:

- Cold weather tends to be very dry. Make sure you stay hydrated. Drink hot beverages or even plain hot water.
- Stay warm during the day by taking care of needed chores. Stay moving and active.
- Keep your head and hands covered since these are the areas where your body loses the most heat.
- By all means, build a fire if you have a fireplace. Note that heaters powered by gasoline or other fuels should *never* be used indoors.
- Layer your clothing and avoid wearing cotton if possible. Wool, as well as the more modern micro-fiber fabrics, trap heat around your body. Wool and some of these modern fabrics also tend to stay warm even when wet.
- Don't break a sweat. Remove layers of clothing as necessary when you're active. Sweat, in effect, makes your body wet, and water can move

moisture away from your body more than one hundred times more quickly than air. If you break a sweat, change into dry clothes.

- Take a hot-water bottle with you to bed. This has been done for hundreds of years.
- Limit your fluid intake before bed so that you don't have to answer the call of nature.
- Sleep in the highest level of your home. If you're sleeping on a floor, make sure you have blankets or other insulation between you and the floor.

Make It Fun

If you have children in your care, make a game out of your preparations and get them involved in this as well as in your family's ongoing efforts to stay cool or warm. Ask for their suggestions. Think of this as an opportunity to teach them about our nation's pioneer past and a way of life that most twenty-first-century Americans will never experience.

Generators

Think of a generator as a small-scale power plant, producing electricity for the homeowner from a variety of fuels that may include gasoline, diesel fuel, propane, or natural gas. Generators fall into two basic categories or types: portable and permanent.

Portable generators, because they are reasonably easy to transport, are far more versatile than permanent generators. Some weigh as little as thirty pounds. These generators are often used by contractors and tradesmen to provide power for job sites. Backcountry lodges and hunting and fishing camps also make use of portable generators to run essential equipment from time to time or to provide a few hours of electricity in the evening hours. In addition, portable generators can be far less expensive than permanent generators. Typically they have a fairly small gas or diesel fuel tank that must be refilled every few hours.

Permanent generators, on the other hand, are installed outside the home, typically on a concrete pad, and are designed exclusively for backup power in the case of an outage. Some new homes now include backup generators as standard equipment. Most run on propane or natural gas and can be connected to the municipal natural gas supply or to an above-ground or below-ground fuel tank on the property. Permanent generators tend to be capable of producing more power than portable generators and can be programmed to automatically restore power to all or part of your home within seconds of a power outage, even if you are away.

In deciding whether to purchase a generator, ask yourself these questions:

- Will I be using the generator for anything other than backup power to my home? If so, choose a portable generator.
- What is my budget? Plan on spending at least $3,000 for a permanently-installed generator, and perhaps considerably more. Portable generators start at less than $500.
- In the case of a power outage, do I want to be able to run a few items at a time, or do I want to be able to provide for the normal power usages of my entire house? Because of their additional output, permanent generators are better able to provide for your full home power needs. In addition, because they are "hard-wired" into the home's normal electrical power supply, they can provide a far more convenient power supply.
- Do I want the power to come on automatically if I'm away from home? Permanently installed generators can detect power outages and start automatically. Portable generators require you to start the generator with an electric or pull start.
- Do I want my generator to be able to run for long periods of time without refueling? Permanent generators can be connected to a fuel tank on your property or to municipal natural gas (although natural gas service may also be interrupted in a widespread power outage or natural disaster). Portable generators must be manually refueled every few hours.

Generator Safety

Like all engines, generator engines produce harmful gases including carbon monoxide. Never use a generator indoors, including in an enclosed garage. Generators must be used outside. Use extension cords to run indoor appliances and tools.

Portable generators typically have both 12-volt and 120-volt outlets to which appliances, tools, and so forth can be plugged in. However, if you want to power light circuits, central heating and air conditioning units, well pumps, or any other direct circuits within your home, you'll be required to install a "transfer switch."

A transfer switch is required by code any time a generator is connected to the home. This switch prevents "back-feed" of electricity into the utility lines that serve your home. *Without a transfer switch, electrical current from your generator could flow back into the municipal power supply, causing injury or even death to linemen who are attempting to restore power. Installation of a transfer switch must be done by a professional electrician.*

A transfer switch also provides power management capabilities—enabling you to turn various circuits on and off and to use a smaller generator to meet your power needs.

Generator Fuel

No matter what kind of generator you use, your power will last only as long as your fuel supply. Ideally, install a fuel tank on your property when you purchase your permanent generator. By having your own reserve supply of fuel, you may be able to power your home for weeks or even a few months without assistance from the outside world. Keep in mind that if you use a portable generator, you may burn several gallons of gasoline or diesel fuel each day. If a power outage covers a large area, you may not be able to replenish your fuel supply.

Selecting a Generator

Generator power is rated by wattage, and generators typically have two power ratings: "surge" (or "maximum") watts, and "running" (or "rated") watts. When an appliance or other electrical device is first turned on, it may require a "surge" of power up to three times what it needs to run continuously. The surge wattage rating on a generator refers to the absolute maximum amount of power the generator can produce for a short period of time. The running wattage is what the generator is capable of producing under normal, longtime running conditions.

Honda Power Equipment suggests these guidelines for determining your basic home power needs:

- If you have a well, you'll require at least 3,800 watts to power the pump.
- If you have gas or oil-forced air heating, you may need as little as 2,500 watts to power your system; electric furnaces and heat pumps typically require 15,000 watts or more.
- Gas water heaters require as little as 2,500 watts, whereas electric heaters often require at least 4,500 watts.
- Homeowners can typically power household appliances using between 3,000 and 6,500 watts.
- You can conserve fuel (and money) by purchasing a generator with an automatic throttle that optimizes power output and controls fuel usage.

However, unless you already know very specifically what appliances or circuits you wish to run with your generator—and are knowledgeable in calculating electricity loads—you will probably be happier in the long run if you consult with a licensed electrician before deciding the generator wattage you'll need to power your home.

Facing Specific Natural Disasters

In previous chapters, we've looked at general guidelines for you and your family that apply to a wide variety of situations. Now we'll take a look at the special considerations you'll want to think about in very specific types of disasters—fires, floods, hurricanes, and more.

Every disaster has its own character. Some, like floods, tend to be widespread, while others like house fires are usually more localized. Hurricanes can be predicted many hours and usually many days in advance, while earthquakes virtually always strike with no warning whatsoever. So that you can prepare as well as possible for your family's safety before, during, and after natural disasters, we need to take a more in-depth look at the contingencies you might face before, during, and after each type of event. And in Chapter 13, we'll talk about insurance coverage to make sure you receive full and fair compensation should your property be damaged in a natural disaster.

Fire

In 2005, fire claimed an American life every three hours. That year, fire departments throughout the United States responded to three hundred and eighty-one

thousand home structure fires, resulting in more than three thousand deaths, more than thirteen thousand injuries, and $6.7 billion in property damage. The best ways to protect your family from the devastation of home fires are *prevention* and *preparation*.

Prevention

Prevention is simply the measures we can take in advance to make sure a fire never happens in the first place and to make sure that family members have as much opportunity as possible to escape if a fire should occur. Prevention measures fall into three basic categories: installing and maintaining smoke detectors, having fire extinguishers at the ready, and checking your home for fire hazards.

Smoke Detectors

Smoke detectors give family members more time to escape a home fire, increasing their chances of survival. Between 2000 and 2004, 65 percent of deaths from home fires occurred in homes that did not have smoke detectors or where the smoke detectors were inoperative. Here are some basic tips for using and getting the most protection from smoke detectors:

- Place *at least* one smoke detector on every level of your house. They should be placed in central areas and mounted high on walls or ceilings. Smoke detectors should not be placed near doors, windows, or vents. Your local fire department can also advise you about smoke detector placement.
- Dust your smoke detectors each month.
- If detectors are hard-wired into the home's electrical power supply, make sure they have a battery backup in case your electricity is knocked out.
- Replace batteries twice a year. An easy way to remember this is to replace the batteries when you reset your clocks for daylight savings time in the spring and fall.
- Replace smoke detector units every ten years.
- If you have an alarm system installed in your home, check to see if your provider offers fire monitoring whereby your police and fire department can be notified if a fire is detected, even if you are not home.

Fire Extinguishers

Fire extinguishers give you a chance to prevent a localized fire from spreading. Again, some basic tips:

- Have at least three fire extinguishers in your home, in the kitchen, basement, and garage, and perhaps a fourth in the bedroom area.
- Mount extinguishers near doorways for maximum access, and no more than five feet above the floor. Do not place them too close to stoves, fireplaces, and other areas where fires are most likely to begin, since they may become inaccessible. Like smoke detectors, your local fire department can also advise you about extinguisher placement.
- Purchase ABC rated fire extinguishers that can be used on a wide range of fire types. The "A" rating covers fabrics, wood, furniture, and walls. The "B" rating covers flammable liquids, grease, fats, gasoline, oil, oil paints, and liquids. And the "C" rating covers electrical equipment such as appliances, power tools, small motors, and so forth.

- After purchasing your fire extinguishers, make sure every family member knows *where they are* and *how to use them*.
- Check your extinguishers regularly to see if they are properly charged. The extinguisher will typically have a gauge that shows its condition. If an extinguisher shows signs of low pressure, corrosion, or damage, replace it.

Home Hazards

Smoke detectors and fire extinguishers are designed to alert you to a fire and give you an opportunity to combat it in the early stages. But the best way to prevent a fire is *before* it begins. Here are some things to consider in making your home as safe as possible from fire:

Wiring

- Immediately replace any power cords that are loose or frayed.
- Do not run power cords under rugs in high traffic areas.
- Include a cover on all electrical outlets and switches.
- If you have an older home, have the wiring inspected by a professional. In particular, have two-prong electrical receptacles replaced with three-prong types.
- If a circuit breaker trips or a fuse repeatedly blows, find out the cause and fix it.

Appliances

- Appliance vents, including those on televisions, stereos, and so on, should be open and free of dust.
- Clean the lint trap on the dryer after each use and regularly check the exhaust pipe for excess lint buildup. Dryer vents should be inspected at least once a year.
- Furnaces and portable heaters should be serviced and cleaned regularly. Portable heaters should never be placed near draperies, furniture, or other flammable items.

Chimneys and Fireplaces

- Have your chimney inspected yearly and cleaned if necessary.
- Use a fireplace screen and chimney fire arrester.

Kitchen

- Understand that kitchen fires are the number one cause of fire injuries.
- Be sure that an ABC fire extinguisher is installed in your kitchen for immediate access.
- Keep the stove free of grease and clean the vent hood filter on a regular basis.
- If you have a gas stove, routinely inspect pilot lights to ensure they are lit and clean.
- Use caution when cooking with oil.
- Keep towels, packaging, and other flammables away from the immediate cooking area.
- Never use a turkey fryer indoors or on wooden decks. Use these fryers well away from the house, and make sure turkeys are completely thawed before placing in the fryer.

Outdoors

- Trim trees a minimum of ten feet away from chimneys.
- Avoid having brush piles within one hundred feet of the house.
- Avoid using charcoal grills on wooden decks. Keep gas grills a good distance away from railings, benches, and the house.
- Clear debris and dead branches from under your deck.
- Make sure your house numbers are easily visible from the street so that emergency personnel can easily find your home.

General Fire Safety Precautions

- Never smoke in bed.
- Keep matches and lighters out of reach of children.

- Keep basements, garages, and other areas of the home free of trash, empty boxes, and other combustible items.
- Only refuel kerosene heaters outside, and only after they have cooled off.
- Sleep with bedroom doors closed, as this will keep heat and smoke out and buy time for you to escape.

Preparation: Your Family Escape Plan

There is no way to make any home or structure completely safe from fire. And unlike disasters such as hurricanes and floods where you may have some advance warning of the situation to come, fires often require you to take proper action to protect your family in only a matter of seconds.

In preparing for the possibility of a fire, we can take a lesson from those who keep our country safer every day—our police officers and military personnel. The training these individuals receive includes both planning and practice in order to be able to react instantly to a life-threatening situation. In a fire, every member of your family should *already know* what to do. By making a family escape plan and then *practicing* it, you and your loved ones will have fewer decisions to make in a crisis and a greater likelihood of reacting in the appropriate way. Here is what you need to do:

- Make a plan in advance to teach your family how to react in a fire.
- Ideally, at least *two* escape routes should be designated for each room in your home.
- Choose an outdoor meeting place where all family members should go once they have escaped from the home.
- Designate someone to contact neighbors and the fire department.
- Train youngsters as early as possible in calling 9-1-1, and make sure that they have memorized your street address.
- Practice fire drills two times a year. Include daytime and nighttime drills. Have a family member yell "Fire!" to alert the household. Practice crawling low and preferably blindfolded, since smoke may make it impossible to see during a real fire. Practice the "stop, drop, and roll" technique to extinguish clothing that may have caught fire.

Tornadoes

Tornadoes can occur any time of year, but most take place during the spring and summer, between the hours of 3 p.m. and 9 p.m. No area is completely immune to tornadoes; they have even been reported in Alaska. Tornado season lasts from March through May in southern states, and into late spring and early summer in northern states. Tornadoes can also accompany hurricanes and tropical storms.

Tornadoes develop quickly and can be obscured by clouds, making them difficult to see. Extreme tornadoes can pack winds up to three hundred miles per hour and can cut a path of destruction up to a mile wide and fifty miles long. On average, tornadoes travel at about thirty miles per hour but have been reported stationary or moving as quickly as seventy miles per hour.

In 1971, T. Theodore Fujita of the University of Chicago developed the Fujita Tornado Damage Scale to categorize tornadoes, ranking them from zero to six based on wind speeds and the damage caused. The scale has more recently been "enhanced," and tornadoes are now categorized based on the "Enhanced Fujita" or "EF" scale.

Here are some of the characteristics of each EF category:

EF Scale	Wind Speed (mph)	Damage Description
EF0	65–85	*Minor*: Chimney damage; broken tree branches; uprooted shallow trees
EF1	86–110	*Moderate*: Stripped roof surfaces; overturned mobile homes; moving vehicles knocked off roads
EF2	111–135	*Considerable*: Roofs torn off frame houses; large trees snapped or uprooted; light-object projectiles generated
EF3	136–165	*Severe*: Well-constructed homes have walls and roofs blown off; entire forests can be uprooted; heavy cars can be lifted from the ground
EF4	166–200	*Devastating*: Well-constructed homes leveled; cars and other large objects become flying projectiles
EF5	200+	*Extreme*: Frame houses wiped out completely; car-sized objects hurled at speeds up to one hundred miles per hour

Preparing for a Tornado

No matter its strength, a tornado can develop within seconds and create a life-or-death situation for those in its path. Because tornadoes allow very little reaction time, preparation is key. And like fires and all emergencies, a family plan is essential.

- Designate a location for family members to meet if separated. Select an out-of-state contact whom all family members can call, and make sure family members memorize their contact information.
- Make sure each family member knows where to go if a tornado strikes. Select an area in your home that is as low to the ground as possible, preferably a basement. If you do not have a basement, select an interior hallway or interior room on the lowest floor, such as a bathroom or closet, with as many walls between you and the outdoors as possible. Make sure your safe place is not near glass doors or windows. If you live in an area prone to tornadoes and live in a single-family home, seek advice on how to structurally reinforce your safe place.
- Trim trees to prevent falling branches that can cause damage to your home.
- Contact your local emergency management office, the local National

Weather Service office, and local Red Cross to find out the risks in your area and what community disaster plans are in place.

- Learn the tornado warning signals for your community. Find out when audible warnings are to be tested to see if they can be heard from inside and outside your home.
- Consider purchasing a NOAA (National Oceanic and Atmospheric Administration) radio that has tone alerts to notify you of watches and warnings while indoors.
- If the weather service believes a tornado is likely, bring in any outside items that are likely to be destroyed or become projectiles.

Tornado Watches and Warnings

Tornado Watch. Issued by the National Weather Service, a tornado watch means conditions are ripe for producing a tornado. At this time, you should remind family members of your designated safe place and listen for more information on radio or television.

Tornado Warning. Also issued by the National Weather Service, a tornado warning means a tornado has either been sighted or picked up on radar. At this time, family members should go to their designated safe place. Take a battery-operated radio with you and remain in the safe place until an "all clear" is given.

Potential Tornado Warning Signs

- *A dark sky,* often with a greenish hue
- *Large hail*
- *"Calm before the storm."* Winds may die down, and the air may appear still.
- *A debris cloud.* Not all tornados will be visible as funnel clouds. Often, you may only be able to see the dust and debris swept up by the tornado.
- *A dark, low-lying cloud,* especially one that is rotating.
- *A funnel cloud.* A visible, rotating extension of the cloud base is a sign that a tornado may develop.
- An *unusual roaring noise.* People often report hearing a loud noise similar to a freight train before a tornado emerges.

If a Tornado Strikes

If You're at Home

Immediately go to your safe place. Do not open windows, as wind and debris can cause damage and injury inside the home.

If You're at Work or School

Immediately go to a basement or inside an interior hallway on the lowest level. Do not go into wide rooms such as auditoriums, cafeterias, or large hallways. Crouch under a large piece of furniture using your arms to protect your head and neck.

If You're in a Mobile Home

Even if the home is tied down, get out immediately and go to a building with a strong foundation. If you cannot get inside a building, lie in a ditch or low-lying spot a safe distance away from the mobile home. Use your arms to protect your head and neck. Remember that the main cause of injury and death from tornadoes is flying debris.

If You're Outdoors

Seek shelter in a strong building. If you cannot get inside, crouch near it. If you cannot get near a building, lie in a ditch or low-lying spot. Do not seek shelter under bridges or overpasses—you are safer in a low, flat area. Use your arms to protect your head and neck.

If You're in a Vehicle

Tornado paths are unpredictable, so do not try to outrun a tornado in your car. Get out of your car, as vehicles can be quickly whisked into the air. Follow the "If You're Outdoors" guidelines outlined above.

After a Tornado

Continue to monitor your radio for instructions and updates. Wait for an "all clear," and stay put until emergency management authorities indicate that the danger of additional tornadoes has passed.

Unless it is absolutely necessary, do not enter buildings that show signs of damage. Wear appropriate gear if you are entering a damaged building, including steel-toed shoes, work gloves, and a hard hat. Do not use electrical circuits or lights; use flashlights or lanterns instead. Be alert for electrical appliances and other hazards that may be submerged under debris.

If you suspect leaking gas or wiring damage, open windows and leave the structure immediately. And do not use water from the tap. Instead, use water from your emergency supply kit, toilet tanks, or other clean sources.

Hurricanes

Hurricanes are the most powerful storms on earth. Annually about twenty tropical storms develop over the Atlantic Ocean, Caribbean Sea, or Gulf of Mexico, with six of these developing into full-fledged hurricanes and one or two striking the United States coastline. A devastating storm will strike our coasts every two or three years, on average.

Tropical storms pack wind speeds of up to seventy-three miles per hour and can be dangerous in and of themselves, often including strong wind speeds, heavy rain, and the potential for tornadoes. When sustained wind speeds greater than seventy-three miles per hour are reached, the storm is redefined as a hurricane.

Hurricanes are further classified by the "Saffir-Simpson Scale," based on their wind speeds as follows:

Category One: Sustained winds from 74–95 miles per hour
Category Two: Sustained winds from 96–110 miles per hour
Category Three: Sustained winds from 111–130 miles per hour
Category Four: Sustained winds from 131–155 miles per hour
Category Five: Sustained winds greater than 155 miles per hour

Hurricanes can cause widespread property damage, injury, and death in several ways, as listed below.

Storm Surge

The swirling winds around a storm can force water toward the shore. As more water is forced toward land, a hurricane storm tide can develop, raising normal tides as much as fifteen feet.

Inland Flooding

Inland flooding is responsible for more than half of all deaths associated with hurricanes and tropical storms during the past thirty years.

High Winds

High winds can devastate poorly constructed buildings and mobile homes. Flying debris, including signs, roofing material, and items left outside, can become deadly projectiles during hurricanes.

Tornadoes

Produced by hurricanes, these usually develop in the right-front quadrant of the storm.

Preparing for Hurricanes

To ensure that your family is as prepared as possible, review the guidelines we outlined in Chapters 1 and 2 of this book. Have an emergency supply kit ready, and make a family disaster plan.

In addition to the general steps we outlined in those chapters to help your family prepare for all types of emergencies, here are some additional steps that you should take before, during, and after the storm if you live in a hurricane-prone area.

Preparation before a Hurricane Ever Happens

- Make sure each family member knows where to go for shelter in case of a hurricane.
- Go over flood safety precautions with all family members. Review the information in Chapter 4 of this book regarding floods. Make sure all family members know how to turn off electricity, water, and gas, and make sure houseguests, babysitters, and caregivers know how to accomplish these tasks if they are staying with you as a hurricane approaches.
- Learn about your community's hurricane preparedness plans, including how you will be notified of the latest information, evacuation criteria

and routes, and policies for school closings and evacuations. Your local emergency management office or Red Cross chapter can provide this information.

- Show your children how to find updated emergency information on local radio and television stations.

Evaluating Your Home

Consider investing in hurricane shutters that are tested and approved for impacts and pressure. These shutters provide protection from flying debris and decrease the possibility of damage from the high pressure. If you choose not to purchase hurricane shutters, consider impact-resistant glass windows and sliding doors. Heavier than typical windows and doors, these have met the same tests as hurricane shutters.

Window safety film offers modest protection by keeping the glass together if a window blows in. If you do not have permanent hurricane shutters, you may wish to install anchors in the home for attaching plywood if a hurricane is predicted. Predrill holes in precut half-inch plywood boards so that you can install the plywood quickly. To make sure the plywood will fit when you need to install it, use a "Sharpie" type laundry marker to indicate which side of the plywood goes out, mark the orientation with an up arrow, and indicate which window each piece of plywood fits.

Check for any missing, loose, broken, or cracked materials, and repair or replace them. Make sure the areas around chimneys and vents are properly sealed. Check the attic for signs of roof leakage. Look for water stains, drip marks, and dark spots on roof structures and decking.

Glue any loose shingles down with roofing cement. If you have a tile roof, have a roofing professional replace any missing or loose tiles.

Make sure that porch roofs are adequately anchored with metal straps or other connectors. For carports, your goal is to keep the roof decking attached to the frame of the carport. You may be able add angle brackets that will help anchor the columns to the concrete slab. Anchor storage sheds to their foundations, or make preparations to strap a shed to the ground using ground anchors and ratchet straps crossed over the top of the shed. Large outdoor equipment like heat pumps or air conditioning compressors should be permanently anchored according to manufacturer's specifications.

When wind speeds exceed sixty miles per hour, the likelihood of water entering the home—though cracks, gaps, holes, siding, and around windows and doors—greatly increases. Use a urethane caulk around windows. Sealants can be used to block holes around gas lines, air conditioning pipes, external faucets and waterlines, external electrical outlets, exterior light fixtures, and dryer vents. If you use aluminum duct tape between the frame and sash of windows, make sure it is done from the outside and when the area is clean and dry. Perform regular maintenance on the weather stripping on doors, and remember that doors that swing out allow less water in than doors that swing in. Keep rain gutters and downspouts free of debris.

Have a professional engineer inspect your home and offer advice on how you can improve your home's ability to withstand hurricanes. If you are building a coastal home, consider elevating it. Check with the local emergency management office or the planning and zoning office for guidelines and possible financial assistance.

When a Hurricane Is Predicted or Imminent

A *hurricane watch* will be issued by the National Weather Service if there is a possibility of hurricane conditions reaching your area within the next twenty-four to thirty-six hours.

A *hurricane warning* will be issued *if* hurricane conditions are expected within the next twenty-four hours.

If a *Hurricane Watch* is Issued:
- Keep your car filled with gas.
- Listen to a battery-operated radio, television, or NOAA weather radio for updates and information.
- Review your evacuation plan with your family.
- Heed the advice of local officials if they suggest or mandate an evacuation. If told to evacuate, avoid flood waters and pay close attention to road closings. Evacuations will be discussed in more detail in Chapter 5.
- If instructed, turn off all utilities at their main switch. (Remember that gas utilities must be turned back on by a professional.) Unplug small appliances and turn off any propane tanks.
- Prepare your property. Move lawn furniture indoors, along with trash cans, hanging plants, and anything else that could become flying debris.

- Close hurricane shutters or board up windows.
- Remove outside antennas if possible.
- If you own a boat, make sure it is securely moored or moved to a safe place. Secure boats on trailers with ropes or chains, and use ground anchors and tie-downs to keep the trailer in place.
- If you have time to do so, move furniture and valuables to a higher floor.

If a *Hurricane Watch* is Issued:
- Listen for radio or television updates. Use the battery-operated radio in your emergency supply kit if power goes out.
- Heed the advice of local officials. If you are not told to evacuate, stay indoors on the first floor of your home. Keep away from windows, skylights, and glass doors even if they are covered.
- Keep all interior doors closed.
- If you live in a mobile home, get out and find other shelter, even if the mobile home is tied down.
- Start storing clean drinking water in plastic containers, clean sinks, and bathtubs.
- If you lose power, turn off all major appliances to avoid damage from a power surge when power is restored.
- Remember that the eye of a hurricane can be deceptive. The eye of the storm produces a calm period even though the storm is not over.
- Be on the alert for possible flooding and tornadoes.

Evacuation (More information on evacuation procedures appears later in this book.)

- Gather your emergency supply kit.
- Call your out-of-state contact to let them know of your evacuation and destination.
- Unplug appliances, and turn off electricity and the main water valve.
- Lock up your home.
- Continue to monitor your radio for updated information.
- Follow evacuation routes. Do not take shortcuts as certain roads may be blocked. Stay away from flooded roads, and be on alert for washed out bridges.

After a Hurricane

- If you have evacuated, wait for an "all clear" before returning home.
- Continue to monitor radio or T.V. for updates.
- Unless it is absolutely necessary, do not enter buildings that show signs of damage. Wear appropriate gear if you are entering a damaged building, including steel-toed shoes, work gloves, and a hard hat. Do not use electrical circuits or lights; use flashlights or lanterns instead. Be alert for electrical appliances and other hazards that may be submerged under debris.
- If you suspect leaking gas or wiring damage, open windows and leave the structure immediately.
- Do not use water from the tap. Instead use water from your emergency supply kit, toilet tanks, or other clean sources.
- Pump out flooded basements gradually (about one-third of the water per day) to avoid structural damage.
- Avoid floodwaters. Heavy rain and flooding that follow hurricanes can pose dangers for hours and even days after the storm.

Floods

Floods are not only among the most common of all natural disasters, but are also the most costly in terms of human hardship and economic loss. Sometimes floods can be anticipated hours or days in advance, but peaceful streams and rivers can also dramatically change into turbulent floodwaters in a matter of minutes. Like other specific disasters we've discussed, knowing what to do before, during, and after a flood is the key to keeping your family safe, as well as minimizing your economic loss.

Before a Flood Ever Strikes

- Prepare an emergency supply kit, and prepare a family disaster plan as discussed previously in this book.
- Familiarize yourself with the flood history of the area in which you live. Contact your local emergency management office or public works office to see if you live in an area prone to flooding.

- Install "check valves" in sewer traps to prevent floodwater from backing up into the drains of your home.
- Seal the walls in your basement with waterproofing compounds to avoid seepage.
- Contact community officials to find out what steps are in place, or planned, to stop floodwater from entering the homes in your area.

In addition, you and your family need to understand the various terms that emergency officials will use in describing a flood hazard. A *flood watch* indicates that existing or anticipated rainfall or snowmelt makes flooding possible. Monitor NOAA weather radio or your local news radio or TV station for information updates. A *flood warning* indicates that flooding is already occurring or will occur soon. If advised to evacuate, do so immediately.

A *flash flood watch* indicates the possibility of flash flooding—sudden and violent flooding, typically of short duration. If you live in a flash flood area, be prepared to move to higher ground, and monitor NOAA weather radio. A *flash flood warning* indicates that a flash flood is occurring. Flash floods are immediate, life-threatening emergencies. If you are in a flash flood area, you must seek higher ground *on foot* immediately.

When a Flood Is Predicted or Imminent

- In addition to the water supply in your emergency supply kit, fill plastic containers, bathtubs, and sinks with clean water.
- Move lawn furniture, outdoor decorations, and so on indoors.
- If you have time, move valuables to higher floors or a safe area.
- If told by officials to do so, turn off utilities at the main switch. Remember that if you turn off the gas, only a professional can turn it back on.
- Participate in local sandbagging efforts once you have secured your own home.
- If flooding in your home is going to be unavoidable, allow water to flow easily into your basement, or flood the basement with clean water yourself. This will help stabilize pressure and may help avoid structural damage to your home. Contact your local emergency management office for more guidelines on this procedure.

If You Are Caught in a Flood

Indoors

- Gather your emergency supply kits, and turn on a battery-operated radio to listen for any updated information.
- Go to the second floor or roof and wait for help.
- Do not attempt to drive on flooded roads.
- If your home floods, turn off utilities until authorities say it is okay to turn them back on.
- Do not attempt to pump out your basement until water has receded.

Outside

- Go to higher ground and remain there.
- Do not walk through flooded areas, and avoid downed power lines.
- Remember that levels of water depth can vary and only six inches of water can sweep an individual away.

In a Car

Do not drive on a flooded road. Six inches of water will reach the bottom of most passenger cars, causing loss of control and possible stalling. One foot of water will float many vehicles, and two feet of moving water can carry away most vehicles, including sport utility vehicles and pick-ups.

If You Are Instructed to Evacuate

- Evacuate as soon as possible, before floodwaters rise and/or you run into traffic problems.
- Follow evacuation routes.
- Do not take short-cuts as roads may be flooded or blocked.

After a Flood

- Continue to monitor news updates, and do not attempt to return home until emergency management officials indicate it is safe to do so.
- Be aware of areas where floodwaters have receded. Roads may have weakened and could collapse under the weight of a car.
- Stay out of any building that is surrounded by floodwaters, and use extreme caution when entering buildings since there may be hidden damage to foundations. Standing water may be electrically charged from downed power lines.
- Pump out flooded basements gradually, removing about one-third of the water each day, in order to avoid structural damage.
- Listen for news reports to learn whether your community water supply is safe to drink.
- Check for damage to utilities, and take steps immediately to begin restoring utility services. Report downed power lines to the power company. Service damaged septic tanks, cesspools, pits, and leaching systems as soon as possible. If you suspect that sewer lines are damaged, do not flush toilets.
- Because sewage and chemicals may be present in floodwater, wash or sanitize your hands whenever you have come in contact with floodwater.
- Clean and disinfect everything that got wet, including walls, floors, shelves, and belongings, since mud and residue left from floodwater can also contain sewage and chemicals.
- Foods that are not in waterproof containers and that may have come in contact with floodwater should be thrown out. Likewise, food containers

with twist-off lids, including soda bottles, cannot be disinfected if they come into contact with flood water and should be discarded.

- Wells inundated by flood waters should be tested before the water is used for drinking.
- Take pictures of damage for insurance claims.
- Take steps to dry out your home as quickly as possible to prevent mildew and mold from developing.
- *Check on financial assistance.* Many nonprofit agencies, as well as government and insurance programs, offer assistance to flood victims.
- If you have flood insurance, contact your agent as soon as possible to begin the claims process.
- *If your home must be rebuilt, consider additional flood-proofing measures in your rebuilding decisions.*

Flood Insurance

Most homeowners' insurance policies *do not* cover damages from floods. Contact your insurance agent to inquire about purchasing flood insurance, or call the National Flood Insurance Program (NFIP) at 1-888-379-9531 for an agent referral. Be aware that there is a thirty-day waiting period before your flood insurance takes effect.

If You Need to File a Flood Insurance Claim

- *Sort damaged from undamaged property.* Do not discard damaged property until the adjuster has seen it, unless the property poses a health hazard or hinders clean up by local authorities. If you must throw items out, take pictures of the property and save samples, such as fabric swatches, to corroborate your claim.
- Photograph all standing water inside and outside your home or business, as well as structural damage and high-water marks on building interiors and exteriors.
- *Use your home inventory (more discussion on this in the next section of this book) to create a detailed list of all your damaged or lost property.*
- *Make sure you are aware of legal deadlines in filing Proof of Loss claims and other paperwork.*

Earthquakes

Unlike hurricanes and most floods, earthquakes strike suddenly and without warning. Forty-one U.S. states are at moderate to high risk from earthquakes.

Earthquake magnitudes are measured by the Richter scale. An earthquake rated 3.5 or lower on the Richter scale is rarely felt, and earthquakes measuring between 3.5 and 5.4 on the Richter scale typically do no damage. Earthquakes measuring 5.5 to 6.0 can cause minor damage to well-constructed buildings and significant damage to buildings that are inadequately constructed. A 6.1 to 6.9 earthquake can cause significant damage within a fifty to sixty mile area, with a 7.0 to 7.9 earthquake wreaking havoc over an even larger area. Earthquakes measuring 8.0 or greater cause severe damage spanning several hundred miles.

Advance Preparations

If you live in an area where you are at high risk for moderate to severe earthquakes, consider these advance preparations in order to minimize damage to your home and protect your loved ones.

- Make sure shelves are securely fastened to walls and large, heavy items are placed on lower shelves. Keep any breakables, such as glass food jars, glass items, or china in a closed, latched cabinet.
- Do not hang any heavy wall hangings, such as pictures, mirrors, and so on, near areas where people sit or sleep.
- Brace overhead light fixtures.
- Inspect for potential fire hazards, such as defective or damaged electrical wiring or gas connections, and make appropriate repairs.
- Repair deep cracks in ceilings or foundations anytime they occur.
- Keep pesticides, weed killers, and other hazardous materials in a closed, latched cabinet.

During an Earthquake

- "Drop, cover, and hold." Drop to the ground, seek cover underneath a heavy piece of furniture, and hold on. If you are unable to hold on to an

object, cover your face and head with your arms. If possible, stay in an inside corner of a building, and keep clear of anything that can shatter or fall. Hold on until the shaking has stopped.

- If you are in bed, stay put, and cover your head with a pillow (unless you are under a heavy light fixture or other items).
- Only use a doorway if it is in close proximity and if it is strongly supported.
- Do not use elevators.
- If in a crowded public area, do not run to an exit. Stay clear of display shelves and similar items that could drop. Use the "drop, cover, and hold" technique described above.
- If in a theater or stadium, stay in your seat. Cover your head with your arms or crawl underneath your seat. Wait until shaking has ceased before exiting.
- Stay inside until shaking has stopped and it is deemed safe to go outside.
- Understand that power may go out and fire sprinklers and alarms may be activated.

If You Are in a Vehicle

- Stop the vehicle when it is safe to do so. Do not park near or under buildings, trees, overpasses, or utility wires.
- Stay in the vehicle.
- Once the shaking has stopped, avoid traveling on roads, bridges, and ramps that have been potentially damaged.

If You Are Outside

- Stay put, and keep away from buildings, utility wires, streetlights, and sign poles.
- Stay out in the open until the shaking has stopped.

If You Are Trapped

- Stay still. Moving about can kick up dust and debris.
- Use clothing or a handkerchief to cover your mouth.
- Tap on a pipe or wall to draw attention to yourself for emergency personnel. Try not to shout, as dust and other particles can be inhaled into the lungs.

After an Earthquake

- Realize that aftershocks do happen and can occur hours, days, weeks, or even months after an earthquake.
- Monitor news reports for instructions and updates.
- Do not enter buildings that show signs of damage.
- Use caution when opening closets and cabinets, as items may have shifted during the earthquake and could fall.
- Inspect gas, electrical, and water lines for damage, as well as utility lines and appliances.
- Check for damage to utilities, and take steps immediately to begin restoring utility services. Report downed power lines to the power company.
- Service damaged septic tanks, cesspools, pits, and leaching systems as soon as possible. If you suspect that sewer lines are damaged, do not flush toilets.

- Immediately clean up spilled medicines, bleaches, gasoline, or other flammable liquids. Get out of the area immediately if you smell gas or chemical fumes.

Earthquake Insurance

Earthquake insurance is usually *not* included in standard homeowner's insurance policies. Contact your insurance agent to inquire about purchasing earthquake insurance.

Winter Storms

Most snowfalls cause only minor inconveniences at worst and can offer recreational opportunities for your family that are not available at other times of year. But severe winter storms and blizzards (defined as a snowstorm with winds of at least thirty-five miles per hour and visibility reduced to less than a quarter mile) can be life-threatening. Homes can be isolated from the outside world, without utilities and other services. Motorists can become trapped in their cars.

While motor vehicle accidents are the major cause of death during winter storms, heart attacks from overexertion take a toll, and the prevalence of home fires increases as well. The general ideas for disaster preparedness that we've already discussed will cover most of the concerns you might face if you lose power, heat, or water, but here are some specific ideas for your consideration in the event of a severe winter storm.

Also, you should understand the various terms that emergency officials will use in describing a winter weather hazard. A *winter storm watch* indicates a possibility of a winter storm occurring in your area. A *winter storm warning* indicates that a winter storm is in your area or will occur in your area. A *blizzard warning* means that sustained winds and considerable blowing snow, with visibility reduced to less than a quarter mile, are expected to occur for a period of three hours or longer.

Preparing for Winter Storms

- Carry a bag of non-clumping cat litter in your vehicle to generate traction if you get stuck.

- Have rock salt or other ice-melt products on hand at home.
- Service your snow blower or other snow removal equipment before winter begins.
- Install storm windows before winter begins.

During a Winter Storm

- Know the signs and symptoms of frostbite and hypothermia. You'll find a discussion of these serious medical conditions in Section III of this book, where we talk about safety in the great outdoors.
- Gather pets and bring them indoors.
- Do not travel unless absolutely necessary. If you must travel, make sure to tell someone your destination, route, and expected arrival time, and take a completely charged cell phone with you.
- If you become stranded in your car, do not get out of the vehicle. Foot travel during a blizzard is extremely hazardous. Slightly open a window

away from blowing wind to let in air. Turn the engine on occasionally and huddle with others to stay warm. Newspapers, car mats, and maps can help with insulation. To maintain circulation, perform minor exercises, making sure you drink enough fluids. Be alert for signs of hypothermia and frostbite, taking care not to overexert yourself.

■ Be careful not to overexert yourself when shoveling snow, walking in deep snow, or pushing a car.

■ Review the additional information on extreme cold emergencies in Chapter 19 of this book.

Epidemics and Pandemics

An *epidemic* is defined as a disease outbreak that is showing up in more cases than would normally be expected, while a *pandemic* generally refers to an even more widespread outbreak affecting an even greater percentage of a population.

The "Spanish Flu" pandemic of 1918–1919 was the most devastating outbreak of disease in recorded history, killing an estimated thirty to fifty million people worldwide—far more than the outbreak of bubonic plague that took place in Europe in the fourteenth century. In the United States, approximately 675,000 lives were lost.

One of the medical community's greatest fears today is that a new form of influenza, to which humans have no built-in immunity, could develop and spread quickly around the world before vaccines could be developed and manufactured. Should such an outbreak occur, you will need to take steps to prevent your family from infection and perhaps even keep your loved ones in relative isolation for an extended period of time.

Many of the guidelines already outlined in this book will be applicable for your family in the event of an infectious disease outbreak. But there are additional steps that we should all consider in the event of a disaster involving an outbreak of severe and infectious disease.

Preparing Your Family

■ Keep in mind that, in a severe disease outbreak, commonly available items may be in short supply. If news reports indicate that a pandemic is occurring or likely, you may wish to increase the food and water supplies that would normally be included with your family's emergency supply kit.

- Likewise, at least a one-month supply of all medications used by family members should be on hand, particularly life-saving medications like those used to control diabetes. Include commonly needed items such as pain relievers, stomach remedies, and cough and cold medicine.

- Think about how you would handle caring for your children and elderly or disabled persons if schools and support services are closed.

- Make sure that you have plans in place to assure that your loved ones are taken care of in the event you are stricken with a pandemic disease.

Good Habits to Help Prevent Influenza

- Wash your hands often with soap and warm water for twenty seconds— long enough to sing the "Happy Birthday" song twice. If water is unavailable, use an alcohol-based hand gel. Cleaning your hands is the single best step that can be taken to prevent the spread of influenza.

- Don't touch your eyes, your nose, or your mouth without first carefully washing your hands.

- Get an influenza vaccination. An annual influenza vaccination can reduce your risk of getting seasonal influenza during a pandemic.

- Practice good health habits. By getting plenty of sleep, remaining physically active, managing your stress, eating properly, and drinking plenty of fluids, your body may be better able to fight disease. Look out for your own needs so that you can care for others if necessary.

- If you travel to areas with bird flu, avoid live bird markets, farms, or direct contact with birds or their secretions.

- Use a chlorine bleach mixture to disinfect items that people regularly touch, including door knobs, toys, keyboards, faucets, remote controls, phones, and light switches. Mix one-quarter cup chlorine bleach with one gallon of water to make a solution. Wipe on surfaces and allow ten minutes of contact before wiping off.

During a Severe Pandemic

- Keep your distance from others by avoiding crowds, limiting your travel, and working from home when possible.
- Unless they have already had influenza, only those who are essential for patient care or support should enter a home where someone is ill.

If a Family Member Is Ill

- To avoid infecting others, those who contract the flu should stay at home for about five days after the onset of symptoms. During an influenza pandemic, public health authorities will provide information on how long persons with influenza should remain at home.
- Place tissues used by an ill patient in a bag and throw them away with other household waste.
- Consider placing a bag at the bedside for this purpose.
- Wash dishes and laundry in your normal way. It is not necessary to separate eating utensils or linens and laundry used by influenza patients.

Traveling While Sick

If the ill person must leave home (such as for medical care), he or she should wear a surgical mask, if available, and take these additional steps:

- Wash hands with soap and water, or use an alcohol-based hand cleanser, after blowing or wiping the nose or handling contaminated objects and materials, including tissues.
- Cover the mouth and nose when coughing and sneezing, using tissues or the crook of the elbow instead of the hands.
- Dispose of tissues in the nearest waste receptacle after use, or carry a small plastic bag for used tissues.

5

If You Must Evacuate

In previous chapters, we've taken an in-depth look at the advance planning steps you and your family can take to help prevent and prepare for disasters, and I've tried not to repeat information that is general in nature. In this brief chapter, however, I want to simply provide, in one handy place, a checklist that you can follow at the moment you decide you are going to evacuate from a disaster area. Some of this information will repeat items that we've already covered. But if you need to evacuate from a disaster, I want you to be able to *turn to this chapter first, as a "quick reference" in the hours or moments when you're preparing to leave your home.*

Evacuation Checklist

- Gather your emergency supply kit and pack it in your vehicle, including items for pets and those with special needs.
- Unplug appliances and shut off utilities if instructed to do so.
- Ensure that all pets have proper collars, identification, and carriers.
- Place refrigerated medications in a sealed plastic bag, and put them in a cooler with cold-packs if available.

- Get in touch with your out-of-state "family contact." Let them know that you are leaving your home, where you intend to go, and your intended route of travel. Keep in touch with your family contact as you travel and when you arrive at your final destination.
- Round up all available cell phones in the household and take them with you, including chargers.
- Round up all available cash and take it with you, including quarters for vending machines.
- Pack a few toys, books, or games for children if you have time.
- In cold weather, make sure all family members have adequate, layered clothing.
- Pack sleeping gear such as blankets and sleeping bags in your vehicle if you have time.
- Continually monitor your radio for updated information, including information about evacuation routes.
- Follow evacuation routes. Do not take shortcuts as certain roads may be blocked.

- Take this book with you to begin reviewing the steps you'll need to take when you return home.
- If it becomes necessary to leave home for an extended period of time, file a change of address form with the U.S. Postal service to ensure that your mail will be redirected to your current address.

Safe and Well Web Site

Following the 2005 hurricane season, the Red Cross established the "Safe and Well" Web site, that enables people within a disaster area to let their friends and loved ones outside of the affected region know of their well-being. By logging onto the Red Cross public Web site, a person affected by disaster may post messages indicating that they are safe and well at a shelter, hotel, or at home and that they will contact their friends and family as soon as possible. During large-scale disasters, there will be telephone-based assistance via the 1-866-GET-INFO hotline for people who live within the affected areas and do not have Internet access but wish to register on the Safe and Well Web site.

People who are concerned about family members in an affected area may also access the Safe and Well Web site to view these messages. They will be required to enter either the name and telephone number, or the name and complete address, of the person about whom they wish to get information. Red Cross chapters will provide telephone-based assistance to local callers who do not have Internet access and wish to search the Safe and Well Web site for information about a loved one.

The Web site is secure, and information about the locations where people are staying is not published. The Red Cross does not actively trace or attempt to locate individuals registered on the Safe and Well Web site. For more information, or to link to the Safe and Well Web site, visit www.redcross.org.

6

Terrorism and Civil Unrest

Over the centuries, virtually all civilizations have experienced times of uncertainty and turmoil. But until recently, most Americans had long assumed that our nation was all but immune to great crisis, at least on our own soil. That assumption changed dramatically on September 11, 2001. On that morning, it immediately became clear that the threat of terrorism in the United States is very, very real.

Many of the precautions that we've discussed in previous chapters—and I won't repeat them here—are perfectly suited to help your family remain safe in the event of a terrorist attack. But there are a number of additional considerations that Americans would face in proximity to an attack involving nuclear, biological, or chemical weapons—often referred to as "weapons of mass destruction."

Nuclear and Radiological Attacks

Nuclear and radiological threats tend to fall into two categories—those posed by large nuclear bombs such as those that have been in the arsenals of many nations for several decades, and radiological dispersion devices often called "dirty nukes" or "dirty bombs." This latter type of device is smaller and intended to cause destruction not by destroying buildings and structures but by scattering radioactive material over a large area.

During a nuclear or radiological attack, finding shelter is your best means of protecting yourself. While the prospects of surviving a direct hit from a nuclear attack are minimal, those who seek shelter, especially in a blast or fallout shelter, will have a better chance of survival. Blast shelters are specifically constructed to offer some protection against blast pressure, while fallout shelters are designed to minimize exposure to harmful radiation.

Preparing for a Nuclear or Radiological Attack

- *Make sure you know your community's warning signals and what they mean.*
- Find out what local public buildings are designated as fallout shelters. Check with your local emergency management office for locations, and look for yellow and black fallout shelter signs (like those that were prevalent during the Cold War).
- Consider where you and family members would go if you could not get to a designated shelter—at home, at work, and at your children's school. Consider basements, subways, tunnels, structures without windows, or middle floors of high-rises. Protection is best achieved by heavy, dense materials such as concrete, bricks, and earth. The more of these materials you have surrounding you, the better.
- *If you live in an apartment or high-rise,* ask the building manager to identify the safest place to seek shelter and to explain to you what measures are in place to handle occupants of the building during and after an attack.
- *Review your community evacuation plans.* Know evacuation routes, relocation sites, and transportation plans for those with special needs.

In the Event of an Attack

- *If a warning has been sounded,* take shelter immediately, preferably below ground. Stay put until officials have deemed it safe to go outdoors.
- *If you are outside* and cannot seek shelter indoors, protect yourself with whatever means possible. Cover your head, and lie flat on the ground behind anything that could serve as protection. Take shelter even if you are miles from the attack area, since radioactive fallout can be carried by the winds.
- *If you are at home, stay in the area that affords the most protection,* and monitor official instructions using the radio in your emergency supply kit.

After an Attack

Never exit a shelter until officials have deemed it safe to do so. Understand from the beginning that your stay in a shelter could last up to four weeks.

Chemical and Biological Attacks

Chemical weapons might include a variety of agents, including vapors, aerosols, liquids, or solids that have toxic effects. Potentially, they might be released by bombs, or from aircraft, boats, or vehicles. Some chemical agents may be odorless and tasteless. They may have an immediate effect (a few seconds to a few minutes) or a delayed effect (several hours to several days). While potentially lethal, chemical agents are difficult to deliver in lethal concentrations.

Biological agents include disease-causing organisms such as bacteria or viruses, as well as toxins found in nature.

Preparing for a Chemical or Biological Attack

In addition to your basic emergency supply kit, the following items may be helpful in the case of a biological or chemical attack:

- A roll of duct tape and scissors
- Plastic sheeting to cover your doors, windows, and vents in a designated room to be used for shelter

During a Chemical or Biological Attack

Many of the measures that were discussed in our chapter on epidemics and pandemics may be applicable and helpful, especially against biological attack. In addition, here are some guidelines to follow during a terrorist attack using chemical or biological weapons.

- *Monitor your radio* for updated information and instructions, including whether or not to evacuate or stay inside.
- *If instructed to stay indoors, close all windows and doors.* Place damp towels over door cracks.
- *Shut off all HVAC systems* including furnaces, air conditioners, vents, and fans.
- *Go to an internal room,* windowless if possible, and seal off the room with plastic and duct tape. Ten square feet of floor space per person (an area just 3 1/2 feet square) will provide enough oxygen for one person for up to five hours.
- *Remain in your protected area* until local officials deem it safe.
- *If you are in an unprotected area,* seek shelter immediately and try to stay upwind of the contaminated area.

After a Chemical or Biological Attack

Before assisting others, decontaminate yourself first using the guidelines below. Decontamination as quickly as possible after an attack is the best means to minimize health risks.

After a Chemical Attack

- Know some of the symptoms of exposure. These may include muscle cramping, difficulty breathing, dizziness, nausea, vomiting, eye pain or vision problems, and burning or red skin.
- All clothing and any other items that may be contaminated must be removed. Do not pull clothing over your head but cut it off instead.
- Decontaminate your hands with soap and water.

- Take out contact lenses, and soak eyeglasses in household bleach.
- Use large amounts of water to flush eyes.
- Face and hair should be gently washed and rinsed.
- Blot other areas of the body with a washcloth that has been soaked with soapy water. Do not swab or scrub.
- Put on clean clothes, preferably those in drawers or closets that are less likely to have become contaminated.
- Use gloves and a mask when aiding in the decontamination of others.
- Anyone potentially affected by a biological or chemical attack should immediately seek medical attention.
- In the event of a major chemical attack, monitor official instructions on radio and television.

After a Biological Attack

- Understand that individuals may not realize that they have been exposed to biological agents until symptoms appear.
- If you have reason to believe that you've been exposed to a biological agent, follow the decontamination procedures outlined above, and place clothing and personal items in a sealed plastic bag.
- In the event of a major biological attack, monitor official instructions on the radio and television.

Civil Unrest

From time to time over the past fifty years, and from place to place, we have seen moments in American history where civil authority almost completely breaks down. We saw vast rioting in the 1960s, and rioting and looting in Los Angeles in 1992 after the acquittal of police officers involved in the arrest of Rodney King. And despite the heroism displayed by many citizens after Hurricane Katrina, portions of New Orleans became virtual war zones where criminals preyed on innocent victims almost at will.

Although the possibility of civil unrest is very real, FEMA and other government agencies have provided very little information to the public about protecting themselves and their families in the event of local or widespread riots. Because the threats we'd face during civil unrest would come not from natural causes or even from terrorist enemies but from people from within our own communities, this becomes a more difficult subject and one that requires us to rely more on our own values than would be the case in a natural disaster or terrorist attack.

If your loved ones, home, business, or employees are threatened in a riot, only you can decide whether to use force—including potentially lethal force—for protection. If you choose to own a firearm or have other defensive measures in place in your home or business, you'll find an in-depth discussion of these measures in Section VI of this book. Regardless of your decision when it comes to defensive measures, here are some ideas for diminishing the dangers that civil unrest might pose to you and your loved ones.

- Follow the guidelines outlined in previous chapters for assembling an emergency kit, establishing a family plan, and for evacuations.
- Know the location of your nearest police station.
- Stay abreast of the developing situation through news reports, keeping in mind that news reports will not have up-to-the-minute information.
- *During civil unrest, avoid subways and other areas from which you can't easily escape.*
- Secure your home and business as best you can, and remove small valuables to the extent possible.
- *Watch out for riot control chemicals since these affect criminals and law-abiding citizens alike.*
- If you're caught in a mob, move with the flow of the crowd until you have an opportunity to escape into a doorway, alley, or side street.
- *Do not stop your vehicle* unless it is absolutely necessary. If a crowd blocks your route, honk the horn, and carefully navigate through or around them. Keep your car moving if at all possible.
- Avoid the temptation to watch the riot from windows or balconies.
- Never drive toward police. Confrontations will likely be occurring in areas where police are stationed, and police will not be able to distinguish you from those breaking the law.
- Consider having a predesignated "safe room" in your home. For more information about safe rooms, see Chapter 14 of this book.

A Word for Business Owners

After the September 11, 2001 terrorist attacks, there was a great deal of concern among business owners and their employees about advance preparations for potential future attacks. In the years since, anxiousness about the next attack has faded. For the most part, we have gone back to our day-to-day work and lives. But the need for preparedness remains.

I've therefore decided to include some ideas for business owners in this section. Keep in mind that the responsibility of business owners to their employees extends beyond not just to preparing for terrorist attacks but to all of the other disaster situations that I talk about in this book. Many of the ideas can easily be translated from the home to a business setting.

I'll keep this section fairly brief. However, if you would like to begin putting in place a more detailed action plan for your business in the event of a terrorist attack or natural disaster, let me suggest that you start with the "Emergency Management Guide for Business & Industry," published by the FEMA. The guide can be found online at *http://www.fema.gov/business/guide/index.shtm*. This checklist is largely drawn from this FEMA guide:

- Appoint an individual or group to be in charge of developing your company's emergency management plan.
- Establish planning deadlines.
- Provide a budget for items that might need to be purchased, as well as for training for employees.
- Consider all emergencies, including fires, severe weather, hazardous material spills, natural disasters, terrorism, utility outages, and evacuations.
- Consider risks that might be unique to your business, including proximity to flood areas, earthquake fault lines, or potential disasters involving the products your company produces.
- Make physical enhancements as needed to improve your facility's safety and security.
- Make sure employees know where to find, and how to use, basic emergency equipment like fire extinguishers, First Aid kits, and automatic external defibrillators.
- Distribute an emergency call list to all employees with phone numbers for persons who would be involved in responding to an emergency. Include

numbers for your local emergency management office, utility companies, security companies, contractors, insurance carriers, and so forth.

- Conduct training, drills, and exercises to ensure that employees can respond quickly and properly in a crisis.
- Have a "shutdown" procedure in case your place of business needs to be completely evacuated.
- Have procedures to account for all employees, visitors, and contractors after an evacuation is complete.
- Train your employees in emergency management procedures, and provide additional training as your plan is improved or revised.
- Conduct a review of your entire plan at least once a year.

7

Coping with Disaster

It has long been recognized that those who serve our country in war, even those who escape without a scratch, can suffer psychological consequences of battle for years or even decades after the guns fall silent. This condition has been known from time to time as "shell shock" or "battle fatigue." Now, we call these symptoms "post-traumatic stress disorder" (PTSD). Furthermore, we now recognize that these symptoms can result not just from battle but from a wide range of psychological trauma—including the trauma of a criminal attack or a natural disaster.

Everyone who sees or experiences a disaster is affected to some degree. Many will experience sadness, anger, or anxiety about the future well-being of family or friends. However, those who experience more serious problems or who continue to have anxiety for a long period of time may benefit by seeking help from a psychologist or psychiatrist trained in the treatment of PTSD, or from faith-based organizations.

FEMA has identified a number of potential PTSD symptoms that may be experienced by adults in the aftermath of a disaster, including:

- Difficulty communicating thoughts
- Difficulty sleeping
- Difficulty maintaining balance in their lives

- Low threshold of frustration
- Increased use of drugs/alcohol
- Limited attention span
- Poor work performance
- Headaches/stomach problems
- Tunnel vision/muffled hearing
- Colds or flu-like symptoms
- Disorientation or confusion
- Difficulty concentrating
- Reluctance to leave home
- Depression, sadness
- Feelings of hopelessness
- Mood swings and easy bouts of crying
- Overwhelming guilt and self-doubt
- Fear of crowds, of strangers, or of being alone

Children, too, may experience symptoms of post-traumatic stress disorder, especially if they felt their lives were at risk, experienced the death of a loved one, friend or pet, were displaced, or lost items important to them. Watching repeated scenes from the disaster on television may be distressing for children, especially younger children.

After a disaster, many children will in fact show some mild changes in behavior, which will diminish with time. However, some children can exhibit long-term behavioral or psychological changes that will require help outside of the family. Children who experience a traumatic event before the age of eleven are three times more likely to develop psychological symptoms than are older children. These symptoms might include:

- A change from being obedient and caring to being loud and aggressive
- A change from being outgoing to being shy and afraid
- Nighttime fears, including fear of the dark or sleeping alone
- Becoming easily upset; crying or whining
- Loss of trust in adults who were not able to control the disaster
- Reversion to younger behavior
- Refusal to go to school or day care
- Feelings of guilt—that they caused the disaster

- Fear of wind, rain, or sudden loud noises
- Unusual irritability
- Risk-taking behaviors in older children, such as reckless driving, or alcohol or drug use
- Fear of leaving home, or avoidance of social activity

For the latest information as well as consumer ratings for products mentioned throughout this book, see www.SafeBookProducts.com. In addition, go to this Web site to sign up for a free monthly newsletter on new products to help keep your family safer.

SAFE IN THE HOME

"He is the happiest, be he king or peasant, who finds peace in his home." So said German playwright Johann Wolfgang von Goethe nearly two hundred years ago, and his words are no less true today. Other than our churches, synagogues, and other places of worship, there is no place more sacred to most Americans than the home. But although we as a nation have accomplished a great deal in recent decades in improving workplace safety, making cars more crash-resistant, and building better safety features into our machinery, far too many serious and even fatal accidents still take place right in our homes. In fact, according to the National Safety Council, Americans are eleven times safer at work than they are at home!

In this section of *Safe*, we'll look at ways to protect your loved ones—including your pets—from accidents as well as hidden threats that few Americans are even aware of. At the same time, we'll consider some of the measures that you can take to protect your home, your family, and your property from criminals who burglarize and rob an astounding *thirteen million American homes* each and every year.

By following some of suggestions in this chapter, you can make your home safer, more secure, and a place of even greater peace and happiness, be you peasant or king.

8

Accident Prevention in Your Home

In 2006, accidents accounted for more than 121,000 deaths in the United States, with motor vehicle deaths the most common cause. But falls and poisonings—accidents that typically take place in the home—were not far behind, with these two causes accounting for more than 48,000, or nearly 40 percent of the accidental deaths in America.

In this chapter, let's take a look at some of the most common causes of accidents in and around the home, and at some ideas about improving the safety of almost any household. In the next chapter, we'll consider some additional accident-avoidance measures you can take that are geared specifically for infants, youngsters, teenagers, and older members of your family.

Remember: In the event of any serious accident or emergency in your home, call 9-1-1 immediately.

Falls

For all age groups, falls are the leading cause of home injury and related death. Falls from stairways and ladders tend to be the most serious, but these accidents can and do occur in every room of the house. Here are several ideas that might help you prevent falls in your own home.

- Keep walkways clear, particularly near stairways.
- Use non-skid backing or double-sided tape to secure throw rugs, and use non-skid throw rugs in bathroom and kitchen areas.
- Clean up grease and water spills immediately.
- Install handrails on both sides and down the entire length of stairways.
- Inspect your home for lamp cords or other loose electrical cords that could be tripped over.
- Know the common side effects of medications that family members take. Some medicines, or combinations of medicines, can cause dizziness leading to falls.
- Install bathroom safety equipment such as grab bars for older family members or those with balance problems or who are taking medications that can cause dizziness.
- Use bath mats or slip-resistant stickers in tubs and showers.
- Improve lighting where necessary, especially near stairways.
- Do a home safety "walk through" and look for additional hazards that might lead to falls. If you have toddlers or children, get low and look at your home from their level to see potential hazards from their point of view.
- When leaning a ladder against a wall, position it so that the horizontal distance from the foot of the ladder to wall is about one-fourth of the working length of the ladder.
- Never use a ladder near power lines or other utility lines.
- Keep your ladder free of oil, grease, wet paint, and other slipping hazards.
- For stepladders, make sure that the metal spreader—designed to hold the front and back sections in an open position—is fully locked.
- Don't work from the top, or the top step, of a stepladder.

Poisonings

After falls, poisonings are the second-leading cause of accidental death in the home. But whereas the risk from falls increases as we grow older, youngsters are at far greater risk of poisoning, with half of all poison-related accidents involving children six years of age or younger. Ninety percent of these accidents take place at home, and many involve household products or items that might not be obvious to us, such as personal care products, hand sanitizers, and even household plants.

If you think someone has been poisoned, call the American Association of Poison Control Centers immediately at 1-800-222-1222. Post this number next to your telephone or with your other readily available emergency numbers, and include it in your cell phone address book.

This hotline is a central number for America's sixty poison control centers, which provide around-the-clock poison expertise and treatment advice by phone. All calls are answered by a medical professional and can provide immediate poison exposure management instructions. To the best of your ability, be prepared to describe the name of the product or poison, when it was ingested, and how much was ingested.

Some of the more common household items that cause poisoning emergencies each and every year include:

- Prescription and over-the-counter medicines, including pain relievers and vitamins
- Disinfectants, deodorants, and air fresheners
- Virtually all spray products
- Polishes and cleaning powder
- Hand sanitizers
- Cosmetics
- Soaps, detergents, and shampoo
- Toilet bowl and drain cleaners
- Lye and bleach
- Kerosene and lighter fluids
- Mothballs and pesticides
- Paint remover and turpentine
- Fertilizers and weed killers
- Insect and rodent poisons and slug bait
- Insect repellent

In addition, here are just a few of the household, garden plants, and cut flowers that could be toxic to humans or animals. There are many others.

- Amaryllis
- Asparagus fern
- Chrysanthemum
- Daffodil
- Iris
- Mistletoe
- Tulip

Here are some of the steps you can take to reduce the risk of a poisoning accident taking place in your own home:

- Store medicines and household products locked up where children cannot see or reach them.
- Store poisons in their original containers. Not only will you know what the product is, but you'll be able to describe it more precisely should the product cause a poisoning emergency.
- Use child-resistant packaging, but remember that no container is absolutely childproof.
- Protect yourself as well as your family. Read the precautions on products including those regarding ventilation and protecting your skin and eyes.
- When using any potential poison, store it safely away immediately after use, preferably in a locked cabinet. This includes taking the product or medicine with you to answer the door or pick up the phone if children are around.
- If you take medicine when children are watching, don't refer to it as "candy."
- Preferably, take medications where children—who learn by imitation— can't watch.
- Avoid placing houseplants where youngsters and pets can reach them, unless you know with certainty that the plants are not toxic.
- For any poison exposure to the eyes, call 9-1-1 and begin flushing the eyes with cool water. Continue flushing for fifteen to twenty minutes or until help arrives.
- Do not induce vomiting unless instructed to do so by specific package instructions or a medical professional.

Scalds

A scald is a burn from hot liquid or steam. According to the U.S. Consumer Product Safety Commission, emergency rooms treat more than sixty thousand scald injuries each year, with one of every three cases involving children under fifteen. The most frequent injuries came from tap water, and these injuries can occur with just *one second* of exposure.

Here are some ideas to prevent scald injuries in your home:

- Set your hot water heater to 120°F. Your water heater may be capable of heating water well beyond this point, so don't assume that your heater is set properly. You'll also save money on your utilities by keeping your water heater at this setting.
- Keep hot drinks away from the edge of tables and counters, and remember that young children can pull down tablecloths and placemats.
- Do not hold or carry a child while you have a hot drink in your hand.
- When cooking, turn the pot handle away from the front of the stove, or use the back burners.
- Keep children away from the stove when you are cooking. The Home Safety Council suggests putting tape on the floor to establish a "No Kid Zone" for your youngsters.
- Keep in mind that youngsters and older people have thinner skin and burn more quickly.
- When bathing children, test the water with your hand and stir the bathwater to avoid hot spots.
- Consider installing scald-prevention tub spouts and showerheads that prevent hot water burns. If the water gets hot enough to cause a scald, these special spouts can shut off the water flow.

If you burn or scald your skin, immediately begin cooling the area with running water and keep the area in cool water for at least three minutes. If the burn or scald looks serious, call your doctor or 9-1-1 immediately. Do not use grease, butter, or ointments on a serious scald or burn, and do not remove clothing from the affected area.

Burns

Burns are classified by medical professionals according to their degree of severity. *First degree burns* cause redness and swelling of the skin but *generally* do not require medical attention unless they involve substantial portions of the hands, feet, face, groin, buttocks, or a major joint. *Second degree burns* involve blistering of the skin and often severe pain but generally do not require medical attention unless the burn area is more than three inches in diameter or involves the aforementioned body areas. *Third degree burns* may appear black, or dry and white, and involve all layers of the skin. These burns, large or small, should always be treated as medical emergencies.

More than half a million Americans receive medical treatment for burn injuries each year, and far more suffer less serious but nevertheless unpleasant burn injuries. Many of these injuries, of course, take place in house fires, which have been discussed previously in this book.

Here we'll take a look at a few additional ideas for safeguarding yourself and your loved ones against burn injuries.

- Always keep a pan lid nearby in case of grease fires, and remember that water will make a grease fire worse and can cause the fire to spread. Use a fire extinguisher.
- As mentioned earlier in the book, have fire extinguishers installed in your home, and know how to use them.
- Never leave a hot iron unattended, and unplug heating appliances like irons and heating pads when not in use.
- Use an insulating screen to prevent burn injuries from fireplaces. Keep children away from fireplaces and portable heaters, and remember to close fireplace doors before going to bed.
- To allow sunscreen to take full effect, apply it twenty minutes before going outside.
- Remember that sunburn can occur more quickly when you're on the water or snow.
- When hiking, camping, hunting, or skiing in snow-covered areas on bright days, wear sunglasses, goggles, or glacier glasses to prevent "snow

blindness"—a burn injury to the inner eye which can cause pain, temporary loss of vision, and even permanent scarring of the cornea.

- Refuel power equipment only when the engine has been given an opportunity to cool.
- Store gasoline in approved safety containers, in well-ventilated areas, and preferably in a shed that is not attached to your home.
- Do not handle gasoline near a heat source or indoors, and do not use gasoline to light a fire or barbeque.
- Understand that a very large percentage of gasoline burns occur among fifteen to twenty-four year olds.
- Teach your kids gasoline safety when instructing them in the use of lawnmowers and other power equipment.
- If your clothing catches fire, "Stop, drop, and roll," to try to extinguish the flames.

If you suffer a serious burn, call 9-1-1 immediately. Begin cooling the area with running water and keep the area in cool water for at least three minutes. *However, do not use water for large or severe burns, especially third degree burns*, as this can cause potentially life-threatening complications, including dehydration, shock, infection, and more. Do not use grease, butter, or ointments on a serious scald or burn, and do not remove clothing from the affected area. Severe burns should be covered with sterile bandages from your emergency supply kit, and, if possible, the burned area should be elevated above the level of the heart.

Drowning

On average, drowning kills an average of nine Americans each day, and drowning is the second-leading cause of accidental death among children up to fourteen years of age. But the areas where drowning is most likely to occur change as children get older. Most infant drowning accidents occur in bathtubs, toilets, or buckets, whereas most drowning accidents among children aged one to four occur in pools, and children five to fourteen years old are more likely to drown in open water sites.

In Chapter 21 of this book, where we talk about safety during recreational activities including fishing and boating, we'll look at some additional ideas for preventing drowning and on-the-water accidents. Here, I'd like to focus on safety for our youngsters in and around the water.

In general, keep in mind that drowning can occur in seconds and that even a small container of water can pose a hazard for very young children. In drowning deaths involving children in residential pools, most had been out of sight less than five minutes and were in the care of one or both parents at the time the drowning occurred.

Here are some specific ideas for preventing drowning accidents, with special emphasis on pool safety issues:

- Empty water containers immediately after use, and store these containers out of reach.
- If you have a pool, install a fence at least four feet high to keep the pool area secured. The fence should include a self-latching gate that opens outward and latches on the inside, where the latch cannot be reached by children.

- After using the pool, remove floats and toys that can make the area even more attractive to children.
- Remember that at your home pool, *you are the lifeguard* and that many drowning accidents are completely silent. Don't be distracted with reading, phone calls, or lawn care when you're the lifeguard.
- Teach your children to swim as early as four years of age. Swimming lessons will give your youngsters a great start toward a wide range of lifetime recreational opportunities.
- Know how to perform CPR as discussed previously in this book. CPR has been shown to provide improved outcomes in some potential drowning victims.
- Manufacturers generally recommend that children fourteen and under should not be allowed to operate personal watercraft.
- At the beach, understand rip currents and know how to deal with them. Rip currents occur when two currents moving in different directions meet. The result is an outrushing of water along a narrow path that can move a swimmer away from the shore quickly. If caught in a rip current, do not try to swim directly toward the shore—you will not be able to match the current. Instead, swim calmly in a direction parallel to the beach. Once you are out of the current, swim at an angle, away from the current and toward the beach. If you cannot reach shore, yell for assistance and float or tread water until help arrives.

Deep Water Situations

In deep water situations, do not attempt to rescue a drowning victim unless you have expert training in lifesaving techniques. You are likely not only to endanger yourself, but to create an even more difficult situation for other rescuers. Follow these steps:

- HAVE SOMEONE CALL 9-1-1 and provide an exact location of the emergency.
- REACH with a pole, oar, fishing rod, towel, or anything else handy.
- THROW anything that will float, including a life preserver or ring, a cooler, empty milk jug, or whatever is available.
- ROW. Use a boat to reach the victim. Be extremely cautious about using a motor to approach the victim; use oars if possible.

Hidden Threats in Your Home

So far, we've discussed home safety issues that can be seen and foreseen. However, it's important to understand that some of the dangers we could potentially face in our homes cannot be detected by our five senses. We'll talk about several of these dangers here—how to detect them and how to deal with them.

Carbon Monoxide

Colorless and odorless, carbon monoxide is often called the "invisible killer." Each year, about five hundred Americans die from unintentional carbon monoxide poisoning not related to fires, and another fifteen thousand are poisoned. Any appliance in your home that burns fuel can be a possible origin of carbon monoxide, and proper installation and maintenance of these fuel-burning appliances is the most significant step you can take toward reducing your family's risk. Here are some additional steps to consider:

- Every home with flame-containing appliances or fireplaces should have a carbon monoxide alarm. Alarms that are hard-wired into the home's electrical supply should also have a battery back-up. Change the batteries for these units when you replace those in your smoke alarms. Carbon monoxide detectors should not be placed near fuel-burning appliances (since these may emit a small amount of carbon monoxide on start-up), in very humid areas such as bathrooms, or within fifteen feet of a heating or cooking appliance.

- Regularly check your appliances to make sure they are functioning properly. Check immediately for malfunction if your supply of hot water has decreased, if your furnace is constantly running or not heating the house properly, if soot appears on vents or appliances, or if an appliance has a burning or odd odor.
- Have your heating system (including chimneys and vents) inspected annually.
- Do not run generators in an attached garage or near open windows or doors.
- During a power outage, do not attempt to heat your home with a gas dryer, range, or oven, and never use catalytic (flameless) chemical heaters inside the home.
- Do not use gas-burning tools in a closed room.
- Know the signs and symptoms of carbon monoxide poisoning, which can include headache, fatigue, nausea, shortness of breath, and dizziness. Should you suspect carbon monoxide poisoning, leave the home immediately. Go to a neighbor's house to call for emergency medical attention.

Radon

Radon is responsible for twenty-one thousand lung cancer deaths per year and, in fact, is the second-leading cause of lung cancer. Radon is a tasteless, colorless, and odorless gas created by uranium decay in soil and rock such as granite and shale. The gas enters homes though cracks in walls, basement floors, and foundations, and it can contaminate water, especially in private wells. Unlike carbon monoxide, victims of radon poisoning do not suffer symptoms until after years of exposure.

Radon is measured by picocuries per liter (pCi/L) of air. The Environmental Protection Agency (EPA) recommends that remedial action be taken to decrease home radon levels above four pCi/L, and the American Lung Association believes that up to one-third of radon-related deaths might be prevented by reducing home radon levels below this EPA-recommended threshold.

Several do-it-yourself kits to test radon levels in your home are readily available at hardware and home improvement stores. Begin with a short-term test that will take between two and ninety days. Carefully follow the instructions on the kit, particularly with regard to placement of the testing material. If this test indicates a radon level of two pCi/L or higher, use a long-term test of ninety days or more for confirmation of the results as well as to gain a more accurate picture of your home's radon concentrations. Should you find that you have elevated radon levels in your home, you'll want to take steps to reduce it.

While you cannot entirely eliminate radon, it can be reduced by making repairs to prevent this soil-based gas from entering your home, by sealing cracks in floors and walls that make contact with the soil. In addition, many homeowners employ "sub-slab depressurization" to prevent airflow from the soil into the home. These systems prevent radon from entering your home by drawing the gas from below the structure and venting it through a pipe to the air above the home. To find out more about these systems, talk to a contractor who is certified by your state to perform radon mitigation in the home.

Indoor Air Pollution

In today's modern world—and I believe that this is unfortunate—we Americans spend far more time indoors than any previous generation. What's more, the EPA estimates that indoor air tends to be two to five times more polluted than outdoor air and can in fact be as much as one hundred times more polluted. The dangers posed by this pollution can range from asthma, allergic reactions, and upper respiratory infections to organ damage and even cancer. This pollution can result from a number of sources.

"Biological" pollutants are living or once-living organisms that can include animal dander, dust mites, bacteria, viruses, fungi, mold, and pollen. They need moisture and nutrients to grow, and tend to be found around moist areas (in heating and air conditioning systems, basements, bathrooms, and kitchens), in bedding, or in areas where pets tend to spend their time.

To reduce biological pollutants, particularly if you have family members with respiratory problems, consider some of these ideas:

- To reduce dust mites (microscopic organisms that breed in areas such as sofas, stuffed chairs, carpets, and bedding), wash bedding in hot water every seven to ten days, and regularly vacuum carpets.
- Regularly bathe and groom pets.
- Have furnaces, heat pumps, central air conditioners, and furnace-attached humidifiers routinely inspected and cleaned by a professional.
- Run exhaust fans in bathrooms as needed to prevent moisture buildup.
- Dehumidifiers and air conditioners can help decrease moisture in the home and thereby help reduce biological pollution.
- Immediately take steps to remove any mold growing in your home, particularly after a flood or plumbing problem.
- If your home has water damage, discard items such as mattresses, wicker furniture, and straw baskets that have been damaged by water or may contain mold. Wet insulation should also be replaced. You do not need to discard furniture, carpet, drapes, or stuffed toys if they can be restored through a thorough washing in hot water or by steam cleaning.

A variety of air cleaning devices is also available to help you combat indoor air pollutants. Air cleaners can be incorporated into the heating and air conditioning system of the home, and portable units are available to improve air quality in individual rooms.

These cleaners are classified by the means in which they trap particles from the air. Mechanical filters move air through some type of filter, trapping the particles in the filter. Electronic filters induce an electric charge into airborne particles and cause to them to be attracted to room surfaces.

When choosing an air-cleaning device, look at the minimum size of the particle that they are capable of removing from the air in your home. One of the best qualities you can look for is a HEPA (high-efficiency particulate air) certification, which indicates that the device can capture at least 90% of all particles as small as 0.3 micron (1 micron = 1 millionth of a meter). You may also want to look for a HEPA certification when purchasing a vacuum cleaner.

10

Accident Prevention and Safety for Specific Family Members

Common sense tells us that different age groups have different accident risk profiles. Poisoning accidents are more common among toddlers, while teenagers are more prone to motor vehicle accidents, and older people are more susceptible to falls.

In the last chapter we focused on preventing major types of accidents. Without repeating what we already covered there, this chapter of *Safe* will provide you with some added safety ideas that are tailored to specific members of your family: infants, youngsters, teenagers, and the elderly.

Safety for Infants

For children less than one year of age, the single leading cause of accidental death is suffocation due to choking (an obstruction in the airway) or strangulation (a constricting of the windpipe due to an external cause). Parents therefore need to understand that vigilance about choking hazards—including checking age labels on toys—is one of the most important ways in which we can provide a safe home for our infants. In fact, many of the items mentioned here, and in the next section on safety for young children, will be focused on preventing suffocation.

Crib Safety Tips

- Evaluate the condition of the crib in which your infant will be sleeping. Make sure there is no broken or missing hardware, and do not use cribs that are old, broken, or modified since these cribs may not meet the safety standards your infant requires.
- There have been many crib recalls over the years. Check with the U.S. Consumer Product Safety Commission (www.cpsc.gov) to make sure your crib is not subject to any recall action.
- Carefully follow the manufacturer's instructions when assembling new cribs.
- Place cribs away from windows, curtains, and blind cords.
- Crib mattresses should be firm. Make sure the crib mattress and sheet fit snugly inside the crib and that there are no more than two finger widths between the crib side and mattress.
- Do not place stuffed animals, pillows, toys, or soft bedding in a crib.
- Some studies indicate that crib bumpers are unsafe, and many safety organizations, including SIDS awareness groups (see Sudden Infant Death Syndrome below), recommend against their use.
- If you use a crib toy that attaches to the side of a crib, carefully follow the manufacturer's instructions when attaching the toy.
- Remove mobiles and other hanging toys from the crib as soon as your child can reach up and touch them.
- Never use an electric blanket in the bed or crib of a small child or infant.

At Bedtime

- Dress infants in one-piece sleepers that fit snugly and are labeled as flame-resistant. Nothing should cover the infant's head.
- Do not use sleep-positioning devices.
- Never place more than one infant in a crib.
- Remember that baby monitors are not perfect. You should always be within earshot of your sleeping infant.

Sudden Infant Death Syndrome

Each year, 2,500 infants die from Sudden Infant Death Syndrome (SIDS). Also called "crib death," the causes of SIDS are unknown, and autopsies of these infants do not show an explainable cause of death.

The National Institute of Child Health and Human Development instructs parents to place infants on their backs when putting them to bed. Infants placed on their stomach are five times more likely to die in their sleep than those placed on their backs, and infants who usually sleep on their backs are eighteen times more likely to die in their sleep when placed on their stomach. Infants do need time on their stomach to strengthen their necks and upper body but should be placed in this position only when they are awake and you can carefully supervise them.

Safety for Young Children

Once children become mobile, our problems as parents increase—because our children are now capable of seeking out and finding their own hazards. Parents walk a fine line. We know that the world is full of risks and that, to learn about those risks, our children will have to experience some of them firsthand. At the same time, we don't want to expose our children unnecessarily to dangers that can easily be controlled without stifling our child's sense of adventure, boldness, and fun.

No home can be completely safe, and no checklist can be complete for every situation or replace common sense. But here are some ideas that might be helpful as you seek to eliminate the key risks that children face in the home. Keep in mind that there are many additional resources on the Internet; search "child-proofing" for more suggestions.

- Install gates at both the top and bottom of all stairways, but do not use accordion gates; these are a strangulation hazard.
- Remember that a window opened just five inches can create a hazard for children. Keep windows closed and locked as appropriate for the age of your children, and remember that window screens do not prevent falls.

- Consider using corner bumpers on hard-edged furniture and fireplace hearth edges.
- Use side railings for children just getting used to "big kid" beds.
- Secure washers and dryers with locks, as children tend to use these as hiding places.
- Bolt any free-standing bookcases to the wall to prevent toppling.
- Avoid loose electrical cords that could present a strangulation hazard or that could enable a child to pull a lamp, appliance, or other item from furniture or counters.
- If stove knobs are easily accessible to children, use protective covers to prevent kids from turning them.
- Store propane grills where children cannot reach the knobs.
- Remember that a child can drown in just one inch of water. Use appropriate products to childproof your toilets and/or bathroom doors.
- Store firearms and ammunition so that they are not accessible to children.
- Install child-resistant covers on electrical outlets.
- Keep matches and lighters out of children's reach.
- Avoid small foam toys that can present a choking hazard.
- Keep plastic bags out of children's reach.
- Shorten curtain and blind cords.
- Remove the plastic end caps on doorstops or replace stops with a one-piece design to prevent choking.
- Place locks on medicine cabinets and in storage units that contain poisons, and remember that vitamins, in sufficient doses, are poison to young children (and even adults).
- Keep all cleaning materials, as well as toiletries such as toothpaste and mouthwash, locked up.
- Place houseplants out of children's reach, and know the names of the plants in your home in case of ingestion.
- Keep on hand activated charcoal (which absorbs some poisons) and Syrup of Ipecac (used to induce vomiting). However, do not use these products unless instructed to do so by the manufacturer's label on the ingested product, or by poison control medical professionals.
- When using a fertilizer or pesticide on your lawn, read the label. The manufacturer may recommend that children and pets be restricted from the area for some period of time.

- For outdoor activities, apply sunscreen to children twenty minutes prior to sun exposure, to allow the sunscreen to build up to full effect. For good eye health later in life, provide polarized, UV-protective sunglasses for children as appropriate.
- Know CPR as discussed in Section I of this book. CPR training also includes the "Heimlich Maneuver," used to clear a blocked airway during a choking emergency.

Safety for Teenagers

As our children become young adults, they'll begin to face entirely new categories of risks, including potential dangers in the online world that have emerged only within the past few years and which will be discussed in Chapters 23 and 24 of *Safe*. As parents, we'll probably want to *encourage* our teenagers to participate in certain activities that involve some risk—like outdoor sports, martial arts, and so forth—to help them along a lifetime path toward self-confidence and good health. However, there are three areas—drug and alcohol abuse and driver safety—where we will want to remain particularly careful in keeping our young adults safe.

Drug and Alcohol Abuse Prevention

Although drug abuse among teens has decreased in recent years, half of all twelfth-graders in the United States still admit to having tried an illegal drug. One-quarter of these twelfth-graders admit to being current drug users, and *one-quarter of fourth-graders* report to having been pressured by peers to try drugs or alcohol.

For more information about teenage drug and alcohol abuse prevention than can be included in this brief chapter, I recommend that you visit the Web site of the Drug Abuse Resistance Education (DARE) program at www.dare.org. Founded in Los Angeles in 1983, the DARE program is offered cooperatively between local schools and police departments and is now available in 75 percent of America's school districts. The DARE Web site also offers important advice for any parent seeking to help a child avoid the dangers of drug and alcohol abuse. Here are some basic suggestions for all parents to help protect young people from the dangers of drugs and alcohol:

- Help your kids develop the tools and confidence they need to get out of alcohol-related or drug-related situations and stand up to peer pressure from those who abuse drugs.
- Make sure that the parties your teenagers attend will be alcohol-free and supervised by adults.
- Set curfews and enforce them with clearly defined penalties.
- Encourage open dialogue with your children about drug and alcohol abuse. Make sure your children understand that they can ask you anything and that you will give them an honest answer.
- Get your kids involved in adult-supervised after-school activities.
- Set down a firm no-use rule for alcohol and drugs, making sure your child understands that the consequences will be severe, long-term, and non-negotiable.
- Be aware that prescription and over-the-counter (OTC) medications have tremendous potential for abuse. Commonly abused prescription drugs include pain relievers (OxyContin, Vicodin, Percocet, Lortab, etc.), tranquilizers (Valium, Xanax, etc.), stimulants (Adderall, Concerta, Ritalin, etc.), hypnotics, and sedatives. Commonly abused OTC drugs include sleep aids such as Tylenol PM, motion sickness remedies such as Dramamine, and cough medicines containing dextromethorphan.
- Be aware of changes in your child's behavior that could be warning signs of drug abuse.
- Stay involved in your child's life, and sit down for dinner as often as possible. Use the time to talk instead of eating in front of the T.V. You'll not only have a better relationship with your child, but you'll be more likely to notice behavior or mood changes that could indicate a problem with alcohol or drugs.

Teenage Driving

As a parent, your first line of defense to keep your teenager safe behind the wheel, or as a passenger in a vehicle driven by another teenager, is to know the facts.

- Motor vehicle crashes are the leading cause of death for U.S. teens, accounting for more than one in three deaths in this age group.

- Teenage drivers are four times as likely as older motorists to be involved in a car crash.
- The presence of teenage passengers increases the crash risk of unsupervised teen drivers, and this risk increases with the number of passengers.
- Crash risk is particularly high during the first year that teenagers are eligible to drive.
- Teens are more likely than older drivers to speed and tailgate, and the presence of male teenage passengers increases the likelihood of these risky driving behaviors. Sadly, 39 percent of young male drivers and 26% of young female drivers were speeding at the time of their fatal crash.
- Compared with other age groups, teens have the lowest rate of seat belt use.
- About 25 percent of crashes killing young drivers involve alcohol. In a national survey conducted in 2007, nearly three out of ten teens reported that within the previous month they had ridden with a driver who had been drinking alcohol. One in ten teenagers reported having driven after drinking alcohol within the previous month.
- Teen crash risk is particularly elevated when driving at night or when fatigued.
- 40 percent of sixteen to nineteen year olds killed in passenger vehicles in 2005 were riding as passengers. Keep in mind that your responsibility as a parent extends beyond your teenage *driver* to include your teenage *passenger*.

There are proven methods to helping teens become safer drivers. Mostly these involve two broad ideas: imposing driving restrictions on your teen that can be eased gradually as he or she gains more driving experience, and imposing strict ground rules on your teenage driver when it comes to obeying traffic safety rules and avoiding drug and alcohol use.

Driving Restrictions

Many states have now implemented "graduated driver licensing" (GDL) programs that introduce driving privileges in stages and allow teens to get their initial driving experience under lower-risk conditions. Two commonly imposed restrictions include limits on nighttime driving and limits on the number of passengers who may be in the vehicle. Some of the ideas listed below may be appropriate for your teenage driver if your state does not already have a GDL program in place. Keep in mind also that a child's readiness to take on the responsibility of driving should be determined by you, not by a birthday. Consider your child's level of responsibility as you grant him or her extended privileges behind the wheel.

Here are some ideas that you may wish to implement in granting driving privileges to your teen as well as protecting your young adult who is a passenger in another vehicle driven by a teenager:

- Have your teen driver log one thousand miles, or sixty hours, behind the wheel before driving alone.
- For the first three to six months, do not allow your teen to use the radio while driving.
- Limit night driving until your teen gains greater experience behind the wheel.
- Do not allow your teen to carry teen passengers until he or she has been licensed for six months, and likewise do not allow your teen to ride with a driver who has been licensed for less than six months. After the initial six-month period, allow no more than one passenger for another six months.
- Mandate seatbelt use by all persons in the vehicle.
- Require your teen to pull over before using the cell phone. According to the Governors Highway Safety Association, twenty-one states and the District of Columbia already ban cell phone use by novice drivers.
- Some parents find it helpful to have a contract clearly stating the policies and expectations regarding driving, spelling out clear consequences for drinking and drug use, traffic tickets, and infringement of other driving rules. In any case, make sure your teen understands there will be severe, long-term, and non-negotiable consequences for any drinking or drug use while driving.
- Have your teen participate financially in the costs of driving to help underscore the responsibility the teen is undertaking.
- Make sure your teenager knows how to respond and whom to call in case of an accident, including an accident involving injuries.
- Remember that, in extreme cases, parents have the right to request that a child's license be revoked.

Safety for the Elderly

Americans aged sixty-five and over account for the largest number of home injury-related deaths. Without repeating some of the general ideas that we've discussed previously, here are some ideas for making your home safer for older family members who live with you or who may visit from time to time.

- For older family members, pay very special attention to the discussion on falls in the previous chapter. Be especially careful to take precautions in bathroom, tub and shower areas, and near stairways.
- A simple change in footwear—to sturdy shoes with non-slip soles—can improve fall safety among the elderly.
- If you're getting older yourself (and all of us are), stay active to maintain balance, strength, and flexibility.
- Be certain that elderly family members are able to hear smoke alarms while asleep. Test the alarm and, if your family member is not awakened, purchase smoke alarms that use strobe lights and/or vibration to signal the presence of smoke or fire.
- Understand that taking the wrong medication, or taking too much medication, are two of the key causes of poisoning among older adults. While a simple pillbox may help keep track of medications, there are several products and services available that provide a more thorough approach to monitoring medication. Contact your family doctor or gerontologist for more information about these products and services.
- Maintain a written list of all medications your elderly family member is taking, including dosage, and take this list with you when visiting the doctor or having a prescription filled.

Security for Your Pets

For many of us, pets are simply part of the family. These special family members have special considerations when it comes to staying safe.

Preventing the Loss of Your Pet

- Make sure that your pet has a collar that provides your contact information if the lost pet is found. Keep the collar updated if you move or change your phone number.
- Consider a fence for your dog, or an electronic pet containment system such as Invisible Fence®. Electronic systems work by delivering a mild shock to your pet if he or she tries to cross the fence boundary. An audible warning signal indicates to your dog or cat that the boundary is close by. Test your system to make sure you can hear the audible signal, and understand that the system will no longer work in the event of a power outage.
- Have your pet microchipped by your veterinarian. These small chips, implanted under the animal's skin, can be read by animal shelters and animal control officials to locate pet owners. Be sure to register the microchip using the paperwork your veterinarian provides.

- New technology offers pet owners GPS pet tracking capability using a device attached to the animal's collar. Available through companies such as ZoomBak and Global Pet Finder, these products generally require a monthly service fee.
- If your pet is lost, remember that animals are capable of traveling great distances and that someone who finds your pet may take it to a shelter that is not the nearest to your home. Continue checking shelters frequently for your pet.

Fire and Disaster Safety for Pet Owners

- Be sure that your pets are part of the family disaster plan we discussed in this book, and include provisions for your pets in your emergency supply kit.
- In rehearsing your family's fire safety preparations, include your pets in your drills.

- Pay attention to your pets if they act strangely. Cats and dogs can smell fire before you can.
- Consider placing stickers on your doors that indicate what pets are inside so that responders will be aware of them in case of fire or other emergency. Give your neighbor a key to your home in case your animals must be removed quickly for any reason.

12

Home Security and Crime Prevention in the Home

So far we've talked mostly about threats presented by the natural and man-made world—everything from disasters to the products we use in our home every day. In this chapter, we'll turn our attentions to an entirely different type of threat, posed by other human beings who choose not to live by our laws.

The harsh fact is that, every few seconds, another burglary takes place in America. Each year almost thirteen million homes in the United States are burglarized, with an average of $1,300 in individual property loss.

Some of these burglaries are carried out by "spur of the moment" criminals, or drug users looking for quick and easy cash. They are carried out with no prior planning. Instead, the criminal sees an object in plain view inside a home or vehicle, breaks a window, and takes it. Or he sees a garage door open and no one else in sight, grabs something quickly, and leaves.

Other criminals may put a little more forethought into their work, planning their crimes in advance based on a known opportunity.

Professional criminals, on the other hand, will put a great deal of planning into their crimes. They target homes in expensive neighborhoods and evaluate the security and layout of the properties. They may spend many days trying to determine when a home is most unlikely to be occupied and whether or not a security system is in place.

Just as knowledge and planning can help you protect yourself against natural disasters and hazards in the home, knowledge and planning can help you dramatically reduce the risk that your home will be the next to be burglarized. The measures we can take to reduce our risk generally fall into four categories: *Detection measures* that alert homeowners, neighbors, and law enforcement officials to the presence of an intruder; *preventive measures* that make homes more difficult to enter; *deterrent measures* that make homes less attractive to criminals; and *managerial measures* that help protect all properties in a neighborhood and/or help protect your home when you're away.

Detection Measures

Detection measures, simply put, are security systems that detect the presence of an intruder, then alert and notify others. Typically a security system sounds an alarm to alert the occupants of the home and, hopefully, scare the intruder away. In addition, a security system can notify authorities of an unauthorized entry into a home so that law-enforcement personnel can be summoned within moments after a burglary begins.

Homes with security systems are three times less likely to be broken into than homes without security systems. Ninety-six percent of those in law enforcement believe that security systems are beneficial to both police and citizens, and 84 percent of police believe that alarm systems are an effective way to protect citizens and property.

How Security Systems Work

A basic security system is composed of three parts: the control unit (which often includes a keypad where you arm and disarm the system); sensor(s), including contacts on doors and windows, and/or motion detectors; and an annunciator with lights and/or sirens to alert residents and neighbors to the presence of an intruder. When armed, a sensor will detect an intruder and send a signal to the control unit, which will then trigger the annunciator. If the system is monitored by a security company, a signal will also be sent to the monitoring station, which will initially contact the homeowner to rule out a false alarm. If the monitoring station is unable to reach the homeowner or receives an incorrect password, police will be notified to respond. There are two types of security systems: hardwired and wireless.

Hardwired Systems

This type of system requires wires and cables to connect each component of the alarm system. Typically, this wiring will be installed during the construction of a home, and the increasing popularity of these systems has made this wiring almost as common as cable television wiring in new homes. Installing hardwired systems after construction of a home is costly and messy, since drywall, paint, and other structures of the home will be affected during installation.

Wireless Systems

Wireless systems use radio waves to allow communication between the various system components. Because there are no cables and wires to run, these systems can be easily installed into existing homes or apartments, and at a lesser cost. Wireless systems are also upgradeable as your security needs change.

Both hardwired and wireless systems have the ability to provide protection in various ways, starting with the window and doors of your home. At these potential access points, magnetic contacts form a circuit between a door and its frame, or between a window and a sill. If the alarm is on and the door or window is opened, the circuit is broken and sets off the alarm. For full protection, all exterior entry doors (including the door from the garage) as well as all first-floor windows should be armed with these contacts.

Some companies also offer "glass break" detectors designed to sense frequencies emitted by the sound of breaking glass. If this sound is detected, the alarm is triggered. Typically, a sensor is required for each room of the home.

Additional protection can be gained through the use of Passive Infrared (PIR) motion detectors that can detect an intruder who has already entered the home. These detectors can sense the body heat of someone moving about in your house. If your windows are not integrated into your security system, motion detectors can play a pivotal role in detecting an intruder who may gain access to your home. Because motion detectors do not discriminate between an intruder and a pet, many security system companies now offer "pet-immune" detectors that ignore heat movement below a certain height, preventing your pets from causing false alarms.

In addition—because you and your family are far more important than your possessions—you can add "spot protection" to your security system which enables you or a family member to manually set off the alarm in the event of an intruder. Commonly known as a "panic button," this feature can be included on your alarm system keypad or can be purchased as a stand-alone device to be added to your keychain or to a pendant. These devices have the added convenience of enabling you to arm or disarm your system when you pull in or out of your driveway.

Finally, some security systems give you the option to enhance your system with medical alert notification, and detectors for smoke, carbon monoxide, and water leaks that communicate directly with the monitoring station. A "line cut" option will trigger the alarm company if your phone lines are cut. And some companies offer intercom services through which homeowners can communicate directly with the monitoring station from the keypad without the use of a phone.

Obviously you need to be able to trust the people who are monitoring your home. In selecting a security system company, contact the National Burglar and Fire Alarm Association (NBFAA) for a referral to a local company that adheres to that organization's Code of Ethics. You can also ask your insurance agent for referrals.

Once your security system company has successfully installed your system, use it! Many security system owners simply don't arm their system regularly when they leave home, or they assume that burglaries only take place during nighttime hours. Not true. More than 60 percent of all burglaries occur between 6 a.m. and 6 p.m., while most people are at work. If you are home during the day, most systems have "home" and "away" settings. The "home" setting activates the entire system except for the motion detectors, so you can move freely about your home without false alarms and still have the perimeter of your home protected.

Cameras and Surveillance

Again, homes with security systems are three times less likely to be burglarized. But if you live in a high-crime area, you may want to take additional steps for further protection and peace of mind.

Video surveillance is another way to detect intruders and protect your home. Cameras not only deter criminals, they also provide powerful evidence to convict a burglar, vandal, or home invader. Video surveillance also allows you to monitor nannies, babysitters, house cleaners, and other workers in your home. Lower costs and better technology have allowed consumers more choices and affordability for installing video surveillance systems, and more homeowners are including them in their overall home security plan.

Like security systems, camera surveillance can either be hardwired or wireless. Like hardwired alarm systems, hardwired camera systems require wires and cords, and tend to be more time consuming and expensive to install. Wireless systems tend to be less expensive, easier to install, and more versatile.

You may choose to monitor your home overtly, with cameras in plain view to deter criminals, or you may choose to monitor your home covertly, with cameras out of view. If choosing the latter, be sure to check with local law enforcement agencies regarding surveillance laws in your area.

Like many technologies, video surveillance systems have changed greatly in the past few years. While earlier systems relied on VCR tape to record images, newer digital systems allow data to be stored on computer hard drives. In addition, the latest IP-based (Internet Protocol) video surveillance system can transmit images in real time via the Internet or a wireless connection, and several cameras can be monitored from a single remote location. Data can be compressed, easily stored, and encrypted for added security.

Again, for referral to a security professional who can discuss options with you for a video security system, contact NBFAA or your insurance agent.

Preventive Measures

In the end, security systems work because they make it less likely that a burglary will be successful. Preventive measures work in a similar way. Preventive measures include a wide range of precautions that can make a home break-in more difficult and therefore less attractive to a potential criminal. The longer it takes for a potential intruder to gain access to your home, the more discouraged he is likely to become and the more likely he will be to move on to an easier victim.

Here are some of the easier ways to deny a burglar easy access to your home, family, and property.

Secure Your Doors

- Make sure your exterior doors are no less than 1 3/4 inches thick, and in good condition. If you have a hollow core door, replace it with a solid one. If your door shows signs of deterioration, make the necessary repairs. If you have a decorative door, consider opting for security over style. Doors with floating panels can be easily broken when kicked.

- Install peepholes on exterior doors that do not have windows. Make sure the peepholes allow you to see the welcome mat and out to both sides.

- If you are constructing a new home, make sure there is a space of at least forty inches between nearby windows and the door lock, so an intruder cannot easily reach in and unlock the door after breaking a glass window.

- Check the fit of your door. The space between your door and the door frame should not be more than 1/16 of an inch. Doors should not move from side to side when pushed. If necessary, reinforce the door frame, especially where the hinges attach.

- Replace short screws on hinges with screws at least two inches long on the door side and three inches on the frame side. Screws should go through the frame and into wall studs.

- Remember that your door is only as secure as its lock and strike plate (the strike place is where the lock fits into the door). When *Consumer Reports* tested solid wood, steel, and fiberglass doors, they found little difference among the three. In all cases, the first failure usually occurred around the lock. *Consumer Reports* recommends using a reinforced metal strike plate installed with at least three-inch screws that lodge into the framing, beyond the door jamb.

- For garage doors, don't rely on your garage door opener to provide protection. Make sure the door can be locked from the inside.

- For sliding glass doors, make sure that the track clearances don't easily allow a burglar to simply lift your door off its track. You can also place a wood or metal "Charlie Bar" in the track when the door is closed. Or drill a hole through the inside door frame and into the outside door frame (being careful to avoid drilling into the glass) and insert a metal pin into the hole. Some doors included a keyed lock between the inside and outside doors as an added security protection.

Secure Your Keys

- When moving into a new home, have a locksmith rekey your locks.
- Make sure all family members keep track of their keys.
- Keys given to babysitters, cleaners, and so on should always be accounted for.
- Should you lose a key, consider rekeying your locks.
- Never mark your keys with your name or address. Should you use a parking valet at a restaurant or hotel, give the valet your car keys only, not your house keys.

Secure Your Locks

Simple key-in-knob locks are the least secure. Instead, install deadbolt locks on all exterior doors. According to the National Crime Prevention Council, "Deadbolts can withstand the twisting, turning, prying, and pounding that regular keyed knobs can't."

Look for deadbolts where the bolt extends at least one inch in the locked position to resist ramming and kicking, hardened steel inserts to prevent the bolt from being sawed off, and a reinforced strike plate with extra long mounting screws that lodge into the framing, beyond the door frame.

There are three common types of deadbolt locks. "Single-cylinder" deadbolts are opened with a key from the outside and with a thumb latch from the inside. "Double-cylinder" deadbolts must be opened with keys from both sides. Double-cylinder deadbolts provide better security for doors that include decorative windows, or that are near windows, because they prevent an intruder from unlocking the door from the inside simply by breaking a window.

If you use double-cylinder deadbolts, make sure everyone in your household knows where the keys are, and check with local law enforcement agencies. Some jurisdictions prohibit these locks for residential use because they can make it impossible for residents to exit quickly in case of a fire or other emergency.

According to *Consumer Reports*, price may in fact be one of the better indicators of lock security. "For the ultimate in protection, plan on spending more. High security locks may cost about $160 to $200 each, but in testing they were the only ones that could withstand picking and drilling."

Secure Your Windows

The best doors and the best locks may not offer much protection if your windows are not secured as well. Remember that, most of the time, a criminal is looking for an easy opportunity. In fact, approximately 22 percent of burglars gain access to homes through first-floor windows.

It may not be practical to install keyed locks on all windows. Like deadbolt locks, keyed windows can make it more difficult to exit your home quickly in case of emergency, and many jurisdictions prohibit these types of locks for residential use. Nevertheless, there are a number of ways for you to make your windows more secure.

- For *standard double-hung windows*, make a stop rod (a vertical Charlie Bar) from a one-inch dowel. Cut the dowel to sit on the top of your lower sash and extend to the top of the window frame, making it impossible to open the window unless the dowel is removed.
- For *casement windows*, increase security with a chain lock, similar to those used on hotel doors.
- For *sliding windows* (which can be lifted off their tracks just like sliding glass doors), insert screws along the inside of the upper window track to make it more difficult to maneuver the window off its track. As with a sliding door, you can also place a wood or metal bar (Charlie Bar) in the track when the door is closed.
- For *basement windows*—a favorite of burglars because they are usually concealed by shrubs—consider security bars. While these would be an eyesore in most of your home, basement windows are generally out of view. Security bars can be fitted with a quick-release mechanism so that these windows can remain usable as an emergency exit in case of fire.
- For *windows with air-conditioning units*, make sure the unit is firmly bolted in place so that it cannot be pushed in by an intruder.
- For *all windows*, you may wish to consider window security film, a nonvisible polyester sheet that is fitted to the inside of the window. A burglar striking the window with enough force will be able to shatter the glass, but the glass will stay together and prevent entry. Window security film is fairly expensive and should be installed by a professional.

Deterrent Measures

Deterrent measures are steps you can take to convince a potential burglar that your home is not a good target. Most burglars look for homes that appear unoccupied. Deterrent measures can include timed lights, cars in the driveway, and other measures that give the impression that someone is home or that an intruder is likely to be seen by homeowners or neighbors.

Simply by trimming shrubs a few feet away from your house, you can eliminate hiding places and make it more difficult for a burglar to remain concealed while he tries to gain access to your home. Or when planting shrubs near windows, consider thorn-bearing plants such as barberry, hawthorn, or roses that can make your home more attractive to your neighbors but unattractive to potential burglars.

In addition, there are two very common deterrent measures that can make your home a less attractive target for criminals: lighting and dogs.

Lighting

Lighting can be one of the least expensive ways to deter a burglary. Good lighting provides the ability to view visitors or possible intruders on your property, rids your property of potential hiding spots, and deters intruders from moving about the outside of your home.

- Install exterior lights that provide illumination around the complete perimeter of your home. Adjust the direction of bulbs to best eliminate blind spots where a potential intruder could hide without being seen, and make sure there is no gap of darkness at the base of the house. For increased security, install motion-sensing floodlights that illuminate back or side yards when someone approaches your property.
- Install lights at each doorway. Use a one-bulb fixture on each side, or a two-bulb fixture (so that the doorway will still be lighted if one bulb burns out). Consider adding sensors that turn the lights on at dusk and turn them off at dawn.
- Install lights with motion sensors above your garage door and any basement doors so that any movement outside these doors will cause the lights to come on.

Watch Dogs and Guard Dogs

Studies have shown that homeowners with watch dogs or guard dogs are less likely to become victims of a home invasion or burglary, and dogs deter criminals in more ways than one. First, no one likes being bitten by a dog. But even beyond the threat of a bite, a barking dog is bad news for a burglar. Even a small, yappy dog—who will hear a potential intruder long before you do—serves as an early warning system to alert you and your neighbors to the presence of a potential burglar.

"Watch dogs" are dogs that can alert homeowners of an approaching stranger, whereas "guard dogs" are trained to protect their owners by physically restraining or even injuring an assailant.

Almost any breed of dog can be trained as a "watch dog," although breeds more prone to barking might be more appropriate. A few of the more popular breeds in this latter category would include the Akita, Boxer, Dachshund, Irish Setter, Pekingese, Poodle, Samoyed, Shetland Sheepdog, Springer Spaniel, Welsh Corgi, and almost any of the terriers.

Guard dogs, on the other hand, tend to come from a few specific breeds that are more aggressive, aloof, trainable, strong, courageous, and resistant to counterattack. Some of the more popular guard dog breeds include the Belgian Malinois, Doberman Pinscher, German Shepherd, Mastiff, Pit Bull Terrier, Rhodesian Ridgeback, and Rottweiler.

Dogs that are intended to serve as guard dogs require extensive training that is usually better left in the hands of a professional, and guard dog training programs may require that your dog be left at the training kennel for the full length of the program. Guard dogs are also instructed in basic commands and are trained not to accept treats except from the owner or handler. Your entire family will need to participate in the training process so that no family member will be perceived as a threat.

In short, the decision to own and train a full-fledged guard dog should not be made lightly. In fact, should you decide to get *any* dog, make sure that you can give him or her a good home first, and consider your security needs second. Find a breed that not only provides the protection you want, but who will be a beloved member of your family.

Two more tips when it comes to watch dogs and guard dogs: First, keep your dog inside when he or she is performing watchdog or guard dog duties. If left outside, a dog is susceptible to attack from an intruder.

Second, don't install a dog door. Thieves have been known to bring small children with them, send them through dog doors, and have the youngster open the main door. A dog door therefore provides an open entryway to your house that will undermine every other precaution you've taken to protect your home.

Managerial Measures

Managerial measures are precautions that do not physically alter your property but give the impression that your home is occupied and/or that someone is keeping an eye on your property. These include measures taken when the home is unoccupied for extended periods of time, and proactive programs such as Neighborhood Watch.

Neighborhood Watch Programs

Neighborhood Watch programs, like our nation itself, are built on the strength of citizens joining together for a common cause—in this case to provide

greater crime protection for all the homes in a neighborhood or community. Founded by the National Sheriffs' Association in 1972, this program now has more than fifty million participants nationwide and has a proven track record of reducing crime. In some cases, burglaries have plummeted more than 75 percent after Neighborhood Watch programs were initiated. As a result of the September 11, 2001 terrorist attacks and the aftermath of Hurricane Katrina, many Neighborhood Watch groups have now expanded their efforts to include emergency preparedness and preventing terrorism.

Check with local law enforcement to see is there is a Neighborhood Watch near you. If so, join. If not, consider starting a program yourself.

Starting a Neighborhood Watch Program

After the National Sheriffs' Association began Neighborhood Watch, it was left to local law enforcement officials to create local groups. By contacting local law enforcement officials, you can find the officer or deputy who is assigned to help create and support these local watch groups. The officer will provide training for Watch leaders, block captains, and members.

To launch and implement a Neighborhood Watch program, the National Sheriffs' Association recommends these steps:

1. Recruit and organize as many neighbors as possible.

   Again, check with local officials first to see if Neighborhood Watch already exists in your community. If not, talk with neighbors regarding their security concerns. For example, you may find that many local citizens share similar concerns about a local gang or a drug problem in your area. Gauge the interest of local residents in starting a Neighborhood Watch program, and ask if they would be willing to attend an initial planning meeting with law enforcement officials.

   You may also wish to contact local community organizations. Residents who may be hesitant to join a Neighborhood Watch program may be more inclined to do so if the program is working with their church, synagogue, business, association, or club. In addition, these organizations may be able to provide meeting spaces, the use of office equipment, or volunteers.

2. Contact your local law enforcement agency and schedule a meeting.

   Set up a time for an initial meeting with neighbors and law enforcement officials to discuss the program. Hand out flyers and post signs communicating to neighbors the date, time, and place of the meeting. Call neighbors to remind them of the meeting. At the meeting, discuss how law enforcement agencies and local residents can work together to fight crime and resolve community issues in your area.

3. Discuss community concerns and develop an action plan.

   Identify the key issues that are of concern to law-abiding citizens in your community. Prioritize these concerns, and begin outlining concrete action steps that can be taken to address the problems faced by local residents. Law enforcement officials can participate in helping you with these steps.

You'll also want to begin organizing your Neighborhood Watch and begin assigning specific duties to specific members.

4. Hold regular meetings and training.

Once the group has been formed and goals have been outlined, regular meetings should be scheduled where volunteers can receive training in crime prevention. Local law enforcement agencies will be able to suggest and provide many training options.

5. Implement a phone tree and take action steps.

Once your Neighborhood Watch program is up and running, you'll want to have a way of immediately passing along important information to all members of the group, particularly in the event that a crime has taken place or an emergency is in progress. The overall goal is to have neighbors watching out for neighbors and reporting problems to each other through an organized, dependable communications process. In addition, you'll want to take steps to make sure that the initial enthusiasm that helped to launch the program is maintained over the years, through events, newsletters, and other efforts to keep the program visible and to recruit new members.

Note: Much of the material above is drawn from the *Neighborhood Watch Manual* prepared by the National Sheriffs' Association in partnership with the U.S. Justice Department. To learn more about Neighborhood Watch, or as a first step toward starting a program yourself, you may wish to read the full manual at http://www.usaonwatch.org.

Protecting Your Home When You're on Vacation

As a "managerial" measure, Neighborhood Watch is designed to give a potential thief the idea that local residents are vigilant and will report suspicious activity anywhere it takes place in the community. However, when you're away for an extended period of time, you'll want to take extra steps to give the impression that your home is still occupied.

Leaving the same light on all day and night will not convince a potential burglar that you're at home. However, there are many measures you can take that can make it more difficult for a potential burglar to determine that you're not home.

- Use automatic timers on interior lights so that the lighting pattern within your home changes throughout the day. Set the timers so that bedroom lights go on and off in the morning and evening, kitchen and living room lights are on during the afternoon and evening hours, and so forth. You can also use these timers to turn appliances such as televisions on and off.
- Consider motion-activated lights that turn on interior lighting if movement is detected outside your home.
- Stop your mail and newspapers, or ask a friend or neighbor to collect these each day.
- Arrange to have regular chores such as grass mowing and leaf raking done while you're away.
- If you have a security system, let your security company know that you intend to be away.
- Disable your garage door opener and lock the door from the inside.
- On your luggage tags, make sure that your home address is not readily visible to strangers.
- Hire someone you can trust to house-sit while you are away. Particularly in the summer months, you may be able to find a responsible college student to stay at your home at a very reasonable daily rate.
- Let trusted neighbors know that you'll be away and ask them to report any suspicious activity at your home. Provide a phone number at which you can be reached in an emergency.
- Do not change your voice mail recording to indicate that you're away.
- Do not completely shut down your air conditioner in the summer. Turn it down instead.
- Do not close all blinds and shades. Keep window treatments in their usual position.

If You Live in an Apartment

Many of the above measures—including detection, preventive, deterrent, and managerial measures—are perfectly applicable to those who live in apartments. But here are a few ideas, assembled into one place, which might be particularly helpful for apartment residents.

Inside Your Apartment

- Make sure your door has a deadbolt and a peephole.
- Secure any sliding glass doors with a Charlie Bar as described earlier in this chapter.
- When going out, leave a radio or light on.
- When leaving for an extended period of time, let neighbors and the building manager know.
- Make a habit of keeping the door locked, even when you are at home.
- Do not use your first name or initial on mailboxes or doors.

Evaluating Your Existing Building, or When Considering a New Building

- Is there a system in place that controls access to and from the building?
- Is there twenty-four-hour lighting that keeps walkways, entrances, hallways, stairways, laundry rooms, and storage areas well lit?
- Are fire stairs that are on the ground floor only able to be opened from the inside?
- Is the mail center in a common area that is well-lit and secure?

Moving to a New Apartment

- Make sure the locks have been changed.
- If you have a hollow door, ask if you can replace it with a solid-core one.
- Make sure all smoke detectors (in the apartment and common areas) are in working order.
- Familiarize yourself with fire evacuation routes.
- Consider a portable alarm system for doors and windows.

Working with Apartment Neighbors

Get to know your neighbors and consider starting an "Apartment Watch" group similar to the Neighborhood Watch concept. If the complex is large, consider establishing a volunteer tenant patrol to monitor any suspicious activity and provide security escorts for the elderly or handicapped in the event of an emergency. You can also organize social events for tenants to get to know one another. Ask the landlord for help.

13

Protecting Your Valuables

Recording Your Inventory

The measures we've looked at so far are mostly aimed at preventing crime—making your home less attractive to criminals and thereby reducing the chances that your home will be selected as a target. But no countermeasures are 100 percent effective. That's why most security experts also recommend that homeowners create an inventory of the items in their home. If your home is burglarized, an inventory may help with identification of recovered items or may even help convict a thief. If your items are not recovered, your inventory will prove invaluable in filing an insurance claim to receive compensation for your loss.

You can record your inventory by hand, simply writing down a description of each item. But the process will be far easier—and more effective in the long run—if you use a digital camera or camcorder to make a photographic or video inventory of your possessions. Chances are, if your home is burglarized, the thieves will take only items that are easy to carry and easy to convert to cash. However, if your home is destroyed by fire or a natural disaster, virtually everything you own may need to be replaced. To ensure that you receive a full and fair settlement from your insurance company, you need to make a record of *everything* in your home—not just valuables but your books, cookware, and office supplies—everything down to your socks and underwear! Otherwise, you may never receive the full amount you deserve if your home is destroyed.

With digital technology, you can create a recording of everything you own, at almost no cost. A videotape or photographs of your personal property will also make proof of ownership much easier to prove to insurance companies, especially if you do not have an original receipt. Follow these steps to create your digital inventory.

- In each room, start with a photograph or video recording of the entire room (using a still camera, multiple photographs will be needed).
- Record the objects that are immediately visible in each room—furniture items, fixtures, lighting, curtains or window treatments, carpets, artwork, computers, electronics, etc. Make sure that each item is shown in its entirety.
- As necessary, open drawers, closets, and cabinets before moving to the next room. Make a record of jewelry, personal items, books, dishes, silverware, toys, and so forth.
- When photographing small items, you can include a ruler in the photograph if you wish to document the size of the item.
- For especially valuable items, create a written log to accompany your digital records, including a description of the item, any identifying marks, model and serial numbers, color, size, and value.
- *Do not keep the sole copy of these records in your home.* Keep a copy of your video or photographs, along with accompanying written documents as well as other paperwork such as appraisals, in a safety deposit box or at another off-site location.
- Update your inventory as needed when you make major purchases, or every few years.
- Remember that videotapes, CDs, and DVDs may deteriorate after a few years. If you haven't made an entirely new inventory, back up your existing records on fresh digital media.

Common Household Items and Furnishings to be Inventoried:

- Furniture of all types, including beds and lamps
- Windows and doors, if these have been upgraded from standard builder's grade
- Curtains and window treatments
- Carpets and area rugs
- Cabinets
- Shelving
- Lighting fixtures
- Major appliances
- Small appliances
- Exercise equipment
- Recreational equipment (firearms, fishing and camping gear, boat accessories, bicycles, etc.)
- Artwork
- Pots and pans
- Silverware and cooking utensils
- Dishes
- Clocks
- Books
- Electronics
- CDs and DVDs
- Jewelry
- Clothing
- Toys
- Linens
- Luggage
- Garage items such as lawnmowers
- Shop tools
- Garden tools
- Ladders

Tagging Valuables—"Operation Identification"

"Tagging" valuables means placing a unique number on selected items so that they can be positively identified in the event the items are recovered after a theft. By taking this step, you can deter theft (because tagged items are more difficult to resell), and you are more likely to recover items that are stolen. In addition, your tags can help provide hard evidence against a criminal who is caught with your goods.

Law enforcement agencies across the country have used "Operation Identification" programs for more than thirty years, working alongside citizens to tag, identify, and return stolen property. These programs have been shown to dramatically reduce burglaries in areas where they have been implemented. Operation Identification involves a simple four-step process.

First, property owners engrave a specific code on their valuables. Some cities provide a unique thirteen-digit code to citizens in their jurisdiction while others request that citizens engrave their drivers license number. *Do not* use your Social Security number as an ID number on your property. Engraving pens can be purchased for a few dollars from a hardware or home improvement store. Ideally, items should be engraved in an area where the ID number cannot be easily removed.

Here are some examples of items that are commonly stolen and that are easy to engrave:

- Televisions
- Stereo equipment
- Computers
- Automobile wheels
- Outboard motors
- Power tools
- Cameras
- Binoculars
- Bicycles
- Lawnmowers and snow blowers

Second, add the tagging information—including which items were tagged and where the ID code is located on the item—to your home inventory log as described above.

Third, if your local Operation Identification program includes a process for registering specific items, do so.

Fourth, consider displaying stickers on your doors or windows indicating that your valuables have been tagged and registered with Operation Identification. These stickers advertise to potential thieves that your valuable property is marked and will therefore be difficult to resell.

Storing Your Valuables

Generally speaking, thieves are looking for items that have high intrinsic value, that are fairly light and easy to carry, and that are easy to resell. Most burglars head straight for the master bedroom where many homeowners keep expensive items, jewelry in particular. Other items that are attractive to thieves include electronic equipment, silver flatware, coin collections, guns, artwork, and camera and video gear.

Many of these items are used frequently or displayed, and so it's simply not practical to keep them in a safe. In this case, we have to rely on the countermeasures against theft that have been discussed earlier in the book.

However, there are some items, such as jewelry, coins, and guns, where storage in a safe is a practical and effective means to deter theft. In addition, a safe can provide fire-resistant storage for important family documents, stock certificates, wills, heirloom photographs, digital media, and so forth. I'd therefore like to spend a short time discussing how safes are rated for security and fire protection and how to choose a safe that's right for you and your family.

Small, portable safes (sometimes called lockboxes) provide very limited protection. While they may deter casual theft or tampering and might be appropriate for keeping items like handguns out of the reach of children, a thief will simply carry the safe away and access the contents later.

For real protection, you need a safe that is either too heavy to carry or that is bolted to a floor from the inside. Safes are typically tested and rated by Underwriters Laboratories—the same organization that tests and rates all types of consumer equipment—and UL ratings generally fall into two categories.

First, safes are rated for fire resistance. This is especially important if you wish to store documents or electronic media in your safe. Please note that the class numbers below refer to the maximum temperature that the safe contents will reach in a typical house fire. Therefore a safe with a lower number rating will provide more fire protection than one with a higher rating.

- Class 350 safes are designed to provide protection for paper but not digital media. However, cases are available which, placed inside a Class 350 safe, will protect digital media to a Class 125 rating.
- Class 150 safes are designed to provide protection for magnetic computer tapes and photographic negatives or images.
- Class 125 safes are designed to provide protection for modern computer media such as CDs and DVDs.

Second, safes are rated for their resistance to break-in by a determined criminal.

- Class TL-15 safes will resist fifteen minutes of effort by a criminal using devices like hand tools, electric grinders, and drills.
- Class TL-30 safes will resist thirty minutes of effort by a criminal using the above tools, as well as cutting wheels and power saws.
- Class TL-40 safes will resist forty minutes of effort by a criminal using the above tools.
- Class TRTL-30 safes offer resistance to thirty minutes of abuse using the above tools, as well as welding and cutting torches.
- Class TRTL-60 safes will resist the above efforts for sixty minutes.
- Class TXTL-60 safes meet the same requirements as Class TRTL-60 safes and can also withstand high explosive devices.

Obviously, the more fire-resistant and tamper resistant you want your safe to be, the more you'll need to spend. In addition, safes become heavier and heavier as their fire-resistance and tamper-resistance properties improve, making them more difficult to install, move to a new area in the home, or transport to a new home.

Only you can decide what level of protection is right for you and how large a safe you need. But in the end, any safe that is difficult to move and that requires significant effort to break into will be better than no safe at all. As we've said, burglars are generally looking for opportunities where they can get in quickly and get out quickly, to decrease the risk of being caught. Even a mediocre safe may prevent many thieves from gaining access to your most valuable possessions.

Insuring Your Valuables

Too often, victims of natural disasters and theft are dealt a second major blow when they learn that their insurance coverage won't come close to replacing the property they've lost. To protect your family from financial catastrophe in the event of a fire, tornado, or other devastating loss—and to have peace of mind even if disaster never strikes—it's important to make sure you have the right kind of insurance coverage and the right amount.

Your Home

The most basic item that your homeowner's insurance covers is the structure—your home itself. As mentioned earlier in this book, most plans do not cover damage from floods and earthquakes, and coverage for these contingencies must be obtained separately. The most important consideration here is that you have "full replacement value" coverage—enough insurance to rebuild your home from scratch should you suffer a total loss.

You'll also want to make sure that your insurance will cover the cost of living away from home in the event of a disaster. After a fire, for example, it typically takes one year for a homeowner to rebuild. Many homeowners' policies include this coverage, but it's worth a call to your agent to make sure.

Your Belongings

Also included with most homeowners' coverage is insurance for your possessions. Most companies provide coverage for 50 percent to 70 percent of the amount of insurance you have on the structure of your home. This may not be enough. Think about replacing every single item in your home right now—appliances, furniture, everything in your kitchen cabinets, all your clothing, recreational equipment, and everything else you've accumulated over a lifetime. For a few more dollars a year, you may be able to increase this limit to 100 percent of the value of your home, or even more.

You should also look carefully at your policy or speak with your agent to determine whether you have "actual value" or "replacement value" coverage for your possessions. As we all know, the value of a new car drops dramatically the moment you drive it out of the showroom. Likewise, the "actual value" of your possessions—also known as the "depreciated" value—is far less than what it would take to replace them after a disaster. Your television set that is a few years old may have an actual value of only $100, but you might have to spend $500 or more to replace it with a similar model in the event of a fire, theft, or disaster. Make sure that replacement value coverage is included in your homeowners' policy and, if not, upgrade your coverage.

In addition, understand that your basic homeowners' policy may have very specific limits and very low levels of coverage for certain categories of items such as jewelry, collectibles, and firearms. For example, you may only have $1,000 or $2,000 of coverage for all of the jewelry in your home, regardless of the value of your structure. To ensure that you'll be compensated should these items be stolen or destroyed, you can add "Scheduled Personal Property" (SPP) coverage that provides additional insurance for the specific items that you list with your insurance agent or carrier, or you can "blanket" coverage that includes all items.

Items that are typically "scheduled" under SPP coverage include:

- Jewelry
- Furs
- Musical Instruments
- Arts and Antiques
- Collectibles including coins and stamps
- Gold and silver items
- Electronics/Computers
- Firearms

I'll note here that all of our NRA members receive $1,000 in additional coverage for their firearms when they join our Association and that we offer supplementary coverage at very competitive rates. To find out more about this coverage or to compare our rates with your current insurance, please contact the NRA at 1-877-NRA-3006.

Liability Protection

This portion of your homeowners' coverage is designed to protect your family financially if you, a family member, or even a pet causes unintentional property damage or even injury to another person, or if another person is injured at your home or on your property.

Liability limits generally start at about $100,000. In today's legal environment, many insurance advisors recommend that you increase this coverage to at least $300,000, and you can purchase even larger amounts (through "umbrella" policies) if you want to further minimize your risk against lawsuits.

If a Burglary Happens

Should you return home and find anything suspicious, such as a screen door or window slit, an open door, or a lock that appears to be tampered with, *do not go inside*. First, you want to avoid the risk of meeting a violent criminal face to face. Second, you want to give police every opportunity to examine a crime scene exactly as the criminal left it.

For these same reasons, leave your home immediately if you realize it has been broken into. Call police from a neighbor's house and then, while waiting for police, watch your home from a safe distance. If you see someone leaving your property, pay as much attention as possible to the person's physical characteristics: hair, skin color, facial hair, height, weight, and clothing. Note how the intruder left the scene and, if possible, get license plate number from the suspicious vehicle.

Once the police arrive, be patient and allow them to conduct a thorough investigation. When the investigation is completed, police will ask you what is missing. A home inventory will be your best ally. It will not only allow you to give police a complete list of items stolen, but it will benefit you greatly when dealing with your insurance claim.

Talk to your neighbors as soon as possible. Find out if they saw or heard anything that may help apprehend the criminal. If they have potentially helpful information, pass it along to the police or ask your neighbors to do so.

Filing Your Claim

Contact your insurance agent immediately in the event of a theft, and be prepared to provide a full inventory of items that were stolen. Keep in mind that while your agent is likely to be well-meaning, your claim will be handled by an adjuster who is likely to be a complete stranger to you. You need to be proactive in making sure you are paid what your stolen items were really worth, so provide the adjuster with as much information as you can to substantiate your claim.

Should you feel that your adjuster is not willing to reach a fair settlement, you may be able to turn to the "appraisal clause" in your homeowners' policy. This clause allows for an independent evaluation if you and the insurance company disagree on the value of an item. Your state insurance commission, which licenses insurance companies to do business in your state, may also be of assistance. You can find a directory of insurance commissioners at the National Association of Insurance Commissioners Web site, www.naic.org. Finally, the American Arbitration Association (AAA) may also aid in disputes. While insurance companies are not required by law to work with AAA, most do. After providing them with a complaint and registration fee, AAA will appoint an arbiter to your case to listen to both sides, attempt to settle differences, and if needed, rule on the dispute. The cost of the arbitration will be split between you and the insurance company.

Finally, understand that once you are a victim of burglary, your risks for another burglary are much higher. Reevaluate the security of your home for any weak points, and correct them accordingly.

Digital Online Storage of Vital Records: NRAe-Safe

In Section IV of this book, we'll talk about some of the new dangers that all Americans face from our increasingly computerized, digital world. However, in closing this section of *Safe*, I want to talk about one of the ways that the digital revolution has improved our lives—by enabling long-term secure storage of key legal, financial, and medical documents.

In a fire, for example, you could lose all of your most important records. Even worse, in a widespread disaster, your doctor's office, your insurance company, and even your bank may suffer the same fate—with critical, irreplaceable records destroyed.

Today, a number of online storage companies exist that provide homeowners with the option to store vital records digitally so that they're readily accessible in an emergency and immediately available to help in the rebuilding process after a disaster.

The company I'm most familiar with, NRAe-Safe, offers its customers peace of mind in knowing that their most vital records will remain accessible in any emergency and that, should a disaster ever devastate their home, they can immediately begin the recovery effort.

NRAe-Safe enables you to store documents in a single place that is 100 percent secure, and allows you, your family, and anyone else you designate (such as your doctor or lawyer) to access these documents twenty-four hours a day through a secure Internet connection.

Just some of the documents you can store include:

- Insurance policies
- Wills and estate papers
- Advance medical directives
- Powers of attorney
- Receipts for insured items
- Car and boat titles
- Tax returns and other tax information
- Financial records including brokerage, checking, and credit card statements
- Important medical records including lab results, radiology reports, prescriptions, diagnoses, copies of CT scans, MRIs, and X-rays

This service employs the same technology used by companies that handle transactions for many of the nation's top financial firms and Fortune 1000 companies. The process of storing records online can be as easy as sending them over a traditional phone line (a secure method) or via an encrypted Internet link where the user is logged in to a password-protected account. Records are stored at multiple sites at least one hundred and fifty miles apart so that a natural disaster at a single site cannot interrupt your access to your records. NRAe-Safe employees are screened, but they have no access to your records, account information, or password.

In short, NRAe-Safe and its best-in-class competitors offer a safe and convenient way to keep all of your records organized and secure, and provide you with worldwide twenty-four-hour accessibility in the event of an emergency at home or when traveling. For more information, visit www.nraesafe.com, or call 1-(800) 672-3888 and press "2" for details.

14

Home Invasions and Personal Protection in the Home

In the previous chapter, we talked about security measures designed to prevent unauthorized entry into your home by a burglar or other intruder. And we assumed that, if a crime takes place, it would occur at a time when you and your family members are not at home. The prospect of having a stranger enter your home, sort through your possessions, and take your valuables is unpleasant enough. But nothing you own is nearly so valuable as your own life and the lives and well-being of those you love.

In this chapter, we'll focus on three key concepts designed to protect your family from an armed or unarmed intruder. We'll discuss creating and maintaining a "Safe Room" that can be defended more readily and for a longer time than other rooms in your home. We'll talk about personal protection in the home in the event that you find yourself face to face with a criminal. And we'll talk about the use of force in self-defense and in the protection of your loved ones.

Note: Nothing in this chapter or in this book is intended to provide legal advice about self-defense issues or firearms ownership. Any questions about local, state, or federal laws governing the use or ownership of firearms, or the use of deadly force in defending yourself or a family member, should be directed

to law enforcement officials or to your family attorney. While not a substitute for legal advice, the Web sites of the National Rifle Association of America (www. nra.org) and its legislative arm, the Institute for Legislative Action (www.nraila. org), include general information about gun ownership as well as fact sheets regarding federal and state laws.

Your "Safe Room"

A "safe room" is an area of your home that has been predesignated for family members to meet in the event of a home invasion, that can be secured to buy time, and from which you can summon help, wait for law enforcement officials to arrive, and defend yourself if necessary.

Sometimes you will hear the "safe room" concept used to describe an area that will be used for multiple emergencies, including natural disasters. Here, however, we will focus on safe rooms that are intended solely for protection during a home invasion. This may or may not be the room in which your emergency supply kit is stored or which you would use in the event of a tornado, terrorist attack, or any other type of disaster.

Safe Room Location

In the event that an intruder enters your home, you will go immediately to your safe room, secure the door, and call 9-1-1. The room should therefore have only one door and should be quickly accessible from all areas of the house. A master bedroom is a likely candidate. An upstairs room might be a good choice since first-floor windows provide avenues that a criminal could use to reach you.

Once you have identified your safe room, take steps to secure it. Again, one of the key goals in having a safe room is to *buy time* until law enforcement officials can arrive at your home. Like exterior doors, the door should be solid wood, fiberglass, or steel—not hollow construction like standard interior doors. The door should be hinged on the inside of the safe room, with a secure lock such as a single-cylinder deadbolt that can be quickly engaged.

Finally, your safe room needs to be stocked with some essential equipment items, including:

- Cell phone. Even if a landline is installed in your safe room, a cell phone is essential since a determined home invader may try to disable regular phone service into your home prior to entry.
- Flashlight. Very powerful "tactical"-type flashlights are available that can temporarily blind an individual, buying you a few more seconds to disable or escape an attacker. Whether you choose one of these lights or not, a flashlight is essential in case power is out or you want to avoid turning on lights.
- Extra car keys. You may be able to set off your car alarm from your safe room, alerting neighbors as well as potentially scaring an intruder away.
- Door peephole. When police arrive, you want to be able to verify their identity.
- Security system control unit. If your home has an alarm system, you should be able to control it from your safe room and activate the "panic" button to set off the audible alarm and notify your security company.

After you've created your safe room, you need to incorporate its use into your overall family disaster plan that we discussed in Section I of *Safe*. While we don't want to unnecessarily alarm our youngsters, they need to know what to do and where to go if an intruder enters the home, just as they need to know how to deal with other emergencies. Let's take a look at how to respond if such an emergency occurs.

Defensive Measures

Later in this chapter, we'll talk about personal protection in the home, and in Chapter 29, we'll discuss Right-to-Carry laws which allow law-abiding citizens to carry concealed firearms for self-protection. Finally, we'll talk about other defensive measures that might be employed against criminals. Here, I only want to say that if you have defensive weapons in the home—a firearm, pepper spray, and so forth—these should be available in your safe room.

If you have youngsters in the home and you wish to keep a firearm or other defensive weapons readily accessible in your safe room, you may want to consider a small gun safe that can be opened quickly, even in the dark, using a fingertip keypad or even biometric fingerprint recognition. Sources for high-quality firearm storage systems include Fort Knox Security Products (www.ftknox.com), Browning (www.browning.com), Liberty Safe (www.libertysafe.com), Cannon (www.cannonsafe.com), GunVault (www.gunvault.com), and others.

Responding to a Home Invasion

In the event that an intruder enters your home, there is no single or simple way to respond. You cannot read a criminal's mind, and you cannot know his intentions. But protecting yourself and your family boils down to a few basic principles.

Prepare

The possibility of having to face a home invasion in your lifetime is remote. But simply knowing that it could occur, and thinking in advance about the steps you might take, will give you an extra edge. The first few seconds after a home invasion begins are going to be the most important, and the more you rehearse in your mind what you would do in the event of a home invasion, the more likely you'll be to react in a way that can protect your family.

Go to Your Safe Room

If you've prepared a safe room using the guidelines above, try to get to it the moment a home invasion starts. Your safe room is designed to give you extra time. Lock the door, then set off your home and car alarms to alert your security company and make it clear to a home invader that help is on the way. Then call 9-1-1. Tell the operator that a home invasion is in progress and give them your address. Through mental preparation and by rehearsing these steps, you should be able to accomplish these tasks within a matter of seconds.

If You Cannot Reach Your Safe Room

If you are unable to reach your safe room, call 9-1-1 from your cell phone or the nearest phone. Some telephones have a 9-1-1 direct dial button. If you can do so quickly, dial in speakerphone mode so that the police dispatcher can hear what is going on in the room. In most jurisdictions, precisely because home invasions can and do occur, police will respond even if the phone is hung up after 9-1-1 is dialed.

Once these basic options have been exhausted, the next steps may not be so obvious and will depend a great deal on your own values, your physical conditioning and mental preparedness, the availability of potential defensive weapons, and the situation itself. Here are some of the options to consider.

Try to Escape

It goes against our nature to run away from a dangerous situation and leave loved ones behind. But in some cases this may be your best option, or the best option for another member of your family—even a responsible child—who is in a different part of the house when the home invasion begins. If you or another family member are able to escape and call 9-1-1 from a cell phone or neighbor's house, the home invader will have lost a key advantage over your family.

Scream

If you live in an apartment building, you may be able to attract the attention of neighbors who will notify police of a potential crime in progress.

Fight

Should you decide to fight, remember that if you are facing a serious attack, you are fighting for your life and there are no rules. You do not care if the home invader is maimed or even killed. Strike quickly with as much force as possible, aim for a vulnerable area of the body such as the eyes or the neck, and then get help by activating your home security system, calling 9-1-1, or escaping.

Use a Defensive Weapon

Firearms, pepper spray, and Mace have all been used countless times to stop violent crimes. Again, your decision and opportunities to use these products in self-defense will depend on your values and the situation you face.

Comply

You can try to comply with the demands of home invaders and hope they don't hurt you. However, *do not* allow a criminal to transport you to another location unless you firmly believe that you will lose your life if you fail to comply. And, if at all possible, do not agree to be tied up since this takes away all of your other options to notify police, escape, or defend yourself.

No Matter What, Keep a Cool Head

Continue to think and evaluate the situation as it evolves. Even as minutes and possibly hours go by, continue to look for opportunities to activate your home security system, call 9-1-1, escape, or gain access to a weapon.

Personal Protection in the Home

Americans enjoy a basic human right that isn't recognized in many other countries—the right to own firearms for hunting, target shooting, and, more important, the protection of our homes and families. Firearms are owned in nearly half of all U.S. households, and handguns account for more than one-third of America's nearly three hundred million privately owned firearms.

According to award-winning research by professor Gary Kleck of Florida State University, Americans use firearms about two million times each year for defensive purposes, with the vast majority of these instances occurring away from the home. In a separate study, Kleck found that people who use guns to defend themselves are less likely to be injured than people who use other means, or no means, of protection.

In more than 98 percent of these cases of defensive firearms use, the gun is never fired. Simply the sight of a firearm, or a verbal warning, is enough to drive the criminal away. In only a tiny fraction of all defensive firearms use is a criminal actually shot.

As executive vice president of the NRA, I believe strongly in the right of law-abiding Americans to defend themselves, their loved ones, and their homes. And for the most part, our system of laws fully supports this principle.

Later in this book, when we talk about safety while you're away from home, I'll discuss "Right-to-Carry" laws that allow law-abiding citizens to carry a firearm for self-defense. In that chapter, we'll also look at other defensive measures such as pepper spray and Mace that can give citizens a fighting chance against criminals. Here, I simply want to touch on the principle, known as the "Castle Doctrine," that gives citizens like you the legal right to defend yourself in your home if you believe that you or a family member is in imminent danger of death or grave bodily harm.

The "Castle Doctrine" and the Use of Deadly Force

All of us are familiar with the saying that "A man's home is his castle." This expression is derived from an English common law doctrine—now incorporated into American law—that gives you special rights in your home that you may enjoy nowhere else. In fact, the laws that are based on this principle are sometimes called "Castle Doctrine" laws.

These laws vary greatly from state to state. It is not the purpose of this book to provide a lengthy discussion on how these laws vary, nor is there room to do so. But in a true life-or-death situation, when it is clear that you have *no other means* to defend yourself against a criminal, America's state laws do recognize your right to use deadly force in your home.

Here are the basic requirements that must be met in order to justify the use of deadly force to defend your home:

- The attacker must present a real threat. An attacker is usually considered to present a threat to life or limb only if actually capable of causing death or serious injury. For example, a small, elderly, unarmed man generally would not be considered to have the ability to threaten the life and limb of a large, muscular, young man.
- You are entitled to use deadly force against an attacker only as long as he presents a threat. Once the threat has ceased, so must your use of lethal force.
- You must reasonably believe that the intruder intends to inflict death or serious bodily harm on you or another occupant of the home.
- The threat must be imminent, that is, about to occur immediately.
- The attack must be unprovoked. You cannot give a person a reason to attack you and then shoot that person in self-defense.
- Though state laws vary widely, in some situations you have a duty to retreat from a confrontation before you can use deadly force to defend yourself. Duty to retreat simply means that you must attempt to physically escape or evade confrontation if you can do so safely. You are not obligated to retreat if doing so will expose you to greater danger.

Firearms Safety and Storage

With the right to keep and bear arms comes responsibility. It is every gun owner's responsibility to store, operate, and maintain firearms safely. Gun owners should also learn and respect all applicable laws that pertain to buying, possessing, and using firearms in their localities.

In addition, safe gun handling involves the development of both knowledge and skills so that you can use the firearm without causing harm to innocent persons or their property.

For the storage of firearms kept for personal protection, there are two main considerations.

First and foremost, the storage method chosen must provide adequate protection against unauthorized persons gaining access to the firearms. The determination of what is "adequate protection" is a matter of judgment on the part of the gun owner. What is adequate in a home inhabited by a single person living miles from the nearest neighbor, or for a couple with no children, may be wholly inadequate in a home in which children reside. The second requirement is that the storage method must allow the firearms to be easily retrieved as needed to defend against an intruder or an attack. Again, "easily retrieved" depends upon the particular circumstances of the home environment.

There is therefore no single best method of firearm storage. You must choose the firearm storage method that is best for you, given your personal circumstances and preferences. As a gun owner, it is your responsibility to research the variety of storage options available to you.

I strongly recommend the NRA Basic Personal Protection in the Home Course for any American with an interest in keeping firearms in the home for self-defense. This course will help you address the safety considerations you face as a gun owner and will provide you with the practical skills you'll need if you are ever threatened with deadly force in your home. To find a course near you, visit www.nrainstructors.org/searchcourse.aspx.

For the latest information as well as consumer ratings for products mentioned throughout this book, see www.SafeBookProducts.com. In addition, go to this Web site to sign up for a free monthly newsletter on new products to help keep your family safer.

SAFE IN THE
GREAT OUTDOORS

When it comes to outdoor recreation opportunities, America is blessed like no other nation on earth. Unlike in Europe, where in some countries virtually every square inch of recreational land is privately owned, the United States boasts more than two acres of public land for every man, woman, and child in the nation.

Our federal lands alone—including national parks, national forests, national wildlife refuges, national wilderness areas, and more—comprise approximately 650,000,000 acres that are owned by all Americans and entrusted to future generations. Yellowstone National Park, our nation's first national park, was founded in 1872, just a few months after the founding of the National Rifle Association. And today, virtually every American can find recreational opportunities on public lands within an hour's drive of home.

When it comes to hunting and fishing in particular, opportunities for Americans are more plentiful than at almost any time in history. Thanks to conservation efforts led by the NRA and other groups, as well as funds from Pittman-Robertson taxes on sporting goods and from the sale of hunting licenses, fishing licenses, and duck stamps, critical habitats have been preserved. Game species such as turkey and deer, which were virtually extinct in many areas a century ago, are now widespread and flourishing.

Unfortunately, in an age of computers, video games, cell phones, and electronic entertainment, fewer and fewer of our young people are benefiting from these opportunities. And in fact, the results of these lifestyle changes among America's youth have the potential to become a national tragedy in the decades to come.

According to Dr. David Ludwig, writing in the *New England Journal of Medicine*, our children may be the first generation at risk of having a shorter lifespan than their parents.

Already the medical community is documenting alarming health trends among our youth. In large part due to a lack of outdoor activity, the incidence of childhood obesity has now reached epidemic proportions. More than triple the number of children ages six to eleven are considered obese compared to just thirty years ago. These overweight children are at increased risk for diabetes, hypertension, cardiovascular disease, and other serious medical problems. In addition, the sedentary lifestyle of our youth has contributed to health problems that include asthma, attention-deficit disorder, vitamin D deficiency, and more. Clearly, there are few gifts we can give our families—for their physical, mental, and spiritual well-being—that are more precious than time spent in the outdoors.

In addition, if we hope to preserve America's precious outdoor resources in the decades and even centuries to come, we *must* continue to develop an appreciation for those resources among our young people. We teach environmental sciences in schools, yet for many children who have never seen a deer in the wild or a mountain stream, who have never camped under the stars or built a fire, these are just abstract concepts. How can we expect the next generation to cherish, preserve, and protect our environment and America's natural treasures if they have never experienced nature's wonders firsthand?

Whatever form of outdoor recreation you choose for your family, a little forethought and preparation can add not only an extra element of safety to the experience, but also a greater level of satisfaction and enjoyment.

Our NRA members have long known that preparing for their next hunting or fishing trip is a big part of the fun. And preparation means more than just sighting in a rifle or oiling a fishing reel. It means being ready to find your own way in the woods, to deal with unexpected weather, minor injuries, or worse. In this section, we'll look at some of the risks you might face and how you can be prepared.

General Outdoor Safety

Every outdoor recreational pursuit comes with its own set of challenges, rewards, and potential hazards. But there are some general safety guidelines that can be applied to almost all outdoor adventure activities. And as I mentioned in the Introduction to *Safe*, there is great satisfaction in knowing that you can meet your family's needs and take care of yourself, regardless of any unforeseen circumstances you might face. Preparation and knowledge will also give you the freedom to enjoy the great outdoors to the fullest.

As we begin this section of the book, let's look at a few of these general safety guidelines that can be applied to almost any outdoor pursuit.

Leave a Copy of Your Travel Plans

To ensure your safety, leave a copy of your plans with a responsible friend or family member. Include the make, model, and license plate number of your car, an itinerary, and when you plan to return. Your itinerary should be as specific as possible—the trails you intend to hike, the locations where you're most likely to set up camp, the section of river you intend to fish, and so forth. If your plans change or if your return is delayed, contact your friend or family member and let them know your new plans and schedule. Agree in advance that if you do not return as scheduled, or contact your friend or family member within a certain time, he or she will get in touch with authorities to begin looking for you.

Know How to Find Help

Know the location of the nearest help, including the nearest telephone, town, or major highway. In national and state parks, know the location of the nearest ranger station. For a listing of ranger stations in our National Parks, visit the National Park Service Web site at www.nps.gov/index.htm.

Watch the Weather

Keep an eye on the weather and understand the implications of changing weather conditions. For example, if you plan to hike through the canyons in Utah, make sure to check the weather in the surrounding mountainous regions. Rain falling miles away could cause flash flooding even if your area receives no rainfall at all.

Check local weather at www.noaa.gov before you leave home and, in the field, begin to prepare for severe weather before it strikes, making camp early if necessary, moving off ridgelines to avoid lightning, moving boats and tents to higher ground, and so forth.

Know First Aid

Learn basic First Aid, including how to identify and treat injuries and illnesses—especially heat- and cold-related conditions. Have a First Aid kit that will enable you to address common minor injuries, and consider a First Aid training course offered by the American Red Cross and other organizations. We'll talk about First Aid in greater detail shortly.

Stay Found

Staying found is the opposite of getting lost. And although the worldwide Global Positioning System (GPS) has revolutionized the way we keep track of where we are, GPS is no substitute for a traditional compass and paper map. By keeping track of your position on a regular map, you'll have an alternate means to find your way out of the backcountry if your GPS unit is damaged, runs out of battery power, or gets dropped into a river.

If You Become Lost

Should you get lost, stay calm. Panic and fear are your greatest enemies. Try to remember as much as you can about how you arrived at your present location. If you are on a trail, don't leave it. Trust your map and compass, but stay put unless you have a clear plan. If it is late in the day or if you are injured or exhausted, stay put and do not make the situation worse by wandering. Remember that people will be looking for you. As long as you have a water source and can improvise some sort of shelter, you can survive in the woods for weeks without food or outside help.

There are few things more rewarding than exploring the outdoors, and in large part, it was a spirit of exploration that founded and built our nation. Although America's early settlers and pioneers were far more on their own than most of us will ever be in our lifetimes, you can still take a lot of pride in your outdoor skills that enable you to go into remote places, meet your own basic needs, find your way, and return safely.

Backcountry Vehicle Travel

With most outdoor pastimes, the most dangerous activity you'll face is driving to and from your destination. In 2006, for example, motor vehicle accidents in the United States accounted for more than 43,000 deaths. Accidental firearm

deaths in the same year, by contrast, accounted for 642 deaths, and only a fraction of these occurred while hunting.

As with any adventure in the outdoors, general preparedness can allow you to more fully enjoy the experience. While many of the following vehicle safety measures would serve a traveler going only across town, the dependability of your vehicle becomes far more important in remote areas where breaking down or getting stuck might mean a very expensive tow or a very long walk.

Before a backcountry trip or a family vacation, review these basic safety considerations on your vehicle and trailer.

- Confirm that your spare tire is properly inflated and that you have all the needed equipment to change the tire including a jack and lug wrench.
- Check fluid levels (including washer fluid, which can be essential on dirt or snow-covered roads).
- Check belts, hoses, and hose connectors for wear and fit.
- If in doubt, take your car to a mechanic for an overall inspection.
- Inflate tires to the recommended pressure listed on the sidewall.
- Check the function of your lights, including emergency flashers. If you will be pulling a trailer (which are notorious for light malfunctions), check light function a few days in advance so you'll have time to make repairs if necessary.
- Have basic safety equipment in your vehicle, including ice scraper, jumper cables, roadside flares, tire pressure gauge, and a First Aid kit.
- Have appropriate maps, including road maps and topographic maps.
- Check the integrity of tie-downs if you'll be securing gear to the top of your vehicle or a trailer.
- If you have 4-wheel drive, test it.
- If you have a winch, test it.
- If you own a tow strap, bring it.
- Have two extra keys for your vehicle. Keep one with you in your pocket and, if you're traveling with family or friends, ask someone else to do the same.
- Monitor your fuel supply and remember that your mileage will decrease dramatically when traveling on dirt roads or snow-covered roads, or when pulling a trailer.

In addition to the day-to-day hazards we all face on the highway, those of us who travel into more remote areas, away from ready help, will want to consider having certain extra items in our vehicles. In some situations, these items could even be lifesaving. Some of this extra gear might include:

- GPS unit and manual (or cell phone with GPS capability)
- Tire inflator (such as Fix-a-Flat)
- Extra quart of oil
- Extra gallon of antifreeze

- Basic tools, including an adjustable (crescent) wrench, Phillips and flat-head screwdrivers, pliers, multi-tool
- Blankets and extra clothing, especially socks, gloves, and hats
- Flashlight and extra batteries
- Windproof, extreme condition butane lighter, and/or waterproof matches and fire starter or candle
- Small can to melt snow or for boiling drinking water
- Water purification tablets or iodine
- Roll of duct tape
- Granola, nuts, dried fruit or energy bars, beef jerky
- Bottled water
- Knife
- Heavy rope or strap for pulling vehicles from mud, sand, or snow
- 50 feet of light rope
- Small shovel
- Tire chains
- Sunscreen and sunglasses
- Whistle and/or other signaling devices, including a small mirror
- Handheld GPS with mapping capability
- Compass

17

Finding Your Way

Global Positioning System (GPS)

GPS navigation began in the early 1970s as a project of the United States military, and full operational capabilities were completed in 1995 with the launch of the last of twenty-four satellites that GPS uses to determine position. In its early days, GPS positions were accurate only within a hundred yards or so, but today the system is capable of pinpointing positions to within a few feet or even a few inches. For the marine and aviation industries that rely on navigation, GPS is the most ground-breaking development since the invention of radar two generations ago. And for outdoor enthusiasts, GPS is perhaps the most important new navigational device since the invention of the compass more than two thousand years ago.

GPS works by using satellites as reference points to find positions on the earth. By measuring the precise amount of time it takes for a satellite signal to reach a GPS receiver, the distance from that satellite to the receiver can be determined. By measuring the distance to *several* satellites, a "triangulated" position can be determined that pinpoints a particular location, including our longitude (east-west position), latitude (north-south position), and altitude above sea level.

Finding your way with a GPS receiver is as simple as reading the manual, and GPS units have various capabilities that we can put to work. At the most basic

level, we can find our location using longitude and latitude coordinates. This information can be superimposed on a built-in road map or topographic map as well. GPS can also track where we've been, or tell us how to get to another place that we want to go, not just in our vehicles but on the water or in the woods. In addition, GPS-based rescue beacons can be used to pinpoint the location of ships in distress, lost hikers, and even children and pets. Understand that these are special devices; this capability is not included with your standard GPS unit.

Like other technologies, prices for GPS devices have dropped dramatically over the years, with the least expensive units now selling for about $100. More expensive units may include features such as longer battery life, waterproofing, preloaded maps, touchscreen capabilities, and more.

Obviously the operation of GPS units depends on the model. If you rely even partially on GPS to keep track of your location in remote areas, read the manual and practice its use before you need to rely on it to keep track of where you are.

Keep in mind that GPS units can fail, get lost, or run out of power. In the backcountry, there is no substitute for a good old-fashioned map and compass, if only as a backup to your GPS.

Map and Compass

Topographic maps are two-dimensional representations of three-dimensional terrain. These maps include numbers on their edges that represent longitude and latitude, as well as "contour lines" that indicate elevation above sea level. The more closely packed the contour lines, the steeper the terrain. The map will include a scale that indicates how much distance over the ground is represented by the distance on the map, as well as colors and symbols that indicate water features, tree cover, roads, structures, and more.

Topographic maps can be purchased as sheets from outdoor stores as well as from the U.S. Geological Survey (www.usgs.gov), the government agency responsible for creating these maps. USGS also sells maps as downloads from their Web site. In addition, map atlases for an entire state can be purchased from companies such as DeLorme (www.delorme.com), publisher of the "Atlas & Gazetteer" series, which is now available for all fifty states. These large-format topographic atlases also include a wealth of recreation information, such as listings of campgrounds, recreation areas, trails, boat launches, and more.

The other basic equipment item that you'll need is, of course, a compass. A good compass should be waterproof, shatterproof, and should include a lanyard so that you can attach it to a pack or other gear.

"Orienteering"—that is, finding your way in unmarked country using only a map and compass—is a skill that requires training and practice. Waiting until you're lost in the woods is not the best time to learn! Unfortunately, it is beyond the scope of this book to provide you with adequate information to use a map and compass with confidence in unfamiliar terrain. There are many good sources on the Internet for learning map and compass skills, as well as many excellent books. Your local outdoor equipment store may even offer classes. I highly recommend that you use these resources to develop your skills if you enjoy travel and recreation in remote areas.

Weather

In thinking about safety issues posed by weather when we're in the outdoors for an extended period of time, we need to look beyond the forecast of rain, snow, or a hot spell. Instead, our key consideration is the adverse impacts that weather might have on our comfort and health.

Simply put, there are four elements with which you as an outdoorsman must learn to contend: cold, hot, wet, and dry. Each of these conditions can lead to specific problems associated with your comfort and health, and in the next chapter we'll focus on First Aid considerations including emergency care and treatment for victims of weather extremes. After that, we'll look at some basic outdoor survival techniques, many of which are intended to help protect us against the weather. Here, we'll look at some general ways to prevent health emergencies caused by weather.

Cold

When exposed to cold temperatures, your body may begin to lose heat faster than it can be produced. Over time, your body temperature may begin to drop, a condition known as hypothermia. Eventually hypothermia begins to affect coordination and the ability to use hands and feet, as well as the ability to communicate or even think properly. This makes hypothermia particularly dangerous because the victim may not even recognize that a serious medical condition is setting in.

Hypothermia is most likely to occur at very cold temperatures, but it can occur even at cool temperatures (above 40°F) if a person becomes chilled from rain, sweat, or submersion in cold water, is ill, or has been exposed for a lengthy period of time.

There are four basic principles to follow in keeping warm. An easy way to remember these principles is to use the word "COLD":

> C = keep clothing *Clean*
> O = avoid *Overheating*
> L = wear *Layered* clothing
> D = keep clothing *Dry*

At the most basic level, all four of these guidelines are intended to maintain a layer of warm, dry air immediately next to your body. Air simply does not conduct heat very well, but water does. In fact, water can move heat away from your body more than one hundred times faster than air.

Clean clothing provides the best insulation properties. As you wear the clothing, moisture and oils from your body displace the insulating air, and the clothing begins to "wick" heat away from you more quickly. Overheating causes you to sweat, again creating heat-dispersing moisture in your clothing. Layered clothing allows you not only to remove layers in order to avoid overheating, but also to replace layers as needed. And keeping clothing dry, obviously, ensures that clothing retains its full insulating potential.

Outdoorsmen have long known that wool is better than cotton for helping the body retain heat. Cotton, when wet, does more harm than good in terms of preserving your body's heat, but wool tends to remain warm, even when wet.

Modern fabrics are even better. These fabrics, often made of recycled plastics and including polyester, fleece, and wool blends, actively move moisture away from the body. For outerwear, choose products such as those made with Gore-Tex® or similar fabrics that are nearly waterproof but that allow moisture to wick through the fabric and away from the body.

Finally, several layers of light clothing are much better than fewer layers of heavy, bulky clothing. Layered clothing enables you to quickly adjust for changing weather conditions as well as compensate for your level of activity. Remember that breaking a sweat in an extreme cold-weather situation is the first signal of trouble to come. If you sweat, change your clothing or remove damp layers until they dry out. You may also want to vent your clothing—intentionally allowing some cold air to reach your skin and base clothing layer. Cold air removes moisture quickly, and a few seconds of ventilation from time to time will enable you to keep your clothing dry where it counts most, next to your skin.

Remember also that your head, your hands, and your feet have more blood circulating near the skin than other areas of your body, and therefore lose heat much faster. In fact, you may lose up to 40 percent of your body heat through your head alone. Good boots with moisture-wicking sock liners, glove liners combined with a quality pair of gloves, and a fleece or wool hat, combined perhaps with a face mask, will reduce heat loss through these areas to a minimum.

Wet

In and of itself, being wet does us no harm. But wet weather does make it more difficult to stay warm, and can cause hypothermia to set in extremely quickly if our clothing becomes soaked.

Fast, heavy rains can also cause flash flooding, which we discussed extensively earlier in this book. Flash floods can be especially dangerous to backcountry travelers since they may not have access to weather reports and may not know about heavy rainfalls upstream. If you are canoeing or rafting, take care to bring boats well above current water levels in the evening, and check frequently during nighttime hours if you suspect river levels may rise, so that boats can be raised even further if necessary. If you are traveling in slot canyons, be *extremely* aware of weather taking place upstream.

Aside from these hazards, the biggest danger of wet weather is lightning associated with thunderstorms. Lighting kills an average of sixty-two Americans each year, and in situations where we can't reach the safety of an indoor shelter we need to know the best precautions to take against a lightning strike.

First, let's look at some general safety measures for avoiding lightning, then we'll consider some specific suggestions if you're caught in a situation where a lightning strike may be imminent.

General Precautions

- Pitch your tent in areas protected by an abundance of tree growth. This will make it less likely you'll be struck by lightning.
- If thunderstorms are likely, avoid hilltops, open fields, and locations that serve as natural lightning rods.
- Count the number of seconds between flashes and thunderclaps. Divide this number by five to estimate how many miles you are from an approaching storm.
- If the lightning to thunder time is less than thirty seconds, stay where you are if you cannot reach better cover quickly and without moving over open ground.

If You Are Caught in a Thunderstorm

- If your car is nearby, get in. Roll up your windows and be sure that all storm activity has passed before returning to your camp.
- Move away from freestanding trees.
- If you're in a wooded area, lie low near a thick growth of trees as this makes you a smaller target and less likely to be struck.
- If a cluster of trees isn't around, look for a low-lying open place away from trees, poles, or other metal objects. You goal is to avoid being the tallest object in the area, or being near the tallest object in the area.

- Do not cluster in groups if you are with others. Keep space between you and anyone else in your party so that others will be available to help if one person is struck.

If Caught on a Ridgeline or Open Area

- Crouch on the ground with your weight on the balls of the feet with your feet together.
- Lower your head and keep your ears covered.
- Place your hands on your forehead and your elbows on your knees. This will create a path for lightning to travel to the ground through your extremities rather than through the core of your body.

Hot and Dry

The key problems associated with hot, dry weather are heat exhaustion, heat stroke, dehydration, and sunburn. Again, we'll discuss more about First Aid in the next chapter. Our goal here is to prevent these injuries and emergencies in the first place.

Here are some basic hot weather safety tips:

- Drink plenty of fluids and don't wait until you're thirsty to drink. Outdoor activities in hot weather may require you to drink well over one gallon of water per day. If you intend to purify your own water, keep these extra needs in mind as you plan your supplies.
- Heavy sweating removes salt and minerals from the body. These are necessary for your body and must be replaced. Salt tablets and other supplements may be helpful.
- Wear loose-fitting and light-colored clothing that reflects the sun's rays away from your body.
- Remember that sunburn is not only painful but also causes a loss of body fluids and affects your body's ability to cool itself. Apply sunscreen twenty minutes before sun exposure to allow the sunscreen to take effect, and reapply as needed throughout the day.
- Use morning and late afternoon hours for hiking and other activities, and rest in the shade during the hottest midday hours.

- Pace yourself. You will not be able to hike as far or as long on extremely hot days.
- Keep an eye on your companions for any symptoms of dehydration, heat exhaustion, or heat stroke. Remember that younger and older family members, and persons who are overweight, will be more susceptible to these problems.

First Aid

Like orienteering techniques, there is simply not room in this book to provide a full discussion of the First Aid measures you might need in the outdoors or in backcountry situations. In addition to other First Aid courses, the American Red Cross offers a Wilderness First Aid program that is tailored especially to those who might have to deal with a medical emergency far from help, care for a sick or injured friend or family member for a longer period of time, or move an injured person. Even more intensive training is available from the Wilderness Medical Institute, run by the National Outdoor Leadership School (www.nols. edu). A variety of courses is offered, and participants need to be only sixteen years old in order to enroll.

However, since even the most basic knowledge and First Aid techniques could save a life, I want to mention some of the principal medical emergencies that you might face in the field, and some of the immediate steps you should take to address these emergencies. We'll also look at the essential components of a wilderness First Aid kit.

Medical Emergencies and First Aid

Hypothermia

Hypothermia simply means that the body is losing heat faster than it can be replaced and that the core temperature of the body is decreasing. Unless the situation is reversed, it will lead to unconsciousness and death.

Signs and Symptoms
- Shivering, exhaustion
- Confusion, fumbling hands
- Memory loss, slurred speech
- Drowsiness

Immediate Treatment
- Take the person's temperature; anything below 95°F constitutes an extreme medical emergency.
- Get the victim into the warmest possible place.
- Remove all wet clothing.
- Warm the core of the body first: the chest, neck, head, and groin. Use warmed blankets, bottles of warm water, skin-to-skin contact, or anything else available. Wrap the victim in layers of blankets, clothing, towels, or sheets.
- Give warm beverages but not alcoholic beverages. Do not try to give beverages to an unconscious person.
- After the person's body temperature has increased, keep the person dry and wrapped in a warm blanket, including the head and neck.
- Get medical attention as soon as possible.

Frostbite

Frostbite is when body tissue has frozen or is in danger of freezing. It most commonly affects the nose, ears, cheeks, chin, fingers, or toes. Frostbite can cause permanent damage, up to and including the need for amputation of destroyed tissues.

Signs and Symptoms
- A whitish or grayish-yellow skin area
- Skin that feels unusually firm or waxy
- Numbness

Immediate Treatment
- Get the victim into the warmest possible place.
- Unless absolutely necessary, do not walk on frostbitten feet or toes, as this can increase the damage.
- Immerse the affected area in warm water (the temperature should be comfortable to the touch for unaffected parts of the body).
- Also, warm the affected area using body heat. For example, the heat of an armpit can be used to warm frostbitten fingers.
- Do not rub the frostbitten area with meat, snow, or anything else. This can cause more damage.
- Do not use a heating pad, heat lamp, or the heat of a stove, fireplace, or radiator for warming. Affected areas are numb and can be easily burned.
- Get medical attention as soon as possible.

Heat Exhaustion

Heat exhaustion is a relatively mild medical condition that can result from heat exposure and/or the lack of sufficient fluids.

Signs and Symptoms
- Heavy sweating
- Paleness
- Muscle cramps
- Tiredness
- Weakness
- Dizziness
- Headache
- Nausea or vomiting
- Fainting

Immediate Treatment

- Have the person rest in the shade or in the coolest area possible.
- Cool the body with water, especially to the head region and the back of the neck.
- Give plenty of fluids (cold fluids if possible).
- Seek medical attention if the problem persists for more than one hour.

Heat Stroke

Unlike heat exhaustion, heat stroke is an immediate and life-threatening emergency, whereby the sweating mechanism fails and the body loses its ability to regulate its own temperature. Heat stroke has the potential to cause permanent disability or death within ten to fifteen minutes.

Signs and Symptoms

- An extremely high body temperature above 103°F
- Red, hot, and dry skin (no sweating)
- Rapid, strong pulse
- Throbbing headache
- Dizziness
- Nausea
- Confusion
- Unconsciousness

Immediate Treatment

- Call 9-1-1.
- Get the victim to a shady area.
- Cool the victim rapidly using any method you can. Immerse the victim in a cool stream, river, or lake. If the humidity is low, wrap the victim in a cool wet towel, t-shirt, or blanket; and fan him or her vigorously.
- Monitor body temperature, and continue cooling efforts until the body temperature drops to 101–102°F.
- Do not give the victim fluids to drink.
- Get medical assistance as soon as possible.

Dehydration

Dehydration can happen even to fit individuals and, in fact, commonly affects even the best athletes. Dehydration can occur regardless of weather conditions but is most common in hot conditions or after exertion.

Signs and Symptoms
- A decrease in urination
- Dry mouth and throat
- Feeling dizzy when standing up
- Young children and babies may exhibit the symptoms above, may cry without tears, or exhibit unusual drowsiness or fussiness

Immediate Treatment
- Give fluids, including sports drinks if available.
- Move the victim to the coolest area possible.
- Have the victim rest, and monitor him or her for additional signs and symptoms.

Open Wounds/Lacerations

Injuries that cause only minor bleeding can be treated with an antiseptic to prevent infection and bandages to keep the wound closed and clean. A pain reliever may help, but do not give aspirin since this tends to interfere with clotting. For more serious injuries, immobilization of the affected area may help keep the wound closed and the victim more comfortable. Major bleeding, however, requires immediate treatment and medical attention. Keep in mind also that shock, discussed separately below, may accompany major bleeding and is itself a serious medical emergency.

Immediate Treatment
- Attempt to stem the bleeding with direct pressure, using a sterile pad if available. Hold pressure for at least twenty minutes before looking to see if the bleeding has stopped.
- Do not remove the pad or dressing. Apply another on top of the existing dressing if necessary.

- If the bleeding doesn't stop with direct pressure, apply pressure to the artery delivering blood to the area of the wound. Arms pressure points are on the inside of the arm just above the elbow and just below the armpit. Leg pressure points are just behind the knee and in the groin. Squeeze the main artery in these areas against the bone. Keep your fingers flat while keeping pressure on the wound with the other hand.
- Immobilize the injured body part once the bleeding has stopped. Leave the bandages in place.
- Get emergency help as soon as possible.
- In the event of an "avulsion" (a body part that is completely cut off), place the part in a plastic bag, then in a cooler, and transport with the victim. Do not place the avulsed part directly on ice.

Fractures, Strains, and Sprains

In the field, it is impossible even for a trained medical professional to always distinguish between a fracture and a strain or sprain. While most fractures are not life-threatening, some can be, especially if located near an artery.

Signs and Symptoms
- Discoloration, swelling, and pain
- Difficulty of movement
- Difficulty bearing weight
- Deformity when compared to the uninjured limb

Immediate Treatment
- If a bone is protruding or if there is severe bleeding, treat for bleeding first.
- Immobilize the affected area to make the victim more comfortable and prevent further injury.
- Seek medical attention as soon as possible.

Shock

Shock is a dangerous complication that can accompany virtually any serious injury.

Signs and Symptoms
- Cool, clammy skin that may appear pale or gray
- Weak and/or rapid pulse
- Breathing that is slow and shallow, or rapid and deep
- Nausea and/or vomiting
- Weakness, feeling faint, confusion, anxiety, or unconsciousness
- Dilated pupils

Immediate Treatment
- Call 9-1-1.
- Put the victim on his or her back, with feet elevated above the head unless raising the legs is painful or might cause further injury.
- Monitor pulse rate and breathing, and begin CPR if these signs are absent.
- Keep the person warm and comfortable.
- Remove tight clothing.
- Do not give fluids.
- Turn the victim on his or her side if vomiting occurs.
- Continue treatment for other injuries and seek immediate medical attention.

Sunburn

The best treatment for sunburn is, of course, prevention. Keep in mind that sunscreen take twenty to thirty minutes to achieve full affect; apply sunscreen prior to sun exposure and reapply throughout the day as needed. Wear light-colored, loose-fitting clothing and take special precautions with exposed skin areas.

Immediate Treatment
- Apply aloe and cold compresses to already-damaged skin and avoid further sun exposure.
- Use pain medications as needed, including topical sprays.
- Seek the care of a professional for extreme cases of sunburn.

Snakebite

Deaths from snakebite in the United States are exceedingly rare, usually five to ten per year nationwide. However snakebite injuries can be exceedingly painful as well as terrifying for the victim.

Immediate Treatment

- Reassure the victim.
- Immobilize the bitten arm or leg. Apply a splint to reduce movement of the affected area but keep it loose enough so as not to restrict blood flow.
- Have the victim stay as quiet as possible to keep the poison from spreading.
- Remove jewelry before the affected area begins to swell.
- If possible, position the area of the bite so it is below the level of the heart.
- Cleanse the wound, but don't flush it with water; cover with a clean, dry dressing.
- Do not use a tourniquet or apply ice.
- Do not cut the wound or attempt to remove the venom.
- Do not give the victim caffeine or alcohol.
- Do not try to capture the snake, but try to remember its color and shape so you can describe it, which will help in treatment.
- Call 9-1-1 or seek immediate medical attention.

Your Wilderness First Aid Kit

A home First Aid kit, or even the First Aid kit in your car or truck, can have virtually everything you need to provide immediate medical assistance to a sick or injured victim until help arrives. In the backcountry, however, we're faced with a dilemma. We need to be prepared for a full range of medical emergencies, yet we must often transport our First Aid kits on our backs, where space is at a premium and weight becomes a major consideration. We therefore have to compromise—making decisions about the minimal amount of gear we might need while still being prepared to meet any contingency we might face in the field.

Where possible, we'll use what's already available to us. For example, it's quite easy to improvise a splint, for purposes of immobilizing an injured limb, out of a few pieces of clothing, a couple of sturdy tree branches, and a roll of duct tape.

Here are some suggestions for items that might be included in your wilderness First Aid kit. Of course, there also many prepackaged kits available, including kits that are designed specifically for use in a wilderness setting and that weigh only half a pound or so.

- Non-latex medical gloves
- Tweezers
- Small scissors
- Thermometer
- Mylar blanket
- Acetaminophen tablets
- Ibuprofen tablets
- Antihistamine tablets
- Antacid tablets
- Burn relief spray
- Antiseptic wipes
- Antibiotic ointment
- Epi-Pen (epinephrine for acute, life-threatening allergic reactions such as to bee stings)
- Eye wash
- Eye patches
- Butterfly bandages (used to close wounds)
- Adhesive bandages, various sizes
- 5" x 9" sterile dressings
- Conforming roller gauze bandage
- 3" x 3" sterile gauze pads
- Thermometer
- Duct tape or adhesive First Aid tape
- First Aid manual or emergency action cards

20

Basic Survival Techniques

None of us ever expect to find ourselves in a true survival situation where our decisions and actions may make a difference between life and death. But throughout this book, we've talked about preparing for the unexpected, having basic items at our ready, and using these items, as well as common sense, to protect ourselves and our families.

In some ways, a survival situation is no different. But it's important to note, at the very beginning of this chapter, that your knowledge, your skills, and the materials you have with you will be far less important in a survival situation than your *mental attitude*. There have been many instances when experienced outdoorsmen panicked or made poor judgments in survival situations and paid the ultimate price for their mistakes. There are equally as many instances when inexperienced individuals and even children, with virtually nothing on their backs, found ways to make it through dire situations in remote areas. Stress, hunger, thirst, fatigue, and isolation can lead to bad decision-making, panic, or the inability to perform simple tasks. A positive outlook can help increase your chances for a positive outcome.

In fact, one of the best ways to prepare yourself mentally for a survival situation is to read some of the available literature on wilderness survival. There are dozens of books and hundreds of Internet resources. Whether or not you become an expert in wilderness survival, simply knowing that you've taken some steps to prepare will be of great psychological benefit if you ever find yourself in a survival situation.

You should also make a commitment to yourself to carry at least some minimal survival gear with you anytime you go into remote areas. A very simple survival kit could include these items and still weigh barely one pound:

- Small but sharp knife
- Waterproof matches in a waterproof container, preferably one with a flint attached
- Watch
- Waterproof ground cloth and cover
- Small flashlight and extra batteries
- A small supply of high-calorie emergency foods
- Signaling items including mirror and whistle
- Compass
- Mylar blanket for warmth and signaling
- Water purification tablets

Again, there are many fine books and articles covering wilderness survival techniques for all types of situations and climates. However, here are a few basic ideas that could be applicable to a wide range of survival situations.

Food

- Understand that food is the least of your concerns in a survival situation. Human beings can go many weeks without food. Obviously that wouldn't be pleasant, but you're not going to starve to death for a long time.
- If you are without food, do not waste time foraging. Your time is better spent procuring water and shelter, and/or figuring out how to get back to civilization.
- If you do find wild foods, eat only those with which you are familiar. Poisoning yourself or making yourself sick will only compound your problems.

Water

- Use water purification tablets if you have them, or boil water if possible.
- If you have no means of purifying water, drink the cleanest water you can find. Upstream sources tend to be cleaner than downstream sources.

Clothing

- Remember that cotton is less than useless when wet. Use synthetic fibers or wool next to your skin to the extent possible. Dry your clothing over a fire each night or as often as practical. Drying your clothing becomes your first priority if you fall into water or are soaked by rain.
- If you are trapped in your car, the seat material, seat back material, and seat insulation can be used to keep warm.
- Plant fibers can provide good insulation when placed between two layers of clothing.

Shelter

- In deep snow, a snow shelter can provide effective protection against the elements. Dig a tunnel or trench deep enough to protect you from the wind, building up the sides with snow if necessary. Line the floor with pine boughs or clothing, and build a top in the same way.
- In desert conditions, seek out a shaded area if possible and dig a trench to rest below the surface of the sand. The sand just a few inches below the surface is much cooler.
- Create shade conditions by improvising a curtain of clothing or of anything else that is available.
- In wooded areas, you will have many natural tools with which to build a shelter. Try to build your shelter against an object like a fallen tree or large rock. Insulate openings with moss, leaves, or mud. Making your shelter as small as possible will make it easier for you to stay warm.

Staying Warm

- Create a heat deflector behind your fire to reflect more of its heat toward you. A tarp, a rock, or a thick object will help.
- Use anything you can find—pine boughs, leaves, etc.—to add natural insulation when you sleep.
- If you have a can, drink hot water heated over your fire.
- If there are multiple individuals in your party, share body heat when you sleep or when taking shelter from bad weather.

Staying Cool

- In arid or desert climates, rest during the day and move about during the very early or late hours.
- Stay hydrated to keep your core temperature lower.
- Try to keep your clothing moist to produce cooling evaporation.

Self-rescue

Most of the time, if you're lost, staying put is your best option. Someone is looking for you, and in all but the most remote wildernesses, they are likely to find you soon. However, should you decide to self-rescue:

- If you have a map, make every possible effort to determine where you are before you begin moving.
- Think before you move. Where do you think the closest road is likely to be? What is the terrain like in that direction? Is there likely to be water along the way?
- Once you make a plan, stick to it unless there is a very clear reason to change the plan. Making a new plan every day will make the situation worse, not better.
- Follow natural waterways downstream. By staying near water, you solve

one of your most important survival problems. All waterways have to go somewhere eventually.

- If you are not following a waterway, try to move in a straight line as best you can in the hope of finding a road or even a dirt track, which can lead you to safety.

Signaling

- Do anything you can to be noticed. Many people simply forget this. Rescuers have passed within yards of people who have simply crawled up under a pile of branches.
- Three of anything is generally recognized as an SOS signal—three gunshots, three fires placed in a triangle, etc.
- Increase the smoke coming from a fire by placing live pine boughs or other green or wet wood on the fire.
- Using a mirror can be helpful for reflecting sunlight toward an airplane, fire tower, or other distant object.
- Under the right conditions, a whistle can be heard more than a mile away. Use three whistles to indicate that you need help.
- Yelling is the least effective way to signal others, but it can't hurt to yell "Help" from time to time, especially if you believe others may be nearby.

Specific Outdoor Activities

Everything we've covered so far in this chapter has been general in nature and applicable to a wide variety of outdoor activities. In this final chapter, let's discuss some key safety concepts for specific outdoor pursuits.

Hunting

Over the past several decades, hunting accidents of all types have significantly declined, and hunting fatalities have become extremely rare. There is no doubt in my mind that our NRA Hunter Safety courses and other hunter safety programs, now required by many states before a hunting license is issued, have contributed significantly to this decline.

Hunter safety courses are offered in all fifty states each year, and no matter where you are in America, a course will be offered near you soon.

In addition, more than 1.2 million youngsters have now participated in our NRA Youth Hunter Education Challenge (YHEC). The YHEC course builds on basic hunter education, with greater emphasis on firearm safety, marksmanship, and outdoor skills. By enrolling your children in a local YHEC program, you can help them become even more proficient in the skills they need for a lifetime of safe hunting. You can learn more about this program at www.nrahq.org, or by contacting the YHEC program directly at (703) 267-1524.

The most basic hunting safety rules can be boiled down to these four principles: *Treat every firearm as if it were loaded.* Even if you are certain that a gun is not loaded, it is standard practice to assume that there is a round in the chamber. Open the action before you hand a firearm to another person. Make it a habit to routinely and repeatedly check the safety to be sure it's on.

Always keep the muzzle pointed in a safe direction. Pay special attention to muzzle direction when loading or unloading a firearm, as this is when many accidental discharges occur. If a hunting buddy or family member is careless in the direction they point their gun, do not be shy about pointing out their mistake. When crossing fences or traversing difficult terrain, unload your firearm and hand it to a friend. If you are alone, unload your firearm and, leaving the action open, carefully place the gun on the ground under the obstacle, with the muzzle pointed away from you. Cross the obstacle far enough from the firearm so that if you fall, you won't fall on it. Retrieve the firearm by approaching the stock end, not the muzzle end.

Be certain of your target and what is beyond your target. As safe hunters, we must always verify that what we think we see is really what it is. If you're on a deer stand or moving through the woods, know where your safe zones of fire are. Make sure that your shot will fall in a safe area if you miss or if the bullet or arrow passes through an animal.

Keep your finger off the trigger until you're ready to fire. The trigger guard on your firearm is designed to keep your finger (as well as tree branches and other objects) from discharging the firearm until you decide to shoot. Use the trigger guard as it was designed to be used, and make it a habit to keep your finger outside of it.

Here are some additional hunting safety tips beyond these universal rules.

Tree Stand Safety

- Always wear a safety harness. Many hunters believe that they can't possibly fall out of a tree stand. These are the hunters who fall out of tree stands. Tree stands have been known to collapse as well. Avoid homemade wooden stands, which quickly fall victim to rot or which can be compromised by the growth of the tree to which they're attached.

- Inspect your tree stand from top to bottom each year, and replace any worn or rusted hardware. Remember that as trees grow, you'll need to reset the straps. Look for missing, broken, or rusted hardware every time you ascend your stand.
- Use two people when setting up a stand.
- When choosing a tree, watch for dead limbs that could fall on the stand.
- Use a haul rope to bring up and lower your gear, including your firearm or bow.
- Tell someone where you're going and when you'll be back, so that someone will look for you if you're injured.
- If you get drowsy, get out of the stand.

Turkey Hunting Safety

- As with all game, make absolutely sure you are looking at a turkey before pulling the trigger.
- Wear full camouflage. Partial camouflage that leaves white, blue, or black exposed may make you look like a turkey.
- Signal approaching hunters with your voice. Do not wave or whistle.
- When carrying a decoy in or out of the woods, or when carrying a turkey out of the woods, wrap the wings around the body and place an orange vest or band around the turkey.

Fishing

Most fishing accidents are not really fishing accidents but boating accidents instead. Read the ideas for safe boating later in this chapter, and review the discussion of drowning and water safety in Section II of this book, particularly with regard to rescuing a fellow fisherman who gets in trouble in the water. Perhaps it should go without saying, but every fisherman needs to know how to swim. And if you're fishing alone, tell someone where you're going and when you expect to return.

To Remove a Fishhook

If the barb has not entered the skin, simply pull the hook out from the direction it went in. If the barb has penetrated the skin, the hook will be best removed by a medical professional. However, if that isn't possible or practical, use one of these two methods:

- Clean the area around the hook, and apply gentle pressure to continue to push the hook through skin in the circular direction of the hook's bend. When you can see the barb, cut it off and pull the remainder of the hook out from the direction it entered the skin. Sterilize and cover the wound. Seek medical attention later to ensure that the wound does not become infected. Get a tetanus shot if necessary.
- Clean the area around the hook, and tie a loop of fishing line around the bend of the hook so that a quick jerk can be applied. Holding the shaft of the hook, push it in the opposite direction of the barb to disengage the barb as much as possible. Give a sharp jerk to the loop of line to pull the hook out. Seek medical attention later to ensure that the wound does not become infected. Get a tetanus shot if necessary.

Never try to use these methods on a hook that is very deeply embedded, that is near a joint or tendon, or that is near the eye or a main artery. Seek medical attention instead. If the hook is embedded in the eye, place a shield over both eyes (to prevent further eye movement). Call 9-1-1, or transport the victim to emergency care with the head slightly raised.

Backcountry Skiing

Backcountry skiing—where there are no lifts, lodges, patrols, or other comforts—is for experienced skiers who are comfortable with their skills.

Avalanches pose a very serious threat for backcountry skiers. While deep snow and steep terrain pose greater risks, avalanches can and do occur with less than two feet of snow cover, and on moderate terrain. And once a victim is fully buried, there is only a one in three chance of survival.

The best way to stay safe is to know when to avoid skiing in certain areas. If you are not an expert, find someone who is. In regions where backcountry skiing is a popular pastime, find out if there is a telephone hotline or Web site that provides up-to-date, local information about avalanche conditions.

- Always ski with a friend. In risky areas, descend one by one.
- Wear an avalanche rescue beacon that signals your location.
- Carry a shovel and a probe designed for locating buried avalanche victims.
- Learn how to use avalanche equipment and the protocols for avalanche rescue.
- If caught, ski toward the side of the slab. Try to grab a tree. You cannot outrun an avalanche on skis.
- If swept off your feet, use a swimming motion to try to keep yourself on the surface.

Hiking and Camping

Most of the key safety concerns that affect hikers and campers can be found in other sections of this book, from our considerations of First Aid, water purification, and so forth.

As with any activity that takes you out of your regular day-to-day life, planning your journey is part of the process and part of the fun. Get your maps in

advance. Check local weather to help you decide what to pack. Make sure you know where water sources will be located along the way. Have a list of things to pack, and double-check your packing to make sure that you don't get five miles down the trail and discover that you've forgotten your matches.

Most of all, remember that enjoying our great American outdoors is not only a right but a privilege. Exercise your responsibility to ensure that ten years from now, or one hundred years from now, the natural beauty that you enjoy today will remain for future generations.

Boating

Boating safety is a difficult topic because your safety considerations will vary a great deal depending on the type of boat you have and the waters you travel. Even the time of year can make a big difference. A capsize in warm water might not be much more than an inconvenience, whereas a capsize in cold water may become a life-threatening emergency within seconds. However, there are some boating safety concepts that are more or less universal and that we can consider here.

- Keep your trailer in good working order and check the function of your trailer lights each time you move your boat.
- Strictly adhere to all federal requirements for boating safety equipment, including personal flotation devices (PFDs), and make sure that items with an expiration date (such as flares) are updated as needed. Make sure your running lights are functioning if you plan to be out after dark.
- If you have a large boat, where the location of PFDs may not be obvious, make sure all passengers know where they are.
- Require that all youngsters, and anyone who can't swim, wear a PFD while aboard your boat.
- Monitor NOAA marine weather forecasts before heading out and while underway.
- File a "float plan" with a family member or friend to let him or her know your intended destination and when you plan to return.
- Take your cell phone with you and, if appropriate, have a VHF radio as well. Know the protocols for calling in a Mayday or medical emergency as well as basic radio etiquette.
- Know how to troubleshoot basic problems with your boat engine. Check fluids regularly and, on an outboard motor, check the operation of your water-cooling system each time you start the motor.
- Know the basics of reading printed and electronic nautical charts.
- Know the standard sound signals that are used in fog and low-visibility situations.
- Carry printed nautical charts in case your GPS fails or you lose power.

- Give some thought in advance as to how you'd react to a fire, capsize, or man overboard.
- Carry an EPIRB (Emergency Position-Indicating Radio Beacon) if you're going far offshore, to areas where cell phone and VHF communication are unlikely to work, to areas where few other boats go, or when boating in extremely cold water where immediate rescue will be necessary to safe your life.
- If alcohol is consumed on your boat, have a qualified "designated driver" who is not drinking. This is now a legal requirement in most states.
- In the event of a capsize, stick with your boat. Most small to medium-sized boats have "positive flotation"—that is, they float even when swamped or full of water. Staying with your boat will make it easier for rescuers to find you.
- For personal watercraft such as jet skis, provide safety instruction and ground rules for your youngsters, and know the minimal age for jet ski use in your state and when traveling to other states. The age requirements generally range from twelve to sixteen years old.

Canoeing, Kayaking, and Rafting

"There is nothing—absolutely nothing—half so much worth doing as simply messing about in boats." So said Ratty to Mole in Kenneth Grahame's classic, *The Wind in the Willows*. And I believe that canoeing, kayaking, or rafting down an open river, with little sign of civilization to be seen, is exactly what Ratty may have had in mind. There are few things more enjoyable in the great outdoors.

Aside from wearing PFDs as appropriate and adhering to standard boating safety practices, the most important consideration for paddling and rafting safety is to know your abilities and know in advance the challenges you will face along your route.

For popular rivers and streams, printed guidebooks as well as Internet resources are available, describing the overall nature of a river stretch, its put-in and take-out points, and describing the overall difficulty of the river as well as potential trouble spots. Streams and rivers are graded into six whitewater "classes" ranging from Class I to Class VI. These classes have the following general characteristics:

Class I: Short areas of small rapids that require no maneuvering

Class II: Longer areas of whitewater that may include rocks and small drops, requiring some maneuvering

Class III: Significant whitewater and fast currents, with medium waves and drops that require skilled maneuvering and experienced paddling skills

Class IV: Long stretches of whitewater with large waves, continuous rapids, large rocks, and other hazards; scouting may be required to plan routes and maneuvers through these rapids.

Class V: May include large drops and other hazards including "hydraulics" which can trap a boat; rescue may be difficult.

Class VI: Cannot be attempted without serious risk to life

Keep in mind that the nature of a small, placid river can change dramatically after a thunderstorm and can require paddling skills that would not normally be needed on that particular stretch of river. In addition, springtime rains and snowmelt can raise water levels dramatically. River stretches that you have run in the summertime may pose much greater challenges during high water levels in the springtime.

Mountain Biking

Mountain biking is a growing sport that combines the exercise and fun of regular cycling with the ability to venture into more remote areas that could normally be accessed only on foot or on horseback. Even many large cities are now incorporating mountain bike trails into their overall recreational opportunities. Here are some key safety tips for mountain bike enthusiasts:

- Ride under control. Maintain the ability to adjust to the terrain and environment, and avoid obstacles like tree branches and stray rocks.
- Respect the rights of others. Let fellow trail users, including hikers and horseback riders, know you're coming. Slow down and yield as necessary.
- Wear eye protection along with your helmet. Many bikers like to wear knee and elbow pads as well. Eventually, every mountain biker will crash.
- Respect the land by staying on marked trails.

- Make sure you have adequate equipment to make minor repairs and adjustments to your bike, and know how to use it. On a mountain bike, you can often cover a lot of distance away from civilization, and it might be a long walk back. Standard equipment might include a multi-tool, appropriate wrenches and screwdrivers, puncture repair kit and pump, chain breaker, and chain lube.

- Make sure you keep track of where you are. On a mountain bike, you can get disoriented or lost just as quickly as a hiker—more quickly in fact, since you are covering more ground faster. Some of the standard equipment that we've discussed for a variety of outdoor activities—including a map, compass, GPS unit, and cell phone—might be appropriate for certain mountain biking adventures.

ATVs and Off-Roading

All-terrain vehicles (ATVs) are commonly used by hunters and landowners for a variety of chores, as well as used recreationally simply for the thrill of riding. Like any other motor vehicle, their use must be taken seriously.

The tips below, many of which are recommended by the All-Terrain Vehicle Association (www.atvaonline.com), can help you stay safe as well as minimize your impact on trails and the environment. Most of these recommendations would be fully applicable to those who venture off-road in 4-wheel drive vehicles as well.

- Always wear proper safety equipment while operating your ATV. This equipment includes but is not limited to gloves, boots, long sleeves, long pants, goggles or other eye protection, and an approved helmet.

- Take an ATV training course to maximize safety. Many retailers offer a discount for completion of a safety course.

- On slick trails, moderate the throttle and use the clutch to gain maximum traction with minimum wheel-spin.

- If possible, don't use three-wheeled versions of ATV vehicles. In 1988, Congress passed a bill banning the sale of these vehicles due to a poor safety record, but many of these vehicles are still being used.

- If you transport game on an ATV, take special care with handling and speed.

- Transport firearms unloaded and in a secured case or rack.
- Stay on roads, trails, or other areas designated for ATV use.
- Try to stay in the middle of the trail to avoid widening it.
- Cross streams only at designated fording points, where the trail crosses the stream. And approach the stream slowly, crossing at a 90° angle.
- On switchbacks, avoid gouging the trail when climbing or descending.
- Avoid muddy trails when possible.
- Carry a trash bag to pack out what you packed in.

For the latest information as well as consumer ratings for products mentioned throughout this book, see www.SafeBookProducts.com. In addition, go to this Web site to sign up for a free monthly newsletter on new products to help keep your family safer.

SAFE IN THE DIGITAL WORLD

I f this book had been written a decade ago, perhaps even less, this section would have been a great deal shorter or might not have been included at all. But the revolution in computer technology—particularly with regard to communications technology, including cell phones, e-mail, social networking sites, and texting—has opened up new avenues for criminals and predators to cause real harm to our families, especially our children.

The problem is compounded by the fact that many of us, as parents, can't recognize a computer threat when we see it or we don't know where to look in the first place. We know how to prepare for a natural disaster, we know how to make our doors and windows more secure, and we know how to stay out of bad neighborhoods, but we're lost when it comes to taking equivalent steps on the computer to keep our privacy, our finances, and our children safe. In this section of *Safe*, we'll take a broad look at some of these threats and how to combat them. These chapters won't make you a computer expert and they won't substitute for basic computer training or skills, but they will give you some idea of what to look for, and some of the easier steps you can take, to protect your family in the digital world.

22

Data Loss, Viruses, and Spyware

Let's start by looking at some of the most basic protections for your computer. In taking steps to protect our computers from data loss and to prevent unauthorized persons (or other computers) from gaining access to our machines, we can also lay the basic groundwork to protect ourselves from identity theft, misuse of our financial information, and exploitation of our children.

Below are some key steps to protecting your computer from intrusion, as recommended by the FBI and others.

Keep Your Firewall Turned On

A firewall helps protect your computer from outsiders who might try to steal passwords or other information or simply try to delete your data or "crash" your computer. This software is already included with some operating systems or can be purchased as an add-on for individual computers.

Install Antivirus Software and Keep It Updated

Viruses and worms are malicious software programs that try to embed themselves within your computer via the Internet or e-mail. Thousands of viruses have been identified. They may be relatively benign, or they can completely wipe out your data. Most of the time, you will have no idea that a virus has infected your computer. Antivirus software is designed to prevent these viruses from attaching themselves in the first place and to locate and destroy viruses that may already be in your machine. Whatever antivirus software you choose, you should make sure that it updates your computer automatically and on a regular basis.

Install Anti-spyware Software and Keep It Updated

"Spyware" can include a variety of computer programs that, like viruses, install themselves on your computer without your knowledge. These programs allow others to keep track of your activities on your computer and collect information about you without your consent. Some operating systems offer free spyware protection, and inexpensive (and even free) software is readily available for download on the Internet. However, before installing spyware software from the Internet, do your homework. Read reviews and independent reports, and download software only from established, widely used companies. Otherwise, you may install a fake program that actually includes spyware or other malicious code.

Keep Your Operating System Up-to-date

An operating system is the basic platform that your computer uses for all other operations. From time to time, these platforms are updated to meet the latest technology requirements or to fix security problems. Maintaining your computer with the latest operating system updates will help keep your data as secure as possible and ensure that your computer can properly utilize the antivirus and anti-spyware programs you've installed.

Be Cautious About What You Download

Carelessly opening e-mail, or downloading e-mail attachments or "free" software from the Internet, can introduce viruses and other malicious code into your computer. Do not open e-mail attachments from people you don't know, and be careful about attachments that have been forwarded by people you do know. Seemingly harmless downloads like "free" screensavers and music represent some of the biggest dangers since computer hackers know that these downloads will be tempting to a wide variety of computer users. Also be particularly careful about e-mails purporting to be from U.S. government agencies, or banks or brokerage houses asking you to update account information or correct a problem with your account. Remember that it is quite easy for anyone to duplicate an official government seal or form, or create a web address that is similar to that of your bank or financial institution.

Pop-up "security" warnings, indicating that your computer may be infected with viruses, are known as "scareware" in the computer industry. Clicking on these ads could result in downloading viruses or other malicious software.

Turn Off Your Computer When It's Not in Use

Leaving your computer on at all times provides an attacker with a constant connection to your data, as well as the opportunity to use your computer as part of a "botnet"—using your computer as a proxy to attack others.

Back Up Your Data

In some ways, losing computer information can be like a small-scale natural disaster: we can lose our financial records, tax records, critical correspondence and documents, and even priceless family photos. But as the saying goes: "There are only two kinds of computer hard drives—those that have already 'crashed' and those that will crash in the future." All computer drives, including yours, will eventually fail. Sometimes, but not always, lost data can be recovered by a professional who specializes in this area, but even if you can get your data back, the process can be extremely expensive. The best way to make sure your difficulties are minimized when your hard drive crashes is to have a recent backup of your data.

While Online

Here are some additional steps you can take to avoid viruses and spyware and to prevent others from gaining access to your data and computer activities.

- Avoid clicking on pop-up ads and search engine advertisers.
- Some sites and pages may ask you to download software in order to read or access information or a video. Do not do so unless you are certain that the software is safe.
- Periodically clear your "cookies" and browsing history in order to prevent others from tracking your Internet use.

23

What Every Parent Needs to Know

Many parents know far less about computers than do their ten-year-old children. Today's youngsters have grown up with computers, and they tend to be much more proficient in the use of computers as well as cell phone technology than are their parents. Yet it remains the responsibility of parents to ensure the well-being of their children when it comes to the wide-ranging threats that technology can pose.

According to a report issued by the office of U.S. Senator Mike Crapo, 61 percent of youngsters admitted to having used the Internet in an unsafe or inappropriate way. Shockingly, 34 percent of youngsters ages ten to seventeen had been exposed to unwanted sexual material on the Internet, including nudity and sexual acts. Twenty percent of youngsters in kindergarten through twelfth grade had met face-to-face with someone they had first met online, and 31 percent of these same youngsters said that they have the skills to circumvent Internet filtering software that parents use to block inappropriate Web sites.

The first key to keeping your children safe has nothing to do with technology itself but involves your willingness and ability to communicate with your child. Just as you can't watch your child's every move when he or she is at school or playing with friends, you can't easily keep track of your youngster's every move while online. Like every other activity that your child engages in, you're the one

who has to set the ground rules and limits. Never forget that this technology can literally enable anyone in the world to communicate with your child. Here are some guidelines.

- Children should never give out personal information on the Internet, including name, home address, school name, or telephone number, without your direct supervision and permission. *Understand that the dissemination of information posted to the Internet cannot be fully controlled. It is available to anyone who wants it, including predators.*
- Likewise, children should never post pictures of themselves, or other identifying information such as a picture of your home, without your supervision and permission.
- Tell your children never to write to someone who has made them feel uncomfortable or afraid. Ask them to tell you right away if they see or read anything on the Internet or in an e-mail that makes them feel uncomfortable.
- Children should never meet face-to-face with someone they've met online without the direct supervision of parents.
- Understand that people online may not be who they say they are. Someone who claims to be a twelve-year-old girl could really be a forty-year-old man.

Monitoring Your Child's Computer Use

Only you can decide whether it is appropriate for you, as a parent, to keep track of your child's Web activities without his or her knowledge. If you decide that this is right for you, two programs that are commonly used are CyberPatrol (www.cyberpatrol.com) and PC Tattletale (www.pctattletale.com). These programs can block inappropriate content, as well as services like instant messaging and chatroom access. Content filters can be adjusted to match the age and

CyberPatrol

Access Restricted

User Profile:

Reason: The website is inappropriate.

Category: Criminal Activity & Phishing

Instant Override: Click here - Password Required

To change any of the filter settings please speak to your CyberPatrol Headquarters' Administrator.

maturity level of your child, keep track of blocked Web sites that your child tries to access, record keystrokes and find out passwords that your child is using, record files that your child deletes, and even take a picture of the computer's screen at periodic intervals for your review later. These programs can be installed and set so that only you can access the recorded information and so that your child will not know that the program is activated.

E-mail

Unfortunately, the Internet allows sexual predators to operate in an anonymous environment where they can establish an initial contact with children and gain their trust and "friendship." At some point, an online predator may begin to introduce sexual overtones into the conversation, transmit sexual material, and try to set up a face-to-face meeting with a child. If your child's e-mail address is posted to a social networking site like Facebook, a predator can cross-reference the e-mail address to gather additional personal information. In addition, unsolicited e-mail ("spam"), perhaps offering a free gift, can include pornographic material or entice your child to a pornographic or other inappropriate Web site.

The National Center for Missing and Exploited Children and other organizations concerned with Internet safety offer these suggestions:

- Children should never open an e-mail from someone they do not know or reply to an e-mail from someone they do not know.
- Ask your children to show you any suspicious or disturbing e-mails they receive.
- Use an Internet provider that offers age-appropriate filters for Internet content and that attempts to block spam and pornography from ever reaching your child's e-mail inbox. AOL is one provider that offers parental controls.
- Monitor your child's e-mail content by logging in as your child once a week. Set the controls so that deleted e-mails remain on the computer.
- Understand that your child can easily set up multiple e-mail accounts without your knowledge. Allow only one e-mail account per child. Set yourself up as the administrator for the computer to prevent children from creating accounts, changing filter settings, or installing new software.
- Consider a program such as CyberPatrol or PC Tattletale, and learn how to use it. "Stealth" mode will enable you to review your child's Internet usage without his or her knowledge. Keep in mind that, if your child uses the Internet and e-mail extensively, reviewing his or her usage may be a very time-consuming proposition.

Search Engines

Search engines include sites like Google and Yahoo! that are used to find other Internet sites with information that a user wants or needs. Most major search engines have filters that block inappropriate content, but these filters are not always reliable and can be disabled. By doing an Internet search yourself for "search engines for children" or something similar, you can find lists of "kid-friendly" search engines, where search results that children receive are limited to content that has already been screened. Other search engines can then be blocked so that children can't access them.

Some Internet Service Providers, including AOL and EarthLink, provide fairly easy controls and settings that can help parents monitor their children's Internet usage as well as limit access to inappropriate web content. AOL offers downloadable programs that include filters for e-mail and "instant messaging" contacts as well as Internet content. AOL can also send parents periodic "report cards" logging their children's online activities. EarthLink provides parental controls as part of its "Total Protection" toolbar, including online time limits, e-mail screening, and a "kid-safe" Internet search engine.

Instant Messaging

Instant messaging (IM) is a tool that children use frequently to communicate with each other. Think of instant messaging as a phone call over a computer where messages are typed rather than spoken. The messages are viewable in "real time" by two or more persons who are logged into the same IM network.

Although fifteen million youngsters now use instant messaging, this capability may not be appropriate for all children since instant messages are difficult for parents to monitor. One of the keys to instant messaging safety is to make sure that privacy controls are set properly. Here are some guidelines:

- Use a non-gender-specific screen name, not a real name, and do not publish a screen name on a public Web site or social networking site (which might enable a predator to correlate a screen name with a real name). Do not use an e-mail address as a screen name.
- Never give out any personal information while using instant messaging, including a real name, telephone or cell number, home address, etc.
- Set controls to allow only persons known to you to send instant messages to your child. Block new contacts until you can verify who the person is. Just as your child shouldn't accept phone calls from strangers, he or she shouldn't accept instant messages from unknown persons. Yet 71 percent of youngsters ages ten to seventeen have reported receiving messages from someone they do not know.
- Know the acronyms that youngsters use when communicating via instant messaging or cell phone text messages. For example, "ASL" is a request for the other person to provide their age, sex, and location. "BRB" is "be right back," and "IMO" is "in my opinion." There are hundreds of these abbreviations and acronyms, many of which are sexually explicit.

To find out what a particular acronym means, type "Internet acronyms" plus the acronym itself into a search engine.

- Internet chatrooms are essentially public gathering places where any number of people can exchange instant messages simultaneously. These various messages stream down a computer screen as they are entered by the various chatroom participants. Many child welfare organizations and experts recommend that you block access to chatrooms or prohibit your child from visiting them as they can be magnets for predators, gang members, and other criminals.

Social Networking Sites

Social networking sites such as MySpace, Facebook, and Twitter have exploded in popularity among young people, not just in America but around the world. First and foremost, children need to understand that anything they post to these networking sites becomes a matter of immediate and permanent public record that is, with some effort, accessible to anyone in the world who wants to view the information. This can cause embarrassment, adversely affect a college application, or provide useful information for potential predators. Only you can decide whether or not your child has the maturity and common sense to participate safely in social networking sites.

The National Center for Missing and Exploited Children (NCMEC) also offers the following tips for social networking sites:

- Make sure kids and teens have their profile set on "private" where only people on their contact list (people they know) can view their profile.
- Select gender-neutral screen names (not real names), and make sure the screen name does not offer any clues to your child's location.
- Talk about Internet safety with your children, and make sure they understand that information posted to social networking sites can be used against them by "cyberbullies" and predators. The rule to convey is, "Think before you type."
- Make sure your kids know not to respond to any rude or inappropriate messages.

- Make sure you know all of your children's passwords, screen names, and other account information. View their profiles from time to time to make sure they are not posting any identifying information.
- Make sure your kids understand that people on the Internet may not be who they claim to be.
- Make sure that if your child posts a photo to Facebook or another social networking site that it does not include any identifying information such as a landmark, street sign, or school sport jersey.
- Make sure your child knows not to post any identifying information about his or her friends, or photos of friends.
- Understand that downloads and links on social networking sites carry the same risks as other downloads and links.

Cyberbullying

"Cyberbullying" is the use of the Internet by a child to harass, embarrass, threaten, or otherwise intimidate another child. This activity must be taken seriously, and there are documented instances when children have committed murder or suicide after having been involved in a cyberbullying incident. Cyberbullying can take place on social networking sites, via instant messaging on the Internet or cell phones, or personal Web sites often called "blogs" (derived from "Weblogs").

Cyberbullies may send degrading or unflattering pictures of the victim via e-mail or cell phone. They make take pictures of the victim in the locker room or bathroom without the victim's knowledge. Like all Web content, these images are then in the public domain and available to others around the world.

Cyberbullies who have obtained access to passwords can pose as the victim and post embarrassing material or sexual content to the victim's own Facebook or social networking page. Or they can set up a new blog or social networking page posing as the victim to accomplish the same thing. They can sign up victims on Web sites to receive junk e-mail or porn. Or they can impersonate the victim in a chat room to send threatening or embarrassing messages to humiliate the victim or to reveal personal information such as the victim's real name, phone number, and address.

In large part, children become cyberbullies for the same reasons that they might have become regular old schoolyard bullies—because they are frustrated, angry, socially maladjusted, looking for a laugh, or just plain bored.

The National Crime Prevention Council and other organizations have outlined a number of steps that might be helpful for parents in combating cyberbullying:

- Ask your children if anyone has been hateful or mean to them on the Internet or done things to intentionally embarrass them or make them unhappy. Keep in mind that your child may not even know what the word "cyberbullying" means.
- Encourage your child not to retaliate. Escalation will only make the problem worse.
- Understand that cyberbullies have the potential to reach a worldwide audience and the problem can go well beyond the schoolyard and your child's circle of friends.
- Don't hesitate to get authorities involved if you believe the level of harassment warrants legal action. Threats, intimidation, and impersonation are all crimes, even if committed by other children.
- Document cyberbullying incidents to the best of your ability and report them to police. Also, the Web site www.wiredsafety.org is staffed by volunteers who are trained to help in cases of cyberbullying, and the site maintains online forms to help you report these cases to the proper authorities.

"Sexting"

"Texting" simply means sending short text messages or photographs over a mobile phone. "Sexting" is a relatively new term referring to messages that include sexually explicit language and photographs in particular. These photographs can be produced using cell phones, computer Web cams, digital cameras, and even certain game systems. They can not only cause embarrassment but, like everything else in the digital age, can be quickly transmitted around the world to an unlimited number of people.

In 2008, a survey of youth between the ages of thirteen and nineteen, presented by the National Campaign to Prevent Teen and Unplanned Pregnancy, found that 20 percent of teens had posted nude or seminude pictures of themselves online and that 39 percent had sent or posted sexually suggestive messages. In some cases, if photos were produced involuntarily, under duress, or with malicious intent, the production or distribution of these images could rise to the level of criminal activity. If prosecuted, this activity would require the participant to register as a sex offender. In any case, sexually explicit images have the potential to affect a youngster's future, such as his or her ability to be admitted to a college or to get a job.

The issues arising from sexting are complex, and few people are recommending across-the-board, blanket prosecution for sexting participants. However, because of the high potential for unintended consequences—including exploitation, blackmail, harassment, and embarrassment—parents do need to be concerned.

The National Center for Missing and Exploited Children (NCMEC) recommends that the best way for parents to combat the dangers of sexting is to simply stay involved in their children's lives. Talk to your kids, know what they're doing, and set limits. It takes only a few moments for a youngster to take a sexually explicit picture and forward it to a friend. Make sure your youngster understands that once a photo is out there, it can't be taken back.

Should you find that a sexually explicit image of your child has been posted on a Web site, contact the Web site owner to ask them to take the image down. If you believe that conduct has risen to the level of criminal activity, report this activity to NCMEC by visiting www.cybertipline.com. NCMEC is a national clearinghouse, which handles reports about apparent child pornography and forwards them to appropriate law enforcement agencies who will then investigate and decide what action to take. Should your child ever receive a sexually explicit image from an unknown sender, this activity should always be reported to www.cybertipline.com for further investigation by law enforcement.

Sexual Predators Online

The "information superhighway" can run in both directions. The Internet has opened up enormous new educational, entertainment, and communications opportunities that those now in middle age never had as youngsters. But unfortunately, the Internet has also opened up huge new opportunities for the most criminal underclass of all—those who seek to sexually exploit our children.

There is no single profile that can describe all sexual predators. They can be of any age or social standing, and female predators do exist. Some are interested only in explicit conversation with children. Others wish to collect pornographic images, while others will seek face-to-face meetings.

Nor do all predators operate in a similar way. Some will try to slowly "befriend" children, simply giving them attention, affection, or perhaps gifts, and may spend a great deal of time and money in the process. They will learn about the child's interests and slowly introduce sexual context into their communications. Others will try to immediately engage youngsters in sexually explicit conversation.

Predators understand that youngsters, especially adolescents, can be curious about sexuality and sexually explicit material. They are at a vulnerable age when they are moving away from total parental control yet do not fully grasp the potential dangers in the world. Remember also that, even if you have computer safeguards in your home, your child may use other computers at school or the homes of friends, outside your supervision. Find out what safeguards are in place on these computers. Following the other guidelines outlined in the previous chapter can also help insulate your children from sexual predators as well as other computer-based risks.

For more information on sexual predators online and offline, I strongly recommend that you visit the Web site for the National Center for Missing and Exploited Children (NCMEC) at www.missingkids.com. Established in 1984, NCMEC operates under a congressional mandate to help prevent child abduction and sexual exploitation, help find missing children, and assist victims.

Signs That Your Child Might Be at Risk

- Your child spends a great deal of time online, particularly in chat rooms and particularly at night.
- Your child primarily makes new friends online or communicates with friends online.
- You find pornography on your child's computer. Sex offenders often send explicit material to children, with or without the intention of setting up a face-to-face meeting.
- Your child receives phone calls from adults you don't know or is making calls to numbers you don't recognize.
- Your child receives mail or gifts from someone you don't know.
- Your child quickly changes the screen on the monitor when you come into the room.
- Your child becomes withdrawn from the family.

If You Believe Your Child May Be Communicating with a Predator

- Talk to your child. Tell him or her about the dangers of sexual predators and try to determine if a predator has contacted your child.
- Review what is on your child's computer. Consider using a program like CyberPatrol (www.cyberpatrol.com) or PC Tattletale (www.pctattletale. com) to monitor or record your child's online activity.

- Use a telephone or device that displays the phone numbers of calls that have been made to and from your home.
- Review or monitor your child's access and use of all electronic communications, including chat room visits, instant messaging use, and cell phone use.

When to Notify Authorities

To protect your child as well as other children, you should notify local law enforcement officials or the FBI and the National Center for Missing and Exploited Children (NCMEC) should any of these situations arise:

- Your child or anyone in the household has received child pornography.
- Your child has been sexually solicited by someone who knows that your child is under eighteen years of age.
- Your child has received sexually explicit images from someone who knows your child is under the age of eighteen.
- You have any other reason to believe that a predator may have made contact with your child.
- In each case, keep the computer turned off to preserve evidence for law enforcement's use. Do not attempt to copy any explicit images or text unless law enforcement directs you to do so.

25

Internet Scams

Scams of various kinds have been around for all of human history. In ancient Greece, for example, ship captains could purchase a form of insurance against the loss of their vessels. A captain would borrow money from a lender before he set sail. If he made it safely back home, he would pay the money back, plus interest on the loan. But if the vessel sank, he kept the money toward the purchase of another ship. Often, however, captains would over-insure their ships and sink them intentionally, or try to hide the vessel in another port and then claim to the insurer that the ship had been lost at sea.

Scams are nothing new. But the advent of the Internet and e-mail has spawned a new generation of "cyber-scammers" who can now communicate with millions of people in the hope that just one or two will fall for a digital ruse. According to *PC Computing* magazine, cyberfraud recently increased by 600 percent in a single year. In 2008, more than 275,000 cyberfraud complaints were registered with the U.S. Department of Justice's Internet Crime Complaint Center (ICCC). Probably a far greater number of victims did not register complaints at all.

Some people mistakenly believe that seniors are the most likely to be taken in by Internet scammers. However, according to the ICCC, nearly half of those who registered Internet fraud complaints with the Center were between the ages of thirty and fifty.

The best advice for helping you avoid a great many of these scams can be summed up in a couple of short phrases. First, "If it seems too good to be true, it probably is." Businesses simply do not give away money or goods for free with no expectation of return. Legitimate companies do not generally offer work-at-home opportunities that pay tens of thousands of dollars per month to people with no experience. Bona fide lotteries don't require that you send a down payment in order to collect your winnings. And foreign government officials are unlikely to need your help in order to move millions of dollars in cash or gold out of their countries.

The second of these watchwords is "buyer beware." In 2008, complaints about Internet auction fraud and nondelivery of merchandise or payment accounted for nearly two-thirds of all Internet fraud reports registered with the Justice Department.

When it comes to defrauding innocent people, the Internet represents the biggest opportunity ever for scammers of all sorts. To cover the full range of Internet and e-mail scams that are known to the FBI and to international authorities would require an entire book. What's more, by the time this book is published and in your hands, entirely new scams will already be in the offing. But to help you develop a more finely attuned "radar" to detect potential Internet fraud, let's look at some of the more prevalent scams and abuses that are taking place right now.

Auction Fraud

Auction fraud refers to the misrepresentation of a product or service advertised for sale through an Internet auction site, or the nondelivery of products that have been purchased and paid for through an auction site.

In one typical scenario, the seller posts the auction as if he resides in the United States, then responds to the winning bidder with an e-mail claiming that he is outside the country for business reasons or a family emergency. He then requests that the funds for the auction item be sent to him via Western Union or bank-to-bank wire transfer. Once funds are transferred in this way, they are rarely recoverable.

Alternatively, the seller might ask that the funds be transferred to another individual. Romania has become well known for this type of fraud. Auctions are posted as if the seller lives in the United States. Then the seller requests that the winning bidder transfer the payment, via a wire service, to a business partner or family member often located in a European country. Again, once the funds are transferred, the buyer has little recourse.

When Buying from Online Auctions

- Understand as much as possible about how the auction works, what your obligations are as a buyer, and what the seller's obligations are before you bid.
- Examine the "feedback" on the seller, rankings by other buyers indicating whether the merchandise was quickly and property shipped and whether the item matched the advertised description. However, be cautious of a 100 percent feedback rating if the seller has a low number of feedback ratings that were all posted around the same date and time. Don't assume that the seller is legitimate just because they have an attractive Web site.
- Determine what method of payment the seller is asking from the buyer and where he or she will be asking you to send payment.
- Verify the seller's return policy if the merchandise is not as advertised.
- When purchasing antiques, relics, or artwork, have an immediate appraisal done by an independent expert.
- Make sure that shipments of expensive items are insured.
- Find out what safeguards have been put in place by the online auction company to protect buyers.
- Avoid sellers acting as authorized dealers in countries where there are no such dealers.
- Understand that sellers outside the United States are usually not subject to U.S. laws and that American authorities will probably have no jurisdiction over these sellers if a problem occurs.
- Be suspicious if an auction merchant is offering a much lower price on an item than any other online vendor can match.
- Consider using a payment escrow service like PayPal, which can offer some added protection against fraud.

When Selling through Online Auctions

- Avoid buyers who ask that their purchase be shipped using a certain method to avoid taxes or customs duties.
- Be suspicious of any credit card purchases where the address of the cardholder does not match the shipping address. Always wait for bank authorization on credit card purchases before shipping any products.
- Find out what safeguards have been put in place by the online auction company to protect sellers.

Ordering Online: Avoiding Credit Card Fraud and Nondelivery of Merchandise

After auction fraud, nondelivery of merchandise is the most commonly reported Internet complaint registered with the Justice Department. Here are some tips for making sure you get the merchandise you pay for:

- Don't assume that the seller is legitimate because they have an attractive Web site.

- Try to verify that you are purchasing your merchandise from a reputable source. See if the company lists a physical address (rather than merely a post office box) and a phone number, and call the seller to see if the number is correct and working. Check with the Better Business Bureau from the seller's area if you have suspicions.
- Be especially cautious when responding to e-mail offers.
- Understand that foreign merchants are generally immune to U.S. laws or prosecution by American authorities.

- The safest way to purchase items via the Internet is by credit card. You can often dispute the charge if you do not receive the item or if it was misrepresented by the seller.
- Make credit card payments online only through secure Web sites, or use an escrow service such as PayPal. Sometimes a tiny icon of a padlock appears to symbolize a higher level of security to transmit data. This icon is not a guarantee of a secure site but might provide you some assurance.
- Verify that the charge on your credit card statement matches the amount you expected to pay.
- Scan your credit card statement each month to ensure that online merchants you have done business with have not applied additional charges against your account.

The Counterfeit Cashier's Check Scam

This scam targets individuals who sell merchandise on the Internet. A "buyer," typically from outside the United States, will contact the seller and tell him or her that payment for the item will be sent from a third party within the United States via cashier's check. The check will include extra funds to cover shipping of the item, and the seller is asked to wire any remaining funds back to the buyer as soon as the check has cleared. Because a cashier's check is used, a bank will typically release the funds immediately, or after a one- or two-day hold. Falsely believing the check has cleared, the seller wires the money as instructed. Not until later is the seller contacted by his or her bank when the check is discovered to be fraudulent.

Other twists on this scheme have victimized U.S. law firms and other corporations that should know better. In these counterfeit check schemes, law firms are asked via e-mail to collect delinquent payments from third parties in the United States. The law firm receives a retainer check and is instructed to deduct its fee from this check and wire the remainder of the money to a foreign bank. Or a law firm is asked to represent an ex-wife who is owed money by her former husband. When the husband sends a cashier's check for the funds, the law firm wires the money, less its retainer fee, to the "ex-wife" overseas. Of course, in both of these scams, the cashier's checks were fraudulent.

"Phishing"

Phishing scammers send e-mails that appear to come from a legitimate business, such as a bank or financial institution, asking the potential victim to provide sensitive information such as online banking passwords and account numbers, credit card numbers, or other financial information. Or the scammer may ask the e-mail recipient to visit a Web site and provide this information. The Web site may look very authentic and may have an address similar to that of the legitimate financial institution, but is completely fraudulent and is set up only to steal financial information.

Lotteries

In this scheme, the victims initially receives an e-mail notifying them that they have been selected as the winner of an international lottery and are to receive a lump-sum payment of $500,000 or more. To claim the prize, the "winner" is asked to contact a "processing company" and pay a fee, generally $1,000 to $5,000, via wire service. A person who falls victim to the initial ruse will be asked for even more money.

"Fine Print" Scams

"Free trial" offers for diet pills, cosmetics, vitamins, and other consumer products often come with fine print that can lead to a big shock on future credit card statements. Consumers are typically asked to pay just a dollar or two (using a credit card) to cover "shipping and handling" for a free supply of the product. The merchant, however, knows that few of those who order the product will pay attention to the terms and conditions that are written in miniscule type or that require the consumer to click to a new page to read. These terms and conditions may specify that the merchant may begin charging the consumer for a monthly supply of the product to be shipped automatically. In many cases, the monthly shipments and credit card charges may begin even before the consumer receives the free trial.

If you believe you have been the victim of unfair marketing practices, contact your credit card company to dispute the charges that have appeared on your statement. Generally, your credit card issuer will be able to resolve the dispute in your favor. Continue to watch your credit card statements for future charges and, if the problem is not revolved, contact the Federal Trade Commission's Bureau of Consumer Protection at http://www.ftc.gov/bcp/.

Prescription Drug Discounts and Counterfeit Drugs

The criminals operating these swindles send spam that offers prescription drugs at lower prices. This is a simple identity theft scheme in which the products are never delivered but the criminals collect enough personal information to apply for credit in the victim's name, or simply to use the victim's credit card information to make fraudulent purchases.

The advent of the Internet has also opened up opportunities for the counterfeiting of medications. These medicines can be contaminated, contain the wrong dosage of medication, or contain no medication at all. Do not purchase medications in response to unsolicited e-mails. If you choose to purchase medications online, you can contact the National Association of Boards of Pharmacy at www. nabp.net or at 1-847-698-6227 to see whether a mail order pharmacy is licensed and in good standing.

"U.S. Government" E-mail Scams

Internet scammers will often send e-mails purporting to be from the Federal Bureau of Investigation (FBI) or the Internal Revenue Service (IRS), U.S. Customs and Border Protection (CBP), or another government agency. These e-mails will alert the recipient that he or she must pay a fee in order to avoid some type of prosecution or clear up a problem. Or the e-mail may ask for personal information that will then be used to apply for credit in the victim's name. Our government agencies do not communicate with U.S. citizens in this way, and all of these e-mails should be viewed as fraudulent.

When the U.S. government issued its "stimulus" checks, scammers flooded the country with e-mails purporting to be from the IRS and asking for personal information, including bank account information, so that stimulus checks could be delivered more quickly. These e-mails, too, were of course fraudulent.

Fraudulent Relief Agencies

After major natural disasters such as the 2010 earthquake in Haiti, it has become all too common for scammers to set up fraudulent "relief" organizations that exist only as a Web site for purposes of bilking well-meaning individuals of their money.

A healthy skepticism can help ensure that your charitable contributions are used as you wish, and not to line a scammer's pocket. Do not respond to unsolicited e-mails, even if you believe they are coming from a legitimate organization. If you wish to make a gift, visit the group's Web site directly, not by clicking through on an e-mail link. Organizations like GuideStar (www.guidestar.org) and Charity Navigator (www.charitynavigator.org) can help to confirm a group's existence as well as provide general ratings of the group's efficiency in its use of contributions.

Nigerian Letter or "419"

Named for the violation of Section 419 of the Nigerian Criminal Code, a victim of the 419 scam will be contacted via e-mail by a person or persons claiming to represent the Nigerian government. The victim will be offered the "opportunity" to help move large sums of money, usually millions of dollars, from Nigerian bank accounts into accounts in another country and to share in these funds once they are safely out of Nigeria. The victim will be asked for funds to cover such expenses as bribes and legal fees. Increasing amounts will be requested if the victim falls for the initial request. In addition, the victim may be asked for other information, such as bank account numbers. In this case, the victim may not only lose his or her money but become a victim of identity theft.

"Reshipping"

Reshipping is an Internet scam designed to convince innocent people to transfer goods that were purchased with stolen credit cards. Reshippers are "hired" through e-mails or Internet ads and are asked to receive packages at their homes then reship the packages abroad. During the "hiring" process, the victim is asked for personal information, including date of birth and social security number, which will be used to obtain credit in the victim's name.

When the packages begin to arrive, the "employee" reships them to another address, generally overseas. Eventually, the "employee" will be contacted by the credit card companies and questioned about the fraudulent purchases. This can result in a legal entanglement for the "employee," and in the meantime, his or her identity has been stolen so that the scammer can purchase additional products to be reshipped by another victim.

The "Mystery Shopper" Scam

This scam combines the reshipping scam with a cashier's check scam. Employment opportunities are offered via e-mail or Internet ads for "mystery shoppers" who are asked to submit to an extensive background check before being considered for employment.

The mystery shopper is then sent a fraudulent cashier's check by the "employer" and asked to conduct research on a retail store by shopping at the store for a certain length of time, spending a specific amount on merchandise, and making notes about the shopping experience. In addition, the mystery shopper is asked to help evaluate the ease of wiring money from the retail location and to wire a portion of the original cashier's check back to the "employer." As with other cashier's check scams, the mystery shopper will not know that the check was fraudulent until he or she has already wired money to the scammer.

Similar scams involve the "hiring" of victims to "process payments" or "transfer funds" and are also based on the victim depositing a fraudulent cashier's check then sending his or her own real funds to the criminals.

Please note that there are legitimate mystery shopper programs available. Legitimate companies will not charge an application fee and will never ask an employee to send a portion of a payment back.

Fraudulent and Counterfeit Gift Cards

If you wish to purchase a gift card, do so through the merchant, not through an online auction or third-party advertisement. Legitimate-looking gift cards can be counterfeited quite easily, and, if you give the card as a gift, you will not know that you have been defrauded until your friend or family member tries to use the card. In addition, it is not uncommon for gift cards to be purchased with stolen credit cards as a way for the credit card thief to obtain cash from the stolen card. If you buy a gift card that was purchased with stolen credit information, you may not be able to use the card after the fraud is discovered.

Summary

Let's face it. If you're an e-mail user, you're going to be bombarded with Internet scam offers for the rest of your life. In addition to knowing some of the tactics that these criminals use, here are some general guidelines for protecting your privacy and your wallet from scam artists who try to prey on unsuspecting victims online:

- Do not respond to unsolicited (spam) e-mail.
- Do not click on links contained within an unsolicited e-mail.
- Avoid filling out forms contained in e-mail messages that ask for personal information.
- If a business sends you an e-mail and you want to respond or take advantage of an offer, log on directly to the official Web site for that business. Do not "click through" from an unsolicited e-mail.
- If an e-mail appears to be from your bank, credit card issuer, or other company you deal with, use the contact information that is provided on your statements. Again, do not click through from an unsolicited e-mail.
- To receive the latest information about cyberscams, visit the FBI's New E-Scams and Warnings Webpage at http://www.fbi.gov/cyberinvest/escams.htm.

For the latest information as well as consumer ratings for products mentioned throughout this book, see www.SafeBookProducts.com. In addition, go to this Web site to sign up for a free monthly newsletter on new products to help keep your family safer.

SAFE AGAINST IDENTITY THEFT AND FRAUD

n previous sections of *Safe*, we've addressed how to make your family more secure from disasters, accidents, and a diversity of criminals, including those who may try to enter your home and those who might try to use your computer as a vehicle to compromise your security or the security of your child.

In this section, we'll turn our attention to a different kind of threat—the threat that criminals can pose to your family's bank and credit account, your credit rating, and your long-term financial future.

Of course, some of the precautions we discussed in the previous section on computer safety have an important role to play in protecting your family's financial security. Let's now take a more in-depth look at some of the deceptions which have cost American citizens literally hundreds of billions of dollars over the years, including a variety of frauds, scams, and investment schemes, as well as one of the fastest-growing crimes in America—identity theft.

26

Identity Theft

What Is "Identity Theft?"

Legally speaking, "identity theft" is the illegal taking of another person's identifying information, while "identity fraud" refers to the use of this information to commit a financial or other crime. However, both of these terms are broadly used to describe a wide range of criminal behaviors in which a perpetrator uses someone else's personal data to commit a crime. In the vast majority of identity theft crimes, the criminal uses the information for economic gain.

Sometimes identity theft is as simple as stealing a wallet or purse and using the victim's credit cards to make purchases. Other identity theft crimes can be much more elaborate, with criminals virtually assuming the identity of the victim to obtain a driver's license, apply for jobs, drain existing bank accounts and open new credit accounts, rent property, purchase cars and boats and homes, obtain medical benefits, make false insurance claims, and even declare bankruptcy in the name of the victim.

Identity thieves have also been known to commit crimes and then present themselves to law enforcement as another person—resulting in a warrant for the innocent person being issued when the identity thief fails to appear in court or follow through on a legal matter.

Think back to the last time you applied for a credit card. Chances are, you didn't visit the issuing bank in person. Instead, you provided information by mail, over the telephone, or online. A criminal, armed with enough information about you, can do the same thing.

In many cases, the damage inflicted on a victim will go far beyond immediate financial losses. It may take enormous amounts of money, including legal fees, as well as hundreds of hours of work in order for a victim to restore his or her credit rating and financial reputation. In some cases, these processes can take several years to complete. In the meantime, victims may find it impossible to obtain a credit card, car loan, home loan, or student loan; may be denied employment based on their tainted credit reports or defaults; and may be sued by creditors or even arrested for crimes they did not commit.

Each year, approximately nine million Americans are victimized by identity theft. While not all of these frauds are equally serious, the average cost per victim is more than $5,700 and requires six hundred hours of effort by the injured party to repair his or her good name.

Real-life Examples of Identity Theft

In one well-publicized case of identity theft, an already-convicted felon stole a victim's identity to run up more than $100,000 in credit card debt, obtain a federal home loan, and purchase vehicles in the name of his victim. The criminal even called the victim on the telephone, taunting him and claiming he could continue to pose as the victim for as long as he wanted because identity theft was not a federal crime. The criminal eventually filed for bankruptcy in the victim's name. This case, and others like it, prompted Congress in 1998 to create a new federal offense of identity theft.

In Wisconsin, a man at home with his two children heard a knock at his door and was confronted by three sheriffs with a warrant for his arrest on charges of cocaine possession with the intent to distribute. He was arrested and spent the next two days in jail. The victim was not completely taken by surprise since he had already lost his job and his driver's license because of other acts committed by the same criminal impersonator.

In Washington state, an employee at a mortgage company was recruited by an identity theft criminal ring to supply them with personal and financial information about people who had applied for mortgages. Using this information, the criminals created phony drivers' licenses using the names and addresses of the victims, but bearing their own photographs. The criminals were then able to drain money from the victims' bank accounts, as well as open up new credit accounts in their names and run up huge charges.

In Florida, a woman was indicted and pled guilty to federal charges after obtaining a fraudulent driver's license in the name of her victim. The woman used the license to withdraw more than $13,000 from the victim's bank account and to obtain five department store credit cards in the victim's name, charging $4,000 worth of merchandise on the cards.

In Maryland, a retired Air Force officer and his wife suddenly found that they had no ability to obtain credit. In requesting their credit reports, they discovered thirty-three fraudulent accounts and debts totaling $113,000, including loans on five vehicles that had originated in Texas and Oklahoma, more than one thousand miles from their home. Banks, stores, and collection agencies began demanding payments and threatening legal action to collect debts the couple had never incurred. When the couple's lawyer sent sworn affidavits attesting that the couple had not opened the accounts, collection agencies would simply transfer the debt to another agency. Civil judgments were awarded against the couple. They were unable to obtain credit for such items as a badly needed new heating system for their home, and false credit information continued to appear on their records for years.

How Identity Thieves Operate

The most common form of identity theft involves the use of credit cards—using another person's cards to make purchases or applying for cards in the name of another person. However, there are many types of information that can be valuable to an identity thief, including Social Security numbers, banking and investment account numbers, computer records, medical records, and more.

Sometimes this information is obtained from the victim directly; at other times, it is obtained without the victim's direct participation. Once an identity thief has enough information about you, he or she can use that information to access your existing bank accounts, make applications for new credit cards and/or loans, or obtain services like medical benefits.

If the criminal takes steps to ensure that bills for the falsely obtained credit cards, or bank statements showing the unauthorized withdrawals, are sent to an address other than the victim's, the victim may not become aware of what is happening until the criminal has already inflicted substantial damage on the victim's assets, credit, and reputation.

Here are some of the ways in which identity thieves have been known to obtain the information they need to steal identities and perpetrate frauds.

"Cold Calling"

Identity thieves pose as customer service representatives of utility companies, offering to enroll a customer in a plan that will lower monthly bills and asking for personal information in order to put the savings plan into effect.

Claiming False Delinquencies

Identity thieves call a family member at home, claiming that a spouse is behind on credit card or loan payments. The caller then asks the family member to confirm a Social Security number or to provide a credit card account number or other sensitive information.

"Skimming"

Identity thieves can use special hardware or software to record credit and debit account numbers, as well as PIN numbers, when the card is swiped at a retail location.

"Pretexting"

Identity thieves can obtain some personal information about you then use it to obtain additional information from companies you do business with, including financial institutions.

"Shoulder Surfing"

In a public place, a criminal can watch you as you punch in credit card numbers on a telephone, or listen in on your conversation when you provide credit card information to make a hotel or rental car reservation.

"Dumpster Diving"

Identity thieves can go through garbage cans or dumpsters to obtain copies of bank statements, credit card statements, or other financial records that include your name, account numbers, and other personal information.

Redirection of Mail

By simply stealing mail from mailboxes or by filing a false "change of address" form, a criminal can receive credit card statements including account numbers and use these account numbers to make online or telephone purchases. If your mail includes new or replacement credit cards, these will also be delivered directly to the thief.

Retrieving Information from Discarded Computers or Hard Drives

If information hasn't been removed from the computer or hard drive properly, criminals can access the stored information.

Hacking

A criminal can hack (or gain illegal online entry) into computers or databases to steal information.

Security Errors

Security errors by corporations or government agencies can result in sensitive information such as Social Security numbers or credit card account numbers being displayed on public Web sites.

Bogus Job Opportunities

Job opportunities can be advertised in a variety of ways that ask victims to provide Social Security numbers or banking or credit card account details.

Fraud

Fraud can be committed by corporate employees who either use sensitive information or sell the information to others for the purpose of committing identity theft.

Computer "Phishing"

As mentioned in the previous section, identity thieves impersonate a company or government agency and convince a potential victim to disclose information that can be used for identity fraud.

Basic Research

Basic research can be done about a potential victim using public records or social network sites such as MySpace or Facebook.

Old-fashioned Theft

Thieves can steal wallets or purses, or steal checks to be forged or used to acquire bank account numbers and bank routing numbers.

Preventing Identity Theft

Your first and most essential step in preventing identity theft is to recognize that anyone can be a victim. You also need to understand the types of information that would be most valuable to an identity thief who wants to use your identity to commit fraud. Obviously, you wouldn't leave a pile of cash in a public place where anyone could simply pick it up. Yet a few key pieces of information could be far more valuable to an identity thief than a big roll of bills.

Like every other type of criminal we've discussed in this book, identity thieves tend to look for easy opportunities. By making your personal information more difficult to access, you make yourself a less attractive target.

Some of your identifying information—such as your name, address, and phone number—can't be kept completely private. But generally, an identity thief will need more than these items to commit a fraud or other crime in your name. The key to minimizing identity theft is to keep key information out of the hands of other people unless they have a bona fide reason to have the data. Some of these key pieces of information include:

- Social Security numbers
- Driver's license numbers
- Credit card account numbers
- Credit card verification codes (extra numbers that may appear on the front or back of your card)
- Checking account numbers
- Personal identification numbers (PINs)
- Computer passwords
- Dates of birth
- Birth certificates
- Passports and passport numbers

Knowing that any of these items could be of value to an identity thief, here are a number of ideas to keep this information private:

- Don't give out personal information just because someone asks for it. Many of the preprinted forms that you fill out will ask for information that is simply not needed but could be valuable to an identity criminal.
- Be particularly vigilant about your Social Security number, and only provide this number when absolutely necessary. Ask why this information is needed, how it will be used, and what security measures are in place to protect it.
- Do not keep your Social Security card in your wallet.
- Never write your ATM or credit card pin numbers on your cards, and do not keep records of these numbers with your cards.
- Carry only the credit cards you need when you leave your home. Fewer cards in your wallet or purse means fewer cards for a thief to steal, less hassle for you in reporting a loss to banks and card issuers, and less opportunity for a criminal to make fraudulent purchases in your name.
- Do not print or write your Social Security number on your bank checks. Use your driver's license number instead.

- Do not throw bank or credit card statements into the regular trash. Small shredders are now available for well under $50, and some banks and communities now offer free shredding services to consumers on a few specified days each year. Also shred credit and debit card receipts, other financial statements of all types, insurance and medical forms, credit card offers you receive in the mail, and expired credit cards and debit cards.
- To no longer receive prescreened credit offers in the mail, call 1-888-5-OPT-OUT.
- When traveling on business or family vacation, have your mail held at the post office or ask a friend or family member to collect your mail each day.
- Avoid putting outgoing mail in your mailbox. Take it to the post office or a mailbox instead.
- If you fail to receive mail for a few days, check with your post office to see if someone has filed a change-of-address request in your name.
- For your computer and for companies you do business with, do not use obvious passwords like your date of birth, mother's maiden name, pet's name, last four digits of your Social Security number, or strings of numbers or letters like "123456" or "ABCDE."
- Do not give information to unidentified callers who claim to represent your bank, credit card company, investment brokerage company, utility company, and so forth. These companies should already have in their files all of the information they need to know about you. If they have a real need for the information, ask them to mail you a request. Respond in writing and make sure that, if a return envelope is provided, the address matches the real address of the company.
- If someone calls you and offers you the opportunity to apply for a credit card, ask him or her to send you a written application form.
- Likewise, if you are notified by telephone that you have won a sweepstakes or prize, do not provide any personal information. Ask for a written form.
- If you need to mention personal information to someone on the phone (for example, if you've lost a credit card or if your spouse needs your Social Security number for a loan application), don't make the call in an open location where a passerby could listen in. Wait until you're in a less public location to make the call.

- Do not dispose of a computer or hard drive without making sure that all information contained on it is erased or made completely unreadable. Simply deleting files is not enough (this does not erase information; it simply gives the computer permission to overwrite it). Before disposing of a computer, you must physically destroy the drive or use "data shredding" or "data wiping" software to wipe out the information permanently.

- Make sure that others in your family, especially youngsters to whom you may have provided a credit card for convenience, understand the threat of identity theft. Have them read this section of *Safe*, and make sure they know what types of information should not be provided when using the Internet or the phone.

- Consider purchasing identity theft protection. Several companies, as described later in this chapter, offer services to monitor your credit, alert you to changes in your credit report or attempts to open new accounts, and more.

Credit and Bank Accounts

Should you ever become a victim of identify theft or any type of financial scam, early detection is the key to preventing further damage, to minimizing the impact on your credit and your family finances, and to beginning the process of repairing whatever damage may already have been done.

Typically, your bank, credit card, and other financial statements will provide the first indication that your identity has been compromised. Here are some steps you should take:

- Maintain careful records of your banking accounts and other financial accounts. Keep statements for a minimum of one year (you may wish to keep these longer for tax purposes; ask your tax advisor).

- Carefully examine your checking account statement each month, and make sure your account balances.

- Examine your credit card statements before paying your bills. Even if your card is never physically stolen, there are countless ways for a criminal to get his hands on your credit card number. If you see transactions that you were not responsible for, report them immediately to your credit card company and dispute the charges. Generally, you have very good protections against the fraudulent use of your credit cards *provided that you report unauthorized charges promptly.*

- If you do not receive a monthly statement for one of your accounts, call the financial institution or credit card company as soon as you notice the problem.

- If you're told that your statements are being mailed to another address, tell the financial institution or credit card representative immediately that you did not authorize the change and that someone may be improperly using your accounts. In this situation, you should also ask for a new statement as well as transactions that have been posted in the time since that statement was issued.

Credit Reports

There are three major credit reporting companies in the United States: Equifax, Experian (formerly TRW), and TransUnion. Upon your request, each of these companies must provide you with a copy of your credit report each year, or any time you are denied a job, credit, or insurance on the basis of information in your credit report. Additional reports during a twelve-month period can be obtained for a relatively small fee. One way to check your credit reports more often than once a year, without incurring additional costs, is to request a report from each agency about every four months.

Credit reports include four basic types of information, including identifying information, credit information, public record information, and inquiries. Typically, positive and negative information remains on your credit report for seven years from the date on which it is first reported. Bankruptcies are an exception; they remain on the report for ten years. If there is inaccurate information in your credit report, you have the right to dispute it and have it removed. However, in an identity theft case, you may have difficulty removing the information since the burden of proof rests with you to show that you were not responsible for the accounts, loans, or late payments.

Identifying information, used to separate your identity from others, will include:

- Your name
- Your current and previous addresses
- Your Social Security number
- Your year of birth
- Your current and previous employers
- Your spouse's name, if you are married

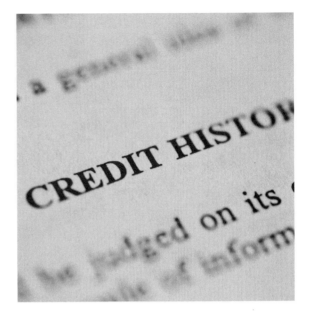

Credit information includes any credit accounts, car loans, mortgages, or other loans that you have with:

- Banks
- Retailers
- Credit card issuers
- Other lenders

Public record information includes any information that is obtained from public court records, such as:

- Bankruptcies
- Tax liens
- Monetary judgments

Finally, *inquiries* indicate applications for credit that you have made, whether or not credit is granted. Inquiries typically remain on your report for two years. In the case of an identity thief applying for credit in your name, you may suffer negative consequences even if the applications were denied. When you apply for a credit or new loan, lenders will look at the inquiries section of the credit report to see if you are applying for a lot of new credit or potentially overextending yourself financially.

To Receive Your Credit Reports

The most efficient and easiest way to receive your free credit reports is by visiting www.annualcreditreport.com, a Web site sponsored and maintained by the three major credit reporting agencies. If you prefer, you can request your credit reports by phone at 1-877-322-8228 or by mail at:

Annual Credit Report Request Service
P.O. Box 105281
Atlanta, GA 30348-5281

Please note that to request a report by mail, you must first download a "request form" at the Web site listed above. Also note that reports requested by phone or mail may take two to three weeks to be delivered to you, while credit reports requested online are viewable immediately upon authentication of your identity.

Not all credit reports will be complete. Nor will each of your three reports necessarily contain the same information. It's therefore important that you check all three reports to ensure that the information is accurate. Even if you haven't been a victim of identity theft, your reports may contain inaccurate information that could affect your ability to obtain new credit or that could force you to pay higher interest rates on your loans or credit cards.

Warning Signs: Detecting Identity Theft Early

No matter how many precautions you take or how careful you are with your personal information, you simply cannot reduce your identity theft risk to zero.

Some of the identity theft methods that we examined earlier, such as "skimming" and security breaches by companies you do business with, are simply beyond our control. Skilled hackers can sometimes penetrate even the most sophisticated protections that we place on our computers. And a determined thief may get his hands on our wallet or purse despite our best efforts.

You therefore need to know the warning signs that your credit or identity has been compromised. Simply because there is incorrect information on your credit report does not mean that you have become a victim of identity theft. Some errors are simply oversights that can be corrected fairly easily. However, here are some of the more typical warning signs that you may in fact have become an identity theft victim:

- You see unauthorized charges on your credit card statements, bank statements, or even on your long-distance telephone bill.
- You receive bills from a credit card account that you did not open, or a loan that you did not apply for.
- Your bank account has been suddenly drained or depleted.
- Your statements from banks or other financial institutions do not arrive on time, or your credit card bills do not arrive on time.
- You see accounts on your credit report that you do not recognize.
- You see credit inquiries on your credit report for credit that you did not apply for.
- A company contacts you regarding merchandise or services that you never agreed to purchase.
- You are contacted by a debt collection agency for a debt you did not incur.
- You are denied credit for a credit card, mortgage, or car loan due to information on your credit report.
- You are not able to obtain the best interest rate on a mortgage, car loan, or credit card, or the credit limit granted on a new card is unusually low.
- You receive credit cards for which you never submitted applications.
- You receive information from your insurance company, or an invoice from a medical provider, for office visits, tests, or procedures that you did not have.

If You Become a Victim—First Steps

To victims of identity theft, the task of restoring their credit and personal reputations can be almost overwhelming. The problem cannot be resolved with a single phone call, and it may take a long period of time to undo the damage caused by an identity criminal. Having said that, here are the steps you should begin taking immediately if you believe you have been a victim of an identity crime.

Report your suspicions to the Federal Trade Commission (FTC) by calling their toll-free hotline, 1-(877) ID-THEFT. This number has been set up exclusively for victims to report these crimes.

Under federal law, the FTC is responsible for processing complaints from identity crime victims, referring those complaints to appropriate entities, including the major credit reporting agencies and law enforcement agencies, and providing additional information to help victims stop the problem and restore their good names. For additional information that will be helpful in the immediate aftermath of an identity theft, I also recommend that you visit FTC's Web site at http://www. ftc.gov/bcp/edu/microsites/idtheft/. The site has several downloadable documents, including an Identity Theft Complaint Form, Identity Theft Affidavits, and other helpful resources such as sample cover letters that you may need to send to creditors and law enforcement agencies. While it isn't required, I highly recommend that you file an Identity Theft Complaint so that this form can be incorporated into the Identity Theft Report to be prepared by your local police (more on this in a moment).

Contact the three major credit reporting bureaus and let them know you have been (or suspect that you have been) a victim of identity theft. Place a Fraud Alert on your credit reports to prevent any more new accounts from being opened in your name, and request a credit report. Placing a fraud alert also allows you to receive a credit report at no charge, even if you have already received your free annual report.

In theory, all three agencies should be notified of the Fraud Alert once you contact any one of the agencies, but it won't hurt to notify all three. I strongly recommend that you contact each agency by telephone to alert them immediately, and then follow up with a letter.

Equifax

To report fraud:
Call 1-800-525-6285
Write to P.O. Box 740250, Atlanta, GA 30374-0250

To order a copy of your credit report:
Call 1-800-685-1111
Write to P.O. Box 740241, Atlanta, GA 30374-0241

To dispute information in your credit report:
Call the number provided in the report.

To opt out of preapproved offers of credit:
Call 1-888-5-OPT-OUT
Write to Equifax Options, P.O. Box 740123, Atlanta GA 30374-0123

Experian (formerly TRW)
> *To report fraud:*
> Call 1-888-EXPERIAN (397-3742)
> Fax 1-800-301-7196
> Write to P.O. Box 1017, Allen, TX 75013
>
> *To order a copy of your credit report:*
> Call 1-888-EXPERIAN (397-3742)
> Write to P.O. Box 2104, Allen TX 75013
>
> *To dispute information in your credit report:*
> Call the number provided in the report.
>
> *To opt out of preapproved offers of credit:*
> Call 1-800-353-0809 or 1-(888) 5-OPT-OUT
> Write to P.O. Box 919, Allen, TX 75013

TransUnion
> *To report fraud:*
> Call 1-800-680-7289
> Write to P.O. Box 6790, Fullerton, CA 92634
>
> *To order a copy of your credit report:*
> Call 1-800-888-4213
> Write to P.O. Box 390, Springfield, PA 19064
>
> *To dispute information in your credit report:*
> Call the number provided in the report.
>
> *To opt out of preapproved offers of credit:*
> Call 1-800-680-7293 or 1-888-5-OPT-OUT
> Write to P.O. Box 97328, Jackson, MS 39238

If you have had checks stolen or bank accounts set up in your name by an identity thief, contact the major check verification companies, including:

CheckRite: 1-800-766-2748
ChexSystems: 1-800-428-9623
CrossCheck: 1-800-552-1900
Equifax: 1-800-437-5120
National Processing Co. (NPC): 1-800-526-5380
SCAN: 1-800-262-7771
TeleCheck: 1-800-710-9898

If you believe an identity criminal has submitted a change-of-address form in your name or has used the mail to commit fraud involving your identity, contact your local office of the Postal Inspection Service as well as your local Post Office.

If you believe your Social Security number has been compromised, call the Social Security Administration at 1-(800) 269-0271 to report the fraud.

If you believe that your tax returns may have been used to commit an identity crime or that tax violations may have occurred as a result of an identity crime, contact the Internal Revenue Service at 1-(800) 829-0433.

If the identity crime involves your telephone service, long-distance bill, or calling card, contact your telephone service provider.

Contact any financial institutions where you have accounts that you know have been compromised. Cancel those accounts and open new ones. Place stop payments on checks that have not cleared. Change your ATM card and your Personal Identification Number (PIN).

Contact your local police department and make an initial contact to report the crime. In a moment, we'll discuss how to work with your local police department to create an official Identity Theft Report that gives you certain legal rights.

If You Become a Victim—Second Steps

Once you have received your credit reports, examine every page and every entry with utmost care. Make sure all identifying information is correct, including your name, current and previous addresses, Social Security number, year of birth, current and previous employers, and your spouse's name, if you are married.

Review the public record information, which includes bankruptcies, tax liens, and court judgments. Also look over any inquiries that have been made, including applications for credit, and determine whether the applications were made by you or by someone else.

Then, begin reviewing the credit information, which includes credit cards and loans, and contact all creditors with whom your identity has been used fraudulently.

If You Become a Victim—Third Steps

Once you have completed your review of your credit reports, contact your local police department to obtain a detailed, valid police report about your identity theft, which is legally known as an "Identity Theft Report." If you filed an Identity Theft Complaint form with the FTC, this form can be attached or incorporated into your Identity Theft Report.

Before visiting your local police department, contact them to ask what documents you will need to present. These are likely to include:

- A printed copy of your FTC Identity Theft Complaint Form
- A government-issued photo identification such as a driver's license or passport
- Something that verifies your address, such as a phone or utility bill or payroll stub—you can mark out financial information if you wish
- Copies of your credit reports that show inaccuracies resulting from the identity theft
- Copies of any credit cards, bills, monthly statements, or collection letters you have received relating to the identity theft
- Any other documentation that you believe provides information about how the identity theft occurred or who committed the crime

Sign your Complaint Form in the presence of the police officer, and ask the officer to sign the "Law Enforcement Report Information" section of your complaint. Once this document is signed, you can include it with communications to creditors and credit reporting bureaus to permanently block fraudulent information from appearing on your credit report, to ensure that debts do not reappear on your credit report, to prevent companies and collection agencies from pursuing you for debts resulting from an identity theft, and to place an extended fraud alert on your credit report.

- Contact all creditors where an identity thief has compromised your account or created an account in your name.
- For each account, obtain the name of a single individual whom you can use as your point of contact.
- For each account, demand a copy of the original application that was completed and used to open the account.

Once you have received and reviewed the application, send a sworn affidavit that you are not the person who opened the account. In your affidavit, point out the false information in the application, including any signature that is not yours. Have the creditor send a statement to all three credit bureaus indicating that they have received this affidavit from you alleging fraud. Ask for a written copy of this statement for your records. In addition, contact the three credit bureaus directly and request that the fraudulent information on your credit report be removed.

Do not try to keep a fraudulent account current by making minimum payments, and do not accept any offer from a creditor or collection agency to settle the account for a reduced amount, no matter how small the amount. Accepting such an offer undermines your identity fraud claim and all but ensures that the fraudulent information will remain part of your credit report for at least seven years.

Stand your ground with creditors and collection agencies. If they accepted a fraudulent application for credit in your name, they bear the financial responsibility, not you.

If any creditor or collection agency becomes aggressive with you on the telephone, demand that all future communications with you be in writing.

Understand that even when incorrect information is removed from a credit report, it can reappear later when similar information is received from a credit issuer. As disputes are resolved, ask each creditor to send you a letter stating that fraudulent debts have been discharged. Retain the letters and send copies to the credit bureaus as needed if false information reappears on your credit report.

If You Become a Victim—Fourth Steps

Order a credit report every month, especially during the first year, to make sure that incorrect information is being removed and does not reappear on your report. Remember that, in the end, you must take the ultimate responsibility for making sure that your credit and reputation are fully restored.

Professional Assistance in Preventing Identity Theft

With the alarming rise in identity theft cases over the past decade, several companies now offer identity theft protection, for a monthly or yearly fee, to help protect sensitive information as well as make this information less usable to potential identity thieves. These companies can:

- Monitor your credit reports and alert you by e-mail or phone when your personal information is being used to apply for credit or services.
- Remove your name from preapproved credit card mailing lists (to reduce the likelihood of having these offers used fraudulently).
- Help you replace the contents of a stolen wallet or purse, and more.

Companies offering identity theft protection services include LifeLock (www.lifelock.com), TrustedID (www.trustedid.com), and Identity Guard (www .identityguard.com).

27

Fraud: Protecting Your Family and Your Finances

Legally speaking, fraud is the intentional use of deceit, trickery, or other dishonest means to deprive another person of his or her money or property. Identity theft, if used to commit a crime, is fraud. Many of the scams, cons, swindles, and rip-offs that we examined in our discussion of security in the digital world could also be considered frauds.

However, there are many types of fraud that don't involve identity theft and that aren't necessarily perpetrated via computer connections. Becoming a victim of fraud can literally ruin our financial lives, with no recourse and, for seniors in particular, no opportunity ever to rebuild.

Most of us, if our home and possessions are destroyed by fire or a natural disaster, will have insurance that can help to replace what we've lost so that we can begin putting our lives back together. But fraud victims, on the other hand, are often left with nothing. The thousands of hard-working individuals whose family assets were tied to the Enron Corporation learned firsthand just how devastating the crime of fraud can be.

Enron was founded in 1985 by Kenneth Lay through a merger of two natural gas companies. Within a few years, Enron became the largest seller of natural gas in the country and was highly touted by Wall Street brokerage firms for its investment potential. The price of Enron stock soared higher and higher. What investors didn't know, however, was that Enron was using accounting loopholes and shaky financial reporting to hide huge liabilities. These frauds were later found to have inflated the company's value by forty-five- to fifty-billion dollars, and, when these irregularities were first revealed in 2001, the company's stock price plummeted, eventually falling to just 1 percent of its previous value. In the end, the company was liquidated. The fifteen thousand employees who held most of their family savings in Enron stock lost nearly everything and were struck with a financial blow that few of us can even imagine. Kenneth Lay was convicted on six counts of securities and wire fraud, and faced up to forty-five years in prison. He died in 2006 before sentencing was scheduled. Others were convicted and sent to jail, but the punishments meted out by the courts did nothing to restore the shattered finances of those whose savings and retirement hopes were demolished by the Enron scandal.

The threat of investment fraud has been of even greater concern to American families since Bernie Madoff was exposed in 2009 for stealing more than $65 billion, mostly from wealthy investors and charitable foundations, in the largest "Ponzi" (named for a Bostonian who bilked thousands of dollars from investors in the 1920s) scheme in human history.

Charles Ponzi was born in 1882 and immigrated to the United States from Europe in 1903. After working at a number of different jobs over the years, Ponzi discovered a little-known way to make money based on purchasing international postage vouchers in Italy and selling them in the United States for a substantial profit. Based on this opportunity, Ponzi launched the "Old Colony Foreign Exchange Company" in 1919 and began seeking investors—promising them extraordinary returns in a short period of time. As more and more money flowed into the company, Ponzi was able to reward his initial investors, but these returns weren't based on profits from the business. Instead, they were paid with money flowing into the scheme from new investors. Seeing an opportunity for easy money, some of these new investors mortgaged their homes and invested their life savings in Ponzi's company. But eventually the money ran out. Ponzi simply couldn't bring in enough new investors fast enough to continue paying the promised returns.

In recent years, Bernie Madoff, of Bernard L. Madoff Investment Securities LLC, took Ponzi schemes to a new and almost unbelievable level. A charismatic con artist, Madoff claimed to investors that his shrewd investment tactics could produce returns far above what most stock investors could ever hope to achieve on their own. His investors received monthly statements indicating that their accounts were indeed growing at the extraordinary rates that Madoff had promised. If an investor wished to cash out of the investments, he or she received a check from Madoff's firm, just like any other broker might send. However, unlike other brokers, Madoff wasn't investing the money in stocks, and the returns that investors received weren't real. Instead, these returns were simply made-up numbers on a piece of paper. But as word spread about Madoff's "genius," he was able to attract more and more money from new investors and to send checks to those who wished to sell their shares. Eventually, however, too many of his investors wanted out, and Madoff couldn't meet their demands. When the scam was revealed and came crashing down, thousands of investors were suddenly face-to-face with financial ruin, and several major charitable organizations were bankrupted.

Both the Enron collapse and Madoff's fraudulent scheme received wide national publicity, and their colossal scale brought about major changes in accounting practices, corporate oversight, and financial regulatory procedures.

As big as these frauds were, they directly affected only a small percentage of American families. For every Enron or Madoff scandal, there are literally hundreds of thousands of smaller frauds that won't make the network news or the front page of your newspaper. *And the potential for these frauds to devastate your family's finances—with virtually no recourse or hope of ever receiving your money back—is just as real.*

The more you know about these frauds and how scam artists operate, the better able you'll be to spot "red flags" that indicate potential rip-offs.

In this chapter, we'll look at some of the ways that honest citizens have been defrauded of literally hundreds of billions of dollars over the years. And although this book can in no way substitute for professional investment advice, we'll also take a look at some of the very general investment guidelines that are widely recommended by financial advisors and other experts in the field.

Health Insurance and Medical Frauds

As we all know, health-care represents a huge portion of our American economy. In addition, the system is enormously complex—involving payments among health-care providers, consumers, labs, equipment companies, nursing homes, insurance companies, state and federal government agencies, and more. For these reasons, scam artists have targeted the health-care industry as a wide-open arena to commit fraud. Of course, not all of this fraud involves consumers directly. For example, a company claiming to provide health-care services can bill an insurance company or Medicare for services that were never performed, or even patients who don't exist.

But too often, consumers do bear the financial brunt of these schemes. Let's look at some of the more common scams that are rampant in the health-care industry and how you can protect yourself.

Medical Equipment Fraud

This scheme involves medical equipment manufacturers or distributors offering medical products to a consumer and offering to bill an insurance company for the equipment, even through the scammers know that the insurance company is unlikely to pay. The consumer is therefore stuck with the bill. In other instances, medical equipment companies have been known to bill insurance companies for products that were never even delivered.

"Rolling Lab" Scams

Rolling lab scams have occurred at health clubs, retirement homes, and shopping malls. These mobile labs offer to perform medical tests on consumers and bill insurance companies. In some instances, the tests are completely bogus. In other cases, the tests are valid but may not be warranted, may not be covered under an individual's insurance plan, or may have already been performed recently under the insurance plan. In all of these instances, the consumer would be liable for the costs of the tests. Not all mobile labs are scams, but consumers need to understand that they may in many cases be required to pay for the tests themselves.

Services Billed but Not Rendered

Con artists can alter existing bills or create bogus bills for medical services that were never rendered and submit these bills to insurance companies for reimbursement.

Medicare Fraud

Any of the schemes listed above, as well as others, would fall into the general category of Medicare fraud if perpetrated against Medicare.

Avoiding Health-care Fraud

- Ask your medical providers what they will charge and what you will be expected to pay out-of-pocket.
- Carefully review your insurer's "explanation of benefits" statement, which is generally provided to you after each medical appointment or procedure. Call your insurer and provider if you have questions, if you see services that were not rendered but appear on the statement, or if you believe that your out-of-pocket costs are more than your insurance provider should ask you to pay.
- Do not sign blank insurance claim forms where additional services, procedures, tests, or equipment could be added to the form after you sign it.
- Do not do business with door-to-door or telephone salespeople who tell you that services or medical equipment is "free."
- Give your insurance or Medicare identification only to those who have provided you with medical services. Understand that medical information can be valuable to identity thieves to obtain medical benefits in your name or to bill your insurance company and/or Medicare for services that were never provided. Protect your medical information as closely as you would guard your credit card and bank account information.
- Know exactly what medical equipment your physician has ordered for your home use.
- Keep accurate records of past health-care appointments.

Avoiding Counterfeit Prescription Drugs

- Closely examine the packaging and physical appearance of prescription drugs and be alert to any changes from one prescription to the next.
- Consult your pharmacist or physician if your prescription drug looks suspicious.
- Alert your pharmacist and physician immediately if your medication causes adverse side effects or if your condition does not improve.
- Use caution when purchasing drugs on the Internet. In the United States, licensed online pharmacies will have a seal of approval called the Verified Internet Pharmacy Practice Site (VIPPS), provided by the Association of Boards of Pharmacy.
- Do not purchase medications from unlicensed online distributors or from those who sell medications without a prescription.
- Special "deals" or discounts on pharmaceutical products may be a warning sign of counterfeit products.

Keeping Your Medical Costs Down

Not all of the following information is directly related to fraudulent practices, but I include it here because this information could save you many thousands of dollars in health-care costs.

- Ask your medical providers what they will charge and what you will be expected to pay out-of-pocket. Few of us would simply hand over our car or truck to a mechanic and tell him to fix any problems he might find and charge us any amount he wanted. But too many Americans seem to believe that, when it comes to health-care, we can't ask about prices beforehand.
- Review your bills. It is quite common to find double billings and errors on health-care invoices. Challenge any fees or charges that you believe to be incorrect.
- Do not pay medical bills that you believe to be fraudulent or unfair. Once you pay the bill, it will be virtually impossible to get your money back.

- If you are faced with a medical bill that you find difficult to pay, continue to pay your most important bills such as your mortgage and credit cards first. Do not use a home equity loan to pay medical bills. Doing so could make it far more likely that you will lose your home if you are sued or forced into bankruptcy.

Any time you can do so, except in a serious medical emergency, make sure that the hospital and doctors accept your insurance. In accepting your insurance, a doctor or hospital agrees to charge only what the insurance company has found to be "reasonable and customary" for the services to be provided. Amounts in excess of the insurance company's payment will have to be written off by the provider. However, if you use a provider who does not accept your insurance, you can be billed for virtually any amount that the doctor or hospital chooses. In this case, your insurance company will generally reimburse you directly for the "reasonable and customary" charges, *and you can be held liable for any amount beyond what the insurance company pays.*

In many cases, the health provider will be willing to lower the fee to an amount closer to what your insurance will pay. Also, your insurance company may be able to help you negotiate a more reasonable fee. If you believe you have truly been unfairly billed for medical services beyond the reasonable and customary fee, you may need to speak with an attorney as a last resort.

Telemarketing Fraud

Telemarketing fraud is rampant in the United States. However, I don't want to give the impression here that all telemarketing is fraud. In fact, many very reputable companies as well as charitable organizations use telemarketing as a key means to reach customers and donors. But it's important that you be able to distinguish legitimate telemarketers from those that are simply trying to defraud you of your money or gain information that could be used for identity theft.

Here are some guidelines, gathered from the FBI and other organizations, to help you weed out scam artists from those who are selling a genuine product or service or who represent a charitable organization that you may wish to support.

- Do not buy products or services over the phone from companies with which you are not familiar. Ask that more information be mailed to you. Most legitimate companies will be perfectly willing to do this.
- Understand that receiving written information as a follow-up to a telephone call does not guarantee that the company is legitimate. Do further research if you have additional doubts or if the amount of money you're being asked to send is particularly large.
- Before making a contribution to a charity, ask what percentage of your donation will actually go to the charity.
- Never pay in advance over the telephone for services such as home maintenance and repairs. Legitimate companies will present you with a written contract describing services to be provided and when payments will be expected.
- As we discussed in the chapter about identity theft, make sure family members know what information should *not* be provided on the phone.
- If you don't fully understand the offer, don't buy the product or service.
- Understand that any information you provide to a telemarketer could be resold to a third party and that, in most cases, this is a legal practice.
- If you believe that you have been contacted by someone who intends or intended to commit fraud, report all the information you have to local, state, or federal law enforcement officials.

Watch for these "catch phrases" which, according to the FBI, should set off warning signals with consumers:

- "You must act now to take advantage of this offer." Legitimate companies will give you time to think things over and make up your mind.
- "You've won a 'free' gift, vacation, or prize." Often you will be asked in the same phone conversation to pay shipping costs, handling fees, or even substantial taxes on the item. You are not only likely to lose this money, but the scammer will then have your credit card information to commit further fraud.
- "You must send money, or provide a credit card or bank account number." Likewise, the caller could simply be looking for information to commit identity theft.

- "As a convenience, we will send a courier to pick up a check." This is standard practice for con artists who wish to avoid leaving a paper trail.
- "You don't need to check out the company with anyone."
- "You don't need any written information about the company or the references."
- "You can't afford to miss this 'high-profit, no-risk' offer."

Advance Fee Schemes

"Advance fee" is a term used to describe a wide range of potential frauds that all have one thing in common—the victim pays money to the scammer, in advance, with the expectation of receiving something of greater value later.

Advance fee schemes can take any number of forms. Con artists have found many ways to dupe their victims by promising to procure a loan or contract for a person or business in exchange for a "finder's fee" to be paid up front. Scammers may claim to have winning lottery tickets that they cannot cash for some obscure legal reason, or funds tied up in a bank account that they need the victim's help to access.

In our section on computer safety, we discussed "Nigerian letter" or "419" scams, where a self-proclaimed government official asks for your help in moving money out of his native country, typically Nigeria. This, too, would be considered an "advance fee" scam since the victim will be asked to pay something in advance to help the "government official" smuggle the money out of his country. This type of scam can be perpetrated by mail as well as e-mail but with the same resulting loss for the victim who falls for the ruse. If you receive a letter from Nigeria asking you to send personal or banking information, or from any suspicious source, do not reply in any manner. Even a joking reply may result in threats being levied against you by the scam artist. Instead, provide a copy of the letter to the U.S. Postal Inspection Service, to your local FBI office, or to the U.S. Secret Service.

The *single best way* to avoid falling victim to advance fee schemes is to remember the old saying: "If an opportunity seems too good to be true, it probably is." Some of Bernie Madoff's victims would have done well to remember this advice.

Here are some other ideas for avoiding advance fee scams. In fact, many of these suggestions that might help you avoid other types of fraud.

- Be skeptical of businesses that use mail drops or post office boxes instead of street addresses and do not have a direct telephone line.

- Be suspicious of individuals who are never in when you call but are always sure to return your call later. Likewise, if your phone calls are never answered but always returned from another phone or cell phone, you may have a reason to be suspicious.

- Ask yourself whether an "opportunity" presented to you follows common business practices. For example, there is little reason to believe that a real lottery winner would have difficult cashing his or her winning ticket.

- Know as much as you can about the people with whom you are dealing. Check with the Better Business Bureau or even an attorney. Search the firm online to see if others have been scammed. The more money involved, the more scrupulous you need to be in your research.

- Beware of business "opportunities" that have an expiration date. Scammers will often insist that you make a fast decision in order to increase sales pressure and limit your chance to catch onto their ruse.

- When purchasing goods and services via the Internet, by phone, or by mail-order catalog, pay by credit card whenever possible. Card issuers give you certain rights when it comes to disputing charges if your order does not arrive or if the goods and services were not as described.

The New Snake Oil: Fraudulent "Anti-aging" Products

Be wary of "secret formulas" or "scientific breakthroughs" that claim to slow down or reverse the aging process or perform other medical miracles. Billions of dollars worth of these products have been sold in recent years, and many have no effect whatsoever in improving skin tone or living up to any of their other claims. Yet because of their appeal of looking or feeling younger, they continue to be snapped up by consumers.

In addition to the ineffectiveness of the products themselves, many of the companies pitching these products have been involved in fraudulent marketing practices that offer a "free" sample of the product but which require (in fine print) that the consumer sign up for a regular shipment of the product, often at exorbitant prices. Should you decide to go ahead and purchase one of these products, use your credit card so that you can dispute the charges if the company begins charging your card for products you did not order.

Debt Reduction and Debt Elimination Plans

There are many legitimate companies and nonprofit organizations that provide credit counseling and debt consolidation services for those who have become overextended on their finances but who wish to avoid bankruptcy. However, the need for these services has also provided criminals and hucksters with new opportunities to commit fraud or just plain "rip off" consumers.

In some instances, these schemes are simply used to gather information to commit identity theft. In others, scammers may charge a fee simply to advise consumers to quit paying their credit card bills, based on a bogus "no money lent" legal argument claiming that banks cannot legally loan money. These victims will not only lose the fee that they've paid to the scammer, but they will be sued by their creditors. Still other debt reduction schemers will charge fees ranging into the hundreds of dollars to provide family budgeting advice that could have been found in any bookstore for a few dollars.

To avoid debt reduction and debt elimination scams, look for a company or agency that is accredited with either the Association of Independent Consumer Credit Counseling Agencies (www.aiccca.org) or the National Foundation for Credit Counseling (www.nfcc.org). These companies will typically charge very minimal up-front fees and provide realistic advice. There are no magic bullets for debt reduction, and a company that offers drastic reductions in your payments or debts is probably not telling the truth.

Lottery and Sweepstakes Scams

Typical lottery and sweepstakes scams involve a potential victim receiving a letter indicating that he or she has won a major prize. The letter includes a check that represents a portion of the winnings. In order to claim the balance of the prize, the "winner" must deposit the check then use a bank wire transfer to send money covering taxes or a fee. Like the various "cashier's check" schemes that we discussed in the previous section on Internet scams, the criminals hope that the victim will wire real money before the "prize" check is discovered to be phony.

Thousands of sweepstakes are carried out each year by reputable product manufacturers, publishers, and charitable organizations, and winners may be required to pay taxes on the winnings. However, this money will be paid to the IRS, not to the sweepstakes sponsor.

Keep in mind also that, under federal law, you are not required to purchase a product or send any money to enter a sweepstakes, nor will purchasing a product increase your chances of winning a prize. Likewise, for sweepstakes carried out by charitable organizations, you are not required to make a contribution in order to enter or win, and a contribution will not increase your chances of winning. In all of these sweepstakes, the sponsors are required to treat your entry just the same as entries from those who have purchased a product or made a contribution.

Contractor Scams

When hiring a contractor for home improvement or repairs, follow a few simple guidelines:

- Ask for references.
- Look at sample of the contractor's work at other homes.
- Make sure that the contractor has a permanent business address, preferably in your own area and not in another state.
- Get everything in writing, including start date, finish date, the scope of work to be performed, and the schedule of payments that will be expected from you.
- Verify that your contractor is licensed and carries liability and worker's compensation insurance.
- Do not make the final payment until all the work has been completed to your satisfaction, including cleanup. Even reputable contractors will have less motivation to complete the final details or fix problems if they've been paid in full.

If you hear these sales pitches or anything similar from a contractor, be cautious:

- "We just did a job nearby and have extra materials. We can use the leftover materials and give you a special price if we can do the work today."
- "You need to make these repairs today to avoid damaging your home and losing your investment."
- "Let's go ahead and sign a contract today at this special price. You can always check our references later."

- "I need payment in cash in order to give you this special price."
- "We need payment up front to cover the cost of materials." A reliable contractor may require some payment in advance but usually no more than one-third.

Auto Warranty Scams

These scams rely on postcards, letters, and phone calls to "inform" consumers that their auto warranty is about to expire (regardless of whether your warranty will expire or when it expired). The mailings are printed to look like they've come from your dealer or automaker, but they actually come from third parties. These warranties have been the subject of a huge number of consumer complaints, are typically very expensive while covering very little, and may be nearly impossible to use. If you wish to purchase an extended warranty for your vehicle, do so through your dealer or automaker.

Investment Frauds

"Stimulus" and Tax Scams

The "stimulus" checks issued by the federal government in recent years have become a prime target for scammers. In addition to Internet scams asking victims to provide Social Security numbers and bank account numbers in order to receive their stimulus checks, fake checks have been delivered in the mail with the promise of "secondary" stimulus money that can be obtained by calling a toll-free number. Callers to the toll-free number are asked to purchase an "information packet" in order to find out about additional financial opportunities available from the government.

Other con artists have defrauded taxpayers by claiming that they can help secure additional tax refunds or share "secret" legal loopholes to pay less tax (or avoid paying taxes at all) in exchange for an advance fee. Those who fall for this scheme can find themselves in even worse trouble when they fail to file tax returns or pay taxes and are then subject to civil and/or criminal penalties from the IRS.

Scammers have also offered to help people submit claims for nonexistent credit in exchange for a fee. Some African-Americans have been targeted by a "reparations" scam and told that they can receive slavery reparations by paying a fee.

There have even been cases when con artists, carrying convincing photo identification, have visited homes and claimed to be IRS field agents. If you have any reason to believe that someone appearing at your home is an imposter, lock the door and call your local police. Then call the Treasury Inspector General's Hotline at 1-800-366-4484.

Finally, when you write a check to the IRS, spell out "Internal Revenue Service" in full. If you write only "IRS," it is very easy for a thief to change "IRS" to "MRS," add a last name, and cash the check that now appears to be written to "MRS Brown," "MRS Smith," or whomever.

Letters of Credit

"Letters of credit" are issued by banks to ensure payment for goods shipped in connection with international trade. Letters of credit are never sold as investments, and any investment "opportunity" offering letters of credit as a vehicle can be assumed to be fraudulent. As a more general rule, be cautious about any investment that offers the promise of extremely high yields.

"Prime Bank" Fraud

"Prime bank" fraud is based on convincing gullible investors that they can gain access to "secret" investment opportunities known only to extremely wealthy families and royalty. The scam may involve claims that, by buying "bank guarantees" from foreign "prime banks" at a discount and then reselling these guarantees, an investor can make a considerable profit in a short period of time. Investors may be required to sign nondisclosure agreements in order to be "allowed" to participate, to discourage anyone from taking steps to verify the investment. The victims are asked to send their investment funds to a foreign bank. Of course, the money is never seen again.

While foreign banks do use instruments called "bank guarantees" in the same manner that U.S. banks use letters of credit, these guarantees are never sold on any kind of market, and these "investments" can be assumed to be 100 percent fraudulent.

Viaticals

Viaticals are investments in which one person purchases the life insurance policy of another—typically a terminally ill person—and takes over the premiums on the insurance policy. The money that the investor provides, less the commission of the viatical broker, is transferred to the terminally ill person so that he or she can pay medical expenses or enjoy a higher quality of life in his or her final days.

Not all viatical investments are frauds, but fraud is rampant in the viatical market. One company alone was alleged by the Securities and Exchange Commission (SEC) to have defrauded thirty thousand viatical investors of one billion dollars. In some cases, the insured person is not even ill, and the investor must make the insurance payments, sometimes for decades, or else lose their original investment. In other cases, the insured person may have purchased the life insurance policy fraudulently (for example, by claiming they were in good health). Some viatical brokers have even sold the same policy to multiple investors. Again, not all viaticals are scams, but the casual investor should approach these investments with extreme caution.

Affinity Scams

Affinity scams use their victim's religious or ethnic identity to build trust and to convince investors to let down their guard. Bernie Madoff convinced many individuals of the Jewish faith, as well as Jewish charities, to invest with him with disastrous results. Be wary of investments that are presented to you because of your faith or ethnicity.

Ponzi Schemes

A Ponzi scheme, as described at the beginning of this chapter, is an investment fraud whereby a scammer attracts investors by promising higher rates of return than might be available through traditional investments. Often, early investors are paid the promised returns, and this attracts even more investors. Eventually, however the scheme collapses when the operator flees with the money or when he or she can no longer attract enough new investors to continue paying the promised returns.

Pyramid Schemes

"Pyramid" schemes, also known as "franchise fraud," are investment scams in which an individual is offered a distributorship or franchise to market a product or service. In addition, the investor is told that he or she can make additional profits by recruiting additional distributors or franchisees.

Keep in mind that there are a great many legitimate "multi-level marketing" programs and companies. Amway distributors, for example, can make money not only by selling products but by recruiting new distributors to sell products as well. However, when the emphasis is on selling new franchises rather than products, the number of potential new investors is eventually exhausted and the pyramid collapses. In general, investors should avoid distributorship or franchise opportunities that require the recruitment of new investors in order to make a profit.

Avoiding Investment Fraud

Remember what we said earlier in this chapter: "If it seems too good to be true, it probably is." Don't put all your eggs in one basket. This is the tragic lesson learned by investors who placed a substantial portion of their assets with Bernard L. Madoff Investment Securities LLC. If possible, do not tie up a large portion of your retirement funds in the company you work for.

If you don't understand an investment or the risks involved, don't invest money. Some of the biggest brokerage houses in the United States were bankrupted not long ago when they failed to comprehend the risks of "credit default swaps" and other exotic investment vehicles—and these guys were supposed to be experts.

- Make sure you fully understand the details of any business agreement that you enter into. If anything is unclear, review the terms with an attorney who has experience in this area.
- Be wary of unsolicited investment offers in which you did not initiate the first contact.
- Don't invest in anything based on appearances. Anyone can create a professional-looking Web site. Anyone can buy an expensive suit or lease an expensive car.

- Be skeptical of anyone who guarantees a particular return. Investment success cannot be guaranteed, even with investments that are considered to have relatively low risk.
- Understand that there are almost no investments that are completely "safe."
- Be wary of any investments that require you to deal with individuals or companies outside the United States. Be aware that U.S. laws usually cannot be enforced outside our borders and that you will have virtually no recourse if you lose your money.
- Trust your own internal radar. If it doesn't "feel" right, don't invest.

Understanding FDIC and SIPC "Guarantees"

Federal Deposit Insurance Corporation

The Federal Deposit Insurance Corporation (FDIC) is an independent agency of the United States government that protects the funds deposited in FDIC-insured banks and other savings institutions. FDIC was created in 1933, in response to bank failures at the beginning of the Great Depression, to restore confidence in America's banking system. Since the inception of FDIC, no investor has ever lost any portion of insured funds as the result of a failure of a member bank.

This automatic coverage extends to checking and savings accounts, money market accounts, certificates of deposit, and certain retirement accounts. The insurance amount is temporarily capped at $250,000 per depositor, per bank. However, this amount will decrease to $100,000 (except for certain retirement accounts) on January 1, 2014.

Note that this coverage does not extend to other financial products that banks may offer, such as stocks, bonds, mutual fund shares, life insurance policies, annuities, or municipal securities.

Securities Investor Protection Corporation

The Securities Investor Protection Corporation (SIPC) is a nonprofit, nongovernment corporation that is funded by its broker-members. SIPC is intended to help return securities and cash to investors, up to $500,000 per customer, if the broker holding these assets fails. SIPC also provides protections against unauthorized trading in a customer's account.

SIPC protections should not be confused with those offered by the FDIC. First, SIPC does not protect investors against market risk. If you invest in a company that goes bankrupt, you will not get your money back. Second, SIPC does not protect you against fraud committed by a broker. For example, Bernie Madoff's firm was an SIPC member, but SIPC will not cover the losses incurred by Madoff's investor clients.

A Special Word to Seniors

Senior citizens constitute just 12% of America's population but represent 35% of fraud victims. You need to be aware that, as you age, you become a more attractive target to those who seek to take advantage of others, and you need to be even more vigilant with your personal information and finances. Here are some of the reasons why.

- Seniors are more likely than young people to have money in the bank as well as to own investments, own their homes, and have excellent credit. This makes seniors a more lucrative target for fraud of all types.
- Seniors were raised during a time when Americans were generally more trusting. Scam artists know this.
- Seniors may be lonely and more willing to talk with a friendly stranger.
- Seniors tend to be at home during the day, making them easier to target, for telemarketing fraud in particular.
- Seniors may be more hesitant to report a crime. They may be embarrassed, or they may fear that their children will deem them unable to take care of themselves or their own finances.
- Age affects memory, and seniors may therefore make less reliable witnesses if a fraud perpetrator is caught. Criminals are aware of this fact. In addition, some seniors may have lost some of their mental sharpness, which once enabled them to more clearly distinguish between legitimate offers and scams.

For Family Members and Caregivers

Because seniors are likely targets for fraud, be aware of these warning signs that may indicate your loved one has been a victim.

- Your family member receives a large number of phone calls requesting contributions or offering special "opportunities."
- Your family member receives a large number of packages, typically useless or cheap items.
- You see unexpected changes in bank account balances or credit card charges.
- Unnecessary improvements or repairs are being performed on your loved one's home.
- New home equity loans or other loans have been entered into with financial institutions you don't recognize.
- Your loved one tells you that he or she has learned about "guaranteed" investment plans or extraordinary new financial opportunities.

Summary

Next to protecting the safety of your loved ones and your home, protecting your family's finances may be one of the most important steps to ensure your quality of life in the years to come. Although the vast majority of businesses and individuals are honest, just one identity thief or scammer can cost you and your family years of hard work and savings. Like other criminals, those who perpetrate identity theft and financial fraud are looking for easy victims and are trying to minimize their chances of being caught. By taking reasonable precautions and maintaining a healthy level of skepticism when it comes to "easy" financial opportunities, you can help maintain the safety and security of your personal information and your family's finances, and make yourself a less attractive target for criminals.

> *For the latest information as well as consumer ratings for products mentioned throughout this book, see www.SafeBookProducts.com. In addition, go to this Web site to sign up for a free monthly newsletter on new products to help keep your family safer.*

SAFE ON THE STREETS

xcept for our section on Safety in the Great Outdoors, most of this book has dealt with safety in the home. Likewise, where we've talked about protecting yourself from criminals, we've talked mostly about crimes that usually take place in the home. But *Safe* would be incomplete without a discussion on protecting yourself and your family from crime on the streets. So that's what this final section is intended to do—to provide you with some concrete information that you can use to protect yourself and your family from specific crimes when you're traveling outside your home.

First, we'll look at specific crimes against your property and your person, and how to prevent them. Next, we'll look at some of the defensive measures that Americans commonly use to protect themselves against violent criminals. Finally, we'll conclude the book by discussing some ideas to help keep your children more secure when you're not there to watch, and to protect every member of your family when you're on the road—whether it's a short hop across town or an extended international vacation.

28

Specific Crimes on the Streets

Purse-snatchers and Pickpockets

Like so many other criminals, purse-snatchers and pickpockets do not choose their victims at random. They look for an easy payoff, where the chances of getting caught are minimal. The key to keeping your purse or wallet safe is to make yourself a less attractive victim.

For Women

- If you are carrying a shoulder bag, place the strap(s) diagonally across your body, as opposed to carrying it on one shoulder. This keeps the purse in front of you, instead of at your side or behind you, and makes the purse more difficult to grab. If you are carrying a handbag, hold it toward the front of your body, not just loosely on your wrist.
- Don't leave your purse unattended on a store counter or in a shopping cart.
- Keep your house keys in a coat or jacket pocket, separate from your purse. This way, if your purse is taken, the thief won't get the keys to your house (since he'll have your address from your stolen identification).

- When using public transportation, leave your purse in your lap or between your feet, not on the seat beside you.
- Use a zippered purse that is more difficult to open.
- If someone takes your purse, yell, "He's got my purse!" There is some chance that a policeman, security guard, or civilian may intervene. If not, at least try to make a mental note of what the thief looked like, including height, build, race, and clothing.

For Men

- Understand that pickpockets don't keep regular hours. They don't always operate at night. Nor do they always operate in crowds.
- The key target areas are back trouser pockets and suit coat and sports jacket pockets, located both inside and out. A pickpocket generally (although not always) will avoid front trouser pockets and buttoned or zippered pockets.
- If you have to carry your wallet in an unbuttoned jacket, coat, or pants pocket, be sure it holds only what you can afford to lose. Keep large sums of money, credit cards, and IDs in your front pocket or a buttoned or zippered pocket.
- Placing a rubber band around your wallet may make it easier for you to detect a pickpocket trying to remove it.
- Don't pat your pocket to see if your wallet is there; this tells a criminal exactly where to look for your valuables.

For Travelers

- On vacation in the United States, and especially abroad, avoid carrying a purse if possible. Having your purse stolen at home is bad enough, but having your purse stolen in a foreign country, along with your ID, money, credit cards, and so forth, is a nightmare. Take only what you need when you leave your hotel, and put these items in an inside pocket. Or purchase a small lightweight travel pouch and wear it around your neck under your blouse or shirt. Or consider a fanny pack, with the pouch turned to the front.

- Pack a photocopy of your airline tickets, passport, credit cards, and any other documents that would be impossible or inconvenient to replace if stolen.
- Keep a list, separate from your wallet, of contact numbers to report lost credit cards.
- Leave expensive jewelry at home.

If You're a Victim

- If you discover that your wallet has been taken, call the police immediately and make a report. Then call your credit card companies. Criminals will try to get as much mileage as possible out of your credit cards as quickly as they can, hoping you won't notice the theft for some time after it occurs.
- If you're traveling internationally when the theft occurs, see Chapter 32 later in this section for more information.

Robbery and Assault

Whereas victims of burglars or pickpockets might not even know that their property is missing for hours or days, robbery is defined as the taking of money or goods from another person, in the immediate presence of the victim, using force, the threat of force, or intimidation. A purse-snatching, for example, would be classified as a robbery if the purse were grabbed off the victim's shoulder but would be classified as a lesser crime if the purse were simply lifted from a shopping cart.

In 2008, over half a million robberies took place in the United States, over half of which were committed by criminals armed with some kind of weapon. In addition to the fact that robbers may be armed, these crimes are made more dangerous by the fact that robbers tend to be desperate people, often under the influence of drugs or alcohol. Desperation, intoxication, and weapons can make for a volatile combination.

Assault, at its most basic level, is defined as a physical attack by one person against another ("aggravated" assault occurs if the victim is seriously injured or if a weapon is used). Over four million assaults took place in the United States in 2008, with approximately 20 percent of these being classified as aggravated assaults.

Your ultimate goal during a robbery or assault should be survival and the protection of your person, since property can be replaced.

If You Are Confronted

- Try to remain calm, since an assailant will be less likely to attack you if you appear controlled and self-confident.
- Determine the criminal's intent. Does the attacker want to take personal items from you? Or does he intend to do you harm? If only your property is at stake, be willing to give it up. However, if an attacker intends to harm you, you may want to employ whatever defensive weapons or physical self-defense techniques are at your disposal and appropriate to the situation (we'll discuss some of these defensive weapons later in this section).
- Try to make mental notes of your assailant's appearance.
- If you decide to flee, try to draw as much attention to yourself as possible. Yelling, "Fire... Fire... Fire!" is one sure way to attract the attention of others.
- Do not try to apprehend the suspect yourself.
- When the attack or robbery is over, go to a safe area and report the crime. Call 9-1-1 immediately. If there is physical evidence of the crime (for example, if the criminal may have left a fingerprint or thumb print on your car), preserve any evidence of the crime. Remember that your quick actions in notifying the police will increase their chance of apprehending the suspect and protecting future victims.
- If you see a robbery or assault in progress, dial 9-1-1 immediately to alert the police. Do not attempt to resolve the situation yourself except to prevent injury to a crime victim.
- Understand that, as we discussed with disaster victims in Section I, crime victims can suffer lasting emotional effects. If you believe you're having trouble dealing with the aftereffects of any violent crime, contact a professional. Do the same for family members who become crime victims.

As with virtually all of the hazards we've discussed in this book, prevention is your best protection against robbery and other violent crimes. We've already discussed a number of measures to prevent robberies in your home, as well as to prevent crimes of opportunity such as purse-snatchings. Without repeating this material, let's look at some additional commonsense ideas for keeping yourself safe on the streets.

When Shopping

- Use a credit card to avoid having to carry large amounts of cash. Your credit card liability will be limited in the event you are robbed.
- Be aware of the surroundings when using an ATM, including potential hiding places like shrubbery. Preferably, use ATMs during the day, not at night.
- Understand that most robberies take place at night. Look for parking in well-lit areas, where vehicles and pedestrians are moving about.
- Put your cash away before leaving the immediate area of the ATM.
- Trust your instincts. If something seems wrong to you, move away from the situation.
- Notify police if you believe the situation calls for it.

On Foot

- Walk on the street side of sidewalks, nearest the curb, to avoid alleyways and building entrances.
- If you walk or jog at night, consider getting a dog that can accompany you. Police interviews with criminals show that a dog is one of the most effective crime deterrents.
- Don't wear headphones, or at least don't turn up the volume so high that you cannot hear what is taking place around you.
- If you work late hours, try to leave at the same time as a coworker.
- Recognize that you are a more attractive target to criminals if you have been drinking or using drugs or appear to be intoxicated.
- If you sense that you are being followed, change directions or cross the street. If the person persists, run to the nearest place where you'll find people.
- Do not allow a stranger to follow you to your doorstep. If you feel threatened, go to a public place where you can call police.

In the Car

- Have your keys in your hand as you approach your car.
- Glance in the back seat for uninvited guests before getting inside your car.
- Keep doors locked as a matter of routine.
- Preplan your travel route if you must enter high-crime areas. Stick to main roads as much as possible. If you become lost, find a public place, such as a service station, to read your map or ask for directions.
- If in doubt, do not stop to assist stranded motorists. Note the next milepost and use your cell phone or the nearest phone to call for help.
- If you are being followed by another car, drive into an open gas station, stay in your car, and ask the attendant to call the police. Better yet, drive straight to the nearest police station for assistance.
- If you are rear-ended by another vehicle, motion for the driver to follow you to a public place. "Bump and rob" artists stage such incidents to lure unsuspecting drivers out of their cars to rob them of their wallets or purses.
- If you feel threatened by a pedestrian while stopped at a red light or stop sign, blow the horn and flash your light to draw the attention of others and make yourself a less attractive target.

Carjacking

Every year in America, according to the U.S. Department of Justice, about 34,000 carjacking incidents take place. Essentially, a carjacking is a robbery where the object of the robbery is a car.

Carjacking is nothing new, nor has it been sweeping the nation in epidemic proportions. Vehicle owners have been victims of this crime for decades. But since the term "carjacking" was coined by the news media, the term itself has raised the fear levels of Americans about the actual probability of becoming a victim. Although these crimes are relatively rare, they have potentially grave consequences for victims. In 74 percent of carjacking incidents, a weapon is used by the criminal, and about 24 percent of carjacking victims are injured as the result of the crime.

Carjackings can happen anywhere: in a parking lot, on a street or freeway, or even in one's own driveway. But your chances of becoming a victim can be decreased by understanding more about carjacking facts and by taking some simple precautions.

How to Reduce Your Risk of Becoming a Carjacking Victim

- Understand that over two-thirds of carjackings occur at night and that carjackers tend to target expensive vehicles.
- Know the area in which you are traveling. Use a map or GPS device to preplan your route when traveling near crime-prone areas.
- In high-crime areas, drive in the lane nearest the center of the road to make it more difficult for potential attackers to reach your car from the sidewalk or roadside.
- When stopped in traffic, leave enough space between your vehicle and the vehicle ahead so that you can move forward or leave the location if someone approaches in a threatening manner.
- If the driver of a vehicle with no markings motions you to pull over to the side of the road, do not pull over. Keep driving to the nearest open business or where other people are present. However, comply immediately when directed by an officer in a marked vehicle. If you sense anything out of the ordinary, request to see identification.
- If you feel you are being followed by another vehicle, do not drive home. Drive to the nearest police or fire station, or to an open business. Do not get out of your vehicle. Instead, honk your horn to attract attention.
- If you are involved in a minor traffic accident and suspect suspicious circumstances, do not check the damage in a remote area or on the freeway. Motion the other driver to follow you to the nearest police or fire station or open business to exchange information.
- Follow your instincts and, if you believe you are in danger, react. Do anything you can to draw attention to yourself and attempt to flee the area.
- If you are attacked and the suspect has a weapon and demands your valuables or vehicle, comply. Your property can be replaced.
- When returning to your vehicle, have your keys in hand and be ready to unlock and enter your vehicle without delay. And, whether walking to or driving your vehicle, convey an attitude of confidence. By giving the appearance that you are totally aware of your surroundings, you can make yourself a less attractive target for criminal predators.

Rape and Sexual Assault

Nationwide, over two hundred thousand rapes and sexual assaults were reported to police in 2008, and an untold number were not reported. In most cases, the person responsible for sexual violence is already known to the victim—a friend, coworker, neighbor, or family member.

Preventing Sexual Assault

- Many of the preventive measures that we mentioned in discussing robbery and assault are also appropriate for lowering your risk of sexual assault.
- Understand that sexual harassment, unwanted touching, intimidation, peeping, and the taking of nude photos can also constitute sexual assault and should be reported to employers or police.
- Recognize that, like other assaults, alcohol and drug use can increase your chances of becoming a victim.
- Remember that the more confident you look, the stronger you appear. Like all crimes, rapes and sexual assaults are often crimes of opportunity, and criminals tend to look for easier targets.
- Self-defense training also helps you present a demeanor of confidence and self-assurance that can make you a less attractive target to criminals.
- Be especially wary of isolated spots, including underground garages, offices after business hours, and apartment laundry rooms.
- Consider employing one or more of the defensive measures we'll discuss in the next chapter.
- Trust your instincts. The *moment* you feel threatened, anytime or anywhere, get to a safe place, attract the attention of others, and call 9-1-1 if the situation warrants.

Resisting Sexual Assault

Many sources advise women to use nonaggressive strategies against sexual assault, and no one can decide for you whether to physically resist a sexual assault. However, some studies have suggested that attempted rapes were completed over 90 percent of the time when women did nothing to resist an attacker, or simply pleaded or cried. By contrast, when intended rape victims responded with loud yelling or screaming, the completion rate for forcible rape dropped dramatically, to approximately 50 percent.

Running away is an even better option, with some studies indicating that as few as 15 percent of women who attempted to flee were raped. And when rape attempts are met with violent physical force, with or without a weapon, the completed rape rate drops even lower. In fact, women who used knives or guns in self-defense were raped less than 1 percent of the time. Studies also indicate that meeting an attack with violent physical force does not increase a victim's chances of being injured during the commission of a sexual assault.

While all resistance strategies have been shown to have some success, a combination of these strategies may be even more effective.

If You Are Attacked

- Yell and scream. Do your best to attract the attention of others and to convince your attacker that he will be caught if he persists.
- Run away if you are physically able and continue to make as much noise as you can.
- If you choose to fight, understand that you are meeting violence with violence for entirely moral reasons and that there are no limits in a life-or-death situation. It is of no concern to you whether your attacker suffers permanent damage. Your goal is to incapacitate your attacker and convince him that you are not a suitable victim. Striking is more effective than pushing or wrestling. Strike hard and fast at vulnerable areas including the eyes, neck, and groin. Kick, gouge, scrape, and use any makeshift weapon at hand.

If You Are Assaulted

- Get away from the attacker and to a safe place as fast as you can.
- Call 9-1-1, then call a friend or family member you trust or a crisis center or a hotline to talk with a counselor.
- Do not wash, comb, or clean any part of your body. Do not change clothes if possible, or touch anything or change anything at the scene of the assault.

- Go to or have police transport you to the nearest hospital emergency room. You need to be examined, treated for any injuries, and screened for possible sexually transmitted infections (STIs) or pregnancy. The doctor or nurse will use a rape kit for any possible evidence that might be helpful in convicting the criminal.

- Ask the hospital staff to connect you with the local rape crisis center. The center staff can help you seek help through counseling and support groups. Understand that feelings of shame, guilt, fear, and shock are normal. Common symptoms will often be similar to those of post-traumatic stress disorder (PTSD) and can include difficulties with interpersonal relations, fear of sex and intimacy, major depression, alcohol or drug abuse, anxiety, obsessive-compulsive disorders, and more. *It is important to get counseling from a trusted professional.*

- Government and nonprofit resources are already in place to assist you. To find assistance in your local area, start by contacting the National Domestic Violence Hotline 1-800-799-SAFE (7233) or 1-800-787-3224 (TDD), or the National Sexual Assault Hotline 1-800-656-HOPE (4673).

Defensive Measures

Self-defense—protecting yourself from violence—is a fundamental human right that is recognized by the Constitution of the United States, forty-four state constitutions, and the laws of all fifty states and the District of Columbia. The U.S. Supreme Court has repeatedly ruled that a person "may repel force by force" in self-defense.

Of course, self-defense can take a variety of forms, and in some sense, virtually everything we've discussed in this book could be considered a form of self-defense—taking steps to avoid natural and manmade hazards in the first place. In this chapter, however, we'll concern ourselves very specifically with defensive measures against violent criminal attack to prevent harm to ourselves or our loved ones.

These measures can take a variety of forms, including the use of hands and feet as taught by a wide range of self-defense and martial arts disciplines, commonly used defensive sprays such as pepper spray and Mace, as well as the defensive use of firearms inside and outside the home.

Boxing, Kickboxing, and Martial Arts

There are literally hundreds of different training disciplines around the world that can be employed in self-defense, and there is no single type of training that

would be considered the best. In fact, there are many good reasons to learn these skills that go beyond self-defense, including cardiovascular fitness, strength and flexibility training, discipline and self-control, improving self-confidence, and so forth.

Most martial arts stress some form of striking ability, blocking aggressive moves from an opponent, and aiming for vulnerable areas on the opponent's body. Beyond that, these disciplines take a wide range of forms. Some of the more popular techniques include:

- Boxing, which provides good overall cardiovascular and strength training. As a sport, boxing has very strict rules, which would not apply to a "street fighting" situation, but the overall techniques would certainly have some applicability to self-defense.
- Kickboxing, which combines traditional western boxing skills with eastern martial arts
- Kung Fu, a broad category of martial arts, all of which originated in China
- Jiu Jitsu, which emphasizes restraint techniques and is used by police and military personnel in many countries
- Karate, which emphasizes striking and is therefore one of the more popular martial arts for self-defense
- Tae kwon do, which places greatest emphasis on kicking techniques
- Krav Maga, developed by Israeli Special Forces, and Ninjutsu, both of which place a heavy emphasis on self-defense
- "Mixed Martial Arts" (or MMA) that blend skills from a variety of disciplines

Although these are some of the more popular self-defense disciplines, there are many others. Many communities offer self-defense training, sometimes at no charge. No matter what kind of self-defense training you choose, the simple fact that you have had this training may help to make you less vulnerable to street crime. If you know how to defend yourself, you convey an intangible but real sense of self-confidence that can make you a less attractive target to a criminal. As we've said many times in this book, criminals look for easy opportunities and try to minimize their risk of getting caught. Half the battle is to let potential criminals know that you're not a good target.

Pepper Spray and Mace

Two disabling chemical compounds are available to civilians for defensive use against criminals (as well as animals like dogs and bears). These are available in small spray canisters for a few dollars and can be very effective in temporarily incapacitating a criminal attacker.

Mace™ is the trademarked name for a form of tear gas that is sometimes used for riot control. This product causes pain and irritation to mucus membranes including the eyes, nose, throat, and lungs, as well as a heavy flow of tears.

In some situations, Mace may be more effective than pepper sprays because it forms a vapor when it hits the air and therefore may have some effect on an attacker even if you do not score a direct hit when spraying the product. However, Mace takes longer to be effective (five to thirty seconds) compared to pepper spray (three to five seconds).

Pepper Spray is made from a chemical called oleoresin capsicum and is derived from natural sources including cayenne and other peppers. Upon contact with eyes or facial areas, it causes intense burning, temporary blindness, and restricted breathing. Because pepper spray causes an involuntary reaction, it may be more effective than Mace against psychotics or drug abusers whose pain response reactions are suppressed. However, pepper spray requires accurate delivery into the eyes or facial area in order to be effective.

Combination sprays include both chemical mace and pepper spray components. The guidelines for safe and effective use of these products are similar:

- Read and understand the instructions. Know how to hold the unit so that you can tell by feel how to deploy the spray in an emergency situation. Choose a unit that has an easy-to-find button that protects against accidental discharge and that is easy to orient and activate by feel.
- Practice with the spray. Buy an extra canister and take it to an open field. Make sure the wind is at your back. Fire it for two seconds and

notice how far the spray traveled and the width of the spray path. Try to visualize how you would spray it into the eyes and face of an attacker. Keep the partially expended canister for further "refresher" practice, and carry a full, fresh canister with you on the street.

- Always keep the spray in the same place in your purse, pocket, or automobile. In a dangerous situation, you won't have time to look for it. From time to time, practice reaching for the unit so that you can access it immediately if needed. Some products include glow-in-the-dark components to make them easier to find and deploy. A small canister that attaches to your keychain can also be convenient when you are approaching or leaving your car.
- Generally, manufacturers recommend short, repeated sprays into the facial area of your attacker.
- Break off your defensive measures as soon as an attacker is incapacitated. Run to an area where other people are, and call 9-1-1.
- Check your state laws regarding these products. Some states allow certain maximum sizes and concentrations, or even require a license to carry a spray. Others may ban Internet sales or allow sales only by licensed firearm dealers. Still others restrict combination sprays that include both pepper spray and Mace components.
- Keep products out of reach of children. While not lethal, these products are designed to be incapacitating and extremely painful.
- Canisters will include an expiration date. Replace the unit as necessary.
- Keep in mind that these products cannot be transported in an airline cabin, including carry-on luggage. You are allowed one canister up to four ounces in your checked luggage only. Be sure to pack the canister in a sealed plastic bag in case it leaks.
- For protection from bear or dog attacks, purchase a spray that is specifically intended for deterring bears or dogs. Bear spray usually comes in a larger canister.

Firearms and the Right to Carry

Across the nation, an estimated five million or more Americans now have state-issued permits to carry concealed firearms for defensive use. Forty states now have laws or procedures that effectively guarantee that law-abiding individuals, usually after taking a safety course or meeting other reasonable requirements, can be issued a permit or otherwise allowed to carry concealed firearms for self-defense. Eight other states make some provision for concealed carry under certain circumstances, and only two—Wisconsin and Illinois—prohibit concealed carry altogether.

Before 1987, only ten states had laws that respected the right of citizens to carry firearms for protection. But in that year, Florida adopted a "shall issue" law that then became the model for other state laws adopted across the country.

Twenty-three states have adopted Right-to-Carry laws since 1991. In many cases, the political opponents of firearms ownership were extremely vocal in predicting dire consequences if the government allowed law-abiding citizens to carry concealed firearms outside their homes.

Obviously, these predictions have not come true; in fact, exactly the opposite has happened. Permit holders are responsible citizens almost without exception and are more law-abiding than the rest of the public. For example, Florida, the state that has issued the most carry permits (based on its large population and having had its Right-to-Carry law since 1987), has revoked only about one in ten thousand permits due to gun crimes committed by permit holders.

Right-to-Carry seems also to have had a very positive impact in reducing crime. From 1991 to 2008, violent crime declined by 40 percent. Murder declined 45 percent. In 2007, Right-to-Carry states had lower violent crime rates, on average, compared to the rest of the country. Overall, crime rates in Right-to-Carry states were 24 percent lower than in non-Right-to-Carry states. Murder rates were lower by 28 percent, robbery rates by 50 percent, and aggravated assault rates by 11 percent.

The simple truth is, criminals fear armed victims. No one, including criminals, wants to run the risk of getting shot. Criminologist Gary Kleck of Florida State University analyzed National Crime Victimization Surveys and concluded, "Robbery and assault victims who used a gun to resist were less likely to be attacked or to suffer an injury than those who used any other methods of self-protection or those who did not resist at all."

A separate study commissioned by the U.S. Department of Justice found that 34 percent of felons had been "scared off, shot at, wounded or captured by an armed victim," and 40 percent of felons had decided against committing particular crimes, fearing that their potential victims might be armed.

As I mentioned in a previous chapter, the sight of a firearm alone is enough to deter most criminal attacks. Ninety-eight percent of the time, the gun is never fired in a defensive situation, and attackers are actually shot in less than 1 percent of all defensive uses involving firearms.

Obviously, gun ownership is not for everyone, and neither I, nor the NRA, recommend gun ownership for everyone, although we adamantly believe that the right to own and use firearms must be protected.

Requirements for obtaining a Right-to-Carry permit vary from state to state but generally involve the filing of appropriate forms, undergoing a criminal background check, taking a training course, and paying an administrative fee. (NRA has worked hard to make sure these fees are reasonable and affordable for all income levels.) Permits are subject to revocation if the holder commits certain crimes and, in nearly all states, must be renewed periodically.

Should you wish to consider firearms ownership or Right-to-Carry as part of your personal protection strategy, pay close attention to these guidelines.

- Employ deadly force only to protect life and limb, and then, only as a last resort. Avoiding a confrontation in the first place, using the other guidelines outlined in this book, is your first and best defense against becoming victim of crime.
- Know and understand basic firearms safety rules (some of these were described in Section III of this book under the heading of hunting safety). If you're new to gun ownership, NRA strongly recommends that you take a course in gun safety. NRA-certified instructors also teach more detailed courses in personal protection both inside and outside the home. For more information or to find a course near you, visit www.nrainstructors.org/searchcourse.aspx.
- Whether in your home or outside your home, store guns safely as appropriate to the situation.
- Know and obey local laws regarding Right-to-Carry and other aspects of transporting firearms outside the home.
- Purchase a firearm that fits your hand and then practice, practice, practice. Should you ever be required to employ a firearm to defend yourself or someone else, the situation will likely evolve almost instantly and be over in seconds. Practicing your skills is the only way to be certain that you will react in the safest and most effective manner possible.

- Break off your defensive measures as soon as an attacker retreats or is incapacitated. Run to an area where other people are, and call 9-1-1.
- Understand that in the aftermath of a defensive shooting you may experience symptoms of post-traumatic stress disorder (PTSD). *It is important to get counseling from a trusted professional.*

Refuse to Be a Victim®

Refuse to Be a Victim is a national crime prevention program, sponsored by the National Rifle Association, that teaches crime prevention and personal safety to Americans from all walks of life. Over 1.2 million citizens have now participated in our three- to four-hour Refuse to Be a Victim seminars taught by NRA-certified instructors, and this number continues to grow dramatically each and every year.

In the beginning, the program was presented only to women, by women. However, the program quickly evolved into an all-encompassing crime prevention program that includes information useful to everyone interesting in protecting themselves and their families against violent and nonviolent crime. Hundreds of federal, state, and local law enforcement agencies across the country have also implemented Refuse to Be a Victim seminars.

Seminar topics address personal safety issues as well as home, automobile, phone, technological, travel, and personal security. Seminar participants are presented with a variety of commonsense crime prevention and personal safety strategies and devices that they may integrate into their daily lives. Please note that firearms use or instruction is not part of these seminars.

For more information about Refuse to Be a Victim, or to find a seminar near you, visit www.nrahq.org/RTBAV.

Child Predators and Child Abduction

Throughout this book, we've talked about some of the safety concerns that parents need to be aware of—special considerations for children in your disaster preparedness plans, in your efforts to provide a safer home, and when your children use computers, cell phones, and the Internet. In this section of *Safe*, as we discuss crime and safety issues outside the home, I want to look at some additional considerations for youngsters when they are away from home or at home without your supervision.

Every day, according to the U.S. Department of Justice, more than two thousand children are reported missing. Most of these cases are resolved quickly, and many involve nothing more sinister than a child's failure to notify parents of his or her whereabouts. About half involve former spouses or other family members taking a child in violation of custody agreements. And a relatively small number of cases involve strangers who abduct children for the purpose of demanding a ransom, committing sexual assault, or otherwise causing harm. The threat cannot be ignored, and any parent whose child has gone missing even for a few minutes knows just how distressing such an incident can be.

When Your Child Is Home Alone

Some experts recommend that children not be left home alone until they are eleven or twelve years old. However, this is a matter that only you can decide, based on your family's needs and the maturity level of your child. In fact, being home alone is one way that children begin to develop decision-making skills and an increased sense of personal responsibility. Although this chapter is concerned mainly with the threat of child predators and child abductions, some of the suggestions below could be important in other emergency situations as well.

Before leaving your child at home for the first time, make sure your child knows:

- His or her full name, address, phone number, and the full names of both parents.
- Phone numbers for both parents, including work and cell numbers.
- When and how to call 9-1-1.
- How to contact another trusted adult if you cannot be reached.
- Instruct your child to keep doors locked when home alone, and not to open the door for people they do not know.
- When answering the phone, your child should not indicate that he or she is home alone. Instead, ask the child to take a message, telling callers that you can't come to the telephone but will call them back.
- Make sure your child knows where to go in a true emergency, such as a fire, so that you can locate the child quickly.

When Your Child Is Outside the Home

- Train your child to let you know when he or she is leaving your home, to let you know upon arriving back home, and to call you to let you know if plans have changed.
- At theme parks, sports arenas, and malls, determine an easily located central meeting place where you can rendezvous with other family members if you become separated. Most of the time, in such a location, it's a

simple case of having lost track of your child. Having a prearranged meeting place can save you hours of worry.

- Teach your children whom to turn to if they get lost, including policemen, store clerks, and so forth. Teach them to look for a badge and similar forms of identification.
- Teach young children not to enter a building or vehicle unless you've said it's OK to do so.
- Make sure your child knows not to accept a ride or a gift from a stranger.
- Make sure your child has memorized the information mentioned above, including *his or her full name, address, phone number, the full names of both parents as well as work and cell numbers, and how to contact another trusted adult if you cannot be reached.*
- Tell your children how to react if someone attempts to grab them. Let them know they should kick, scream, and make a scene to attract the attention of others, then remove themselves from the situation as quickly as possible. Make sure they understand that if someone offers them candy, asks for their help to look for a kitten or puppy, or asks them to go with that person for any other reason, they should say no and get away from that person.
- Tell your children that they must let you know if someone touches them inappropriately, says something that bothers them, or makes them feel uncomfortable in any way.

If Your Child Goes Missing

Should you notice your child missing, the National Center for Missing and Exploited Children (www.missingkids.com) recommends the following immediate action.

- Search your home thoroughly, including closets, laundry piles, in and under beds, inside large appliances, and in vehicles, including trunks, and any other place where a child could crawl or hide.
- If your child disappears in a store or other public building, notify the manager or security office.
- Call 9-1-1 to immediately notify local law enforcement agencies. Provide your child's name, date of birth, height, weight, and any other identifying

characteristics including eyeglasses, braces, and so forth. Tell them when and where you last saw your child, and what clothing he or she was wearing. Ask that this information be placed immediately into the National Crime Information Center (NCIC) Missing Person File.

■ After notifying local law enforcement officials, notify the National Center for Missing and Exploited Children at 1-800-THE-LOST (843-5678).

Custody Battles and Family Abductions

Although estimates vary, "family" abductions of minor children may occur as many as three hundred fifty thousand times each year in the United States alone. About half of these incidents include children who are not returned at the end of an agreed-upon visit (with the children being kept away at least one extra night). The other half include attempts to conceal the whereabouts of a child, to transport the child to another state in violation of a custody agreement, or to keep the child indefinitely.

The U.S. Department of Justice's Office of Juvenile Justice and Delinquency Prevention (OJJDP) has identified several potential risk factors (or profiles) that indicate a family or parental abduction may be more likely, including:

■ A parent who has previously threatened to abduct a child or who has actually abducted a child.

■ A parent who suspects or believes that the other parent has abused the child and has other friends or family members who support these concerns. In this instance, the parent may attempt to "rescue" the child, whether or not the concerns of abuse are substantiated.

■ A parent who is mentally disturbed.

■ A parent who is a citizen of another country in a mixed-culture marriage. These parents may have strong ties to their home country and feel a need to return to their ethnic or religious roots.

■ A parent who feels alienated from the legal system, including those who have little knowledge of custody and abduction laws, who feel unable to have their views represented in the courts, or domestic violence victims who believe that the legal system has been unable to help them or their children.

Family law with regard to parental rights and abductions is extremely complex, and remedies may involve both criminal and civil penalties against the offender. However, if you suspect that the other parent or another family member has abducted your child, or a child is not returned to you in compliance with a legal agreement, the procedures to follow are similar to those in any other suspected child abduction situations.

Please note also that, under certain circumstances, your child's name can be entered into the U.S. State Department's "Children's Passport Issuance Alert Program," enabling you to be notified before a passport is issued for your child. For more information, visit the State Department's "Passport Issuance and Denial to Minors" Web page (http://travel.state.gov/passport/ppi/family/family_866.html).

In the Event of an Abduction

- Understand that immediate action gives you a better chance of recovering your child.
- Call 9-1-1 to immediately notify local law enforcement officials. Provide your child's name, date of birth, height, weight, and any other identifying characteristics including eyeglasses, braces, and so forth. Tell them when and where you last saw your child, and what clothing he or she was wearing. Ask that this information be placed immediately into the National Crime Information Center (NCIC) Missing Person File.
- If you suspect that a family member or another person known to you has abducted your child, provide law enforcement officials with as much information as possible. Include a personal description, place of residence, vehicle description and plate number, previous threats, the presence of known mental illness, country of dual citizenship, and any other information that you believe might be helpful in recovering your child.
- After notifying local law enforcement, notify the National Center for Missing and Exploited Children at 1-800-THE-LOST (843-5678).

For more information, the National Center for Missing and Exploited Children has produced a lengthy brochure entitled *Family Abduction Prevention and Response* that can be ordered by calling the toll-free number above, or downloaded from the Internet at www.missingkids.com/en_US/publications/NC75.pdf.

AMBER Alerts

When a child goes missing, the first minutes and hours after a potential abduction are the most critical in securing the child's safe return. "AMBER Alerts" are named for Amber Hagerman, a nine-year-old girl who was kidnapped in January of 1996 while riding her bicycle in Arlington, Texas. Her body was found four days later, and the kidnapping and murder were never completely resolved.

Subsequent efforts by her parents were instrumental in the passage of the federal Amber Hagerman Child Protection Act, and national standards were later implemented for the issuance of AMBER Alerts.

The goal of AMBER Alerts is to maximize efforts among law enforcement agencies, the media, and the general public to locate an abducted child in the critical first hours after a disappearance takes place. AMBER Alerts notify the public of a missing child through television and radio emergency alert systems that are commonly used for all types of emergency notification, changeable traffic signs, Internet, and wireless services. To date, more than three hundred sixty children have been returned safely through the use of AMBER Alerts.

AMBER Alerts are issued when law enforcement officials are reasonably certain that an abduction of a child seventeen years old or younger has taken place, when the child is believed to be in imminent danger of injury or death, and when there is enough information available to provide a good description of the child.

When a child is reported missing, law enforcement officials determine whether an AMBER Alert is warranted. If so, details of the abduction, the child's description, and other information such as a getaway vehicle description are provided to local radio and television outlets to alert listeners and viewers. Television alerts may also include a photograph of the child. Recently, an effort has been launched to enable citizens to sign up for AMBER Alerts via text message, and citizens can sign up for these alerts at www.wirelessamberalerts.org or at their wireless provider's Web site.

Anyone with helpful information in response to an AMBER Alert should immediately call 1-800-THE-LOST (843-5678) to report the information.

31

Safe Traveling

All of us have heard disturbing stories about travelers in the United States and abroad who have lost their passports or luggage, had their money or camera gear stolen, or who have been victimized by street crime. But by far, these experiences are the exception, not the rule. The vast majority of travelers have safe and wonderful vacations with family and friends, and experience firsthand some of the limitless cultural or natural treasures that others might never see.

By far, the most dangerous situation you're likely to face, whether you're going to the local movie theater or to Timbuktu (there really is such a place), is traveling by motor vehicle. Let's therefore begin our travel safety discussion by looking at a few automobile safety ideas, particularly for children.

Child Safety in and around Vehicles

I won't repeat the statistics and gory details that you've already heard concerning drunken driving and cell phone use while driving. Nor will I repeat the safety tips that we covered in our chapter on backcountry vehicle travel. And although car seats and other child restraints have a vital role to play in keeping youngsters safe, there is already a vast amount of information about these products, which need not be duplicated here.

I do, however, want to discuss some important safety considerations for youngsters that have the potential to save lives but that do not receive nearly as much public attention as these other concerns. We'll start at the first place an accident can happen—right at your garage door.

Garage Doors

Make sure that the photoelectric safety sensor on your garage, required for all doors manufactured since 1993, is working properly. Every garage door is required to have sensors (using a light beam across the door opening) that will reverse the door and send it to the open position if an object is detected by an interruption in the light beam. Doors are also required to reverse if they strike objects before reaching the fully closed position. Test your door by intentionally breaking the light beam as well as by placing an object in the path of the door to see if it reverses properly.

Children around Cars

Every year, children are killed or injured because drivers simply didn't see them while backing up or in the first few feet when moving forward. The typical victim is two years old and struck in a driveway by a parent or family friend. Remember that larger vehicles including SUVs may provide less visibility and have larger "blind spots" than smaller cars and traditional sedans. In addition, the redesign of vehicles for better aerodynamics and fuel efficiency has likewise reduced overall visibility in many vehicles.

- Take time to walk around your car, as well as to look under the vehicle, before you get in.
- If children are nearby, have them move to a place where you can clearly see them.

- Consider a back-up detection device (also known as a vehicle reversing sensor, as well as by other names) on your next car, or have an after-market device installed on your current vehicle.

Power Window Dangers

While power window accidents are rare, dozens of children have been killed as the result of suffocations and other accidents involving power windows, and hundreds of people are treated for injuries each year. Newer vehicles are now required to feature recessed or lever power window switches that are more difficult for small children to operate, but tens of millions of vehicles are still on the road that feature "rocker"-type switches that can be activated by a stray hand or arm leaning on the switch.

Use the locking feature on your power windows when children are in the vehicle, and make sure that hands and arms are inside the vehicle when you close the windows.

Locks and Keys

- Keep your car locked, including your trunk. Remember that young children who manage to get into a car, and then activate the power locks, may not know how to get out. In hot weather, this could be life-threatening. Make sure that older children know how to unlock the doors.
- *Keep keys out of reach of small children*, just as you would medications or any other dangerous items. Stray keys can tempt a child to enter a vehicle and even try to drive it.
- Keep garage door remote controls away from small children.
- Keep rear folding seats closed so that a child cannot find his or her way into your trunk without your knowledge.

Children in Hot Vehicles

Dozens of children die every year as a result of heat-related injuries from being left in a vehicle. Infants and children are more susceptible to the dangerous effects of heat than adults, and their body temperatures can rise three to five times more quickly than that of an adult. Very young children also have less ability than adults to sweat and thereby cool themselves.

In the sun, the temperature in a car rises nearly twenty degrees in just ten minutes. Even with a window cracked open, temperatures inside a vehicle can rise by nearly forty degrees in just half an hour, and children have been known to die of heat-related injuries when temperatures outside the vehicle were as low as 70°F.

- *Never leave a child in a car unattended, even for a few minutes.*
- Too often, parents have accidentally left children in vehicles with tragic results. Make a habit of checking the car seat(s) before leaving your car.
- Use a window shade while driving, particularly for children who are strapped into restraining devices and cannot move out of the sun.

Rental Vehicles

- If you think you may be in or near high-crime areas, consider a rental with a GPS device to help keep you on main roads and avoid getting lost.
- If possible, rent a car that does not include rental car markings, since rental cars can be more attractive to criminals.
- Before leaving the rental lot, check the car for scratches and damages so that you are not held liable for these later. Existing damage should be marked on your agreement by the rental agent.

Airline Travel

Since September 11, 2001, more than ten thousand Americans have died in motor vehicle accidents for every person who perished aboard the four hijacked jetliners. Airline accidents today are so rare that every single one makes national news, even if no fatalities occurred. In short, airline travel is extremely safe. Generally, the biggest hazard we'll face during air travel is the threat of lost luggage. Nevertheless, there are additional precautions you may wish to consider.

Airline Travel with Children

- The Federal Aviation Administration (FAA) recommends that children under forty pounds use a car seat that is approved for airplane use. Check the label or manual to see if your child restraint is suitable for use on airplanes.
- Understand that you may not be able to use a child restraint if you do not purchase a ticket for your infant. Other restraining devices are available for use by parents who wish to keep infants on their laps.
- Carry on enough food, diapers, and medications to last through potential flight delays or lost luggage.

- Seat small children away from the aisle so that they won't be injured by other passengers or serving carts being moved through the aisle.
- If emergency oxygen is activated during a flight, put on your own mask before helping your child or others. Oxygen deprivation can occur in seconds at high altitude; putting on your own mask first ensures that you'll be able to help your child or another passenger.
- If you use medications, place these in carry-on bags, not in checked luggage.

Approved Locks

Special locks that are approved by the Transportation Security Administration (TSA) can be used to discourage pilfering of your checked bags. These locks can be opened by the TSA for inspection of your luggage, then replaced on your bag. Non-approved locks may be cut off by TSA for inspection of bags. If it appears that the contents of your checked bag have been tampered with, check for a printed notice from TSA indicating that your luggage was opened for inspection.

Hotel and Motel Safety

Whether you're traveling to New York City, Rio de Janeiro, or Nairobi, larger and more modern hotels are likely to have better security and safety provisions than older, smaller lodgings. On the other hand, staying in a worldwide chain hotel can mean that you'll miss out on some of the charm and authenticity of a new destination. In some places, modern security and safety features may not be available anywhere or at any price. Only you can decide what's right for your family. But here are some of the safety considerations that you may wish to think about as you travel:

- Again, larger hotels tend to have better built-in safety precautions. Some experts recommend asking for a room on the second through seventh floors, high enough to deter easy entry from outside but low enough for fire equipment to reach.
- Look for electronic "keycard" locks, deadbolts and peepholes on doors, and fire alarms and sprinkler equipment.
- When checking in, ask the receptionist to write your room number on a piece of paper so that persons nearby will not know your room number.
- If in doubt, stay with your luggage instead of having it brought to your room.
- Grab a couple of hotel business cards or matchbooks at the check-in desk so that you'll have the hotel address if you get lost.
- Review the fire safety instructions in your room, and know how to report a fire. Know where the nearest fire exits are located, and count the number of doors between your room and the exit. By doing so, you will be able to feel your way to the exit if you have to crawl through a dark, smoke-filled hallway.
- If you're traveling with small children, look over the room for hazards such as lamp cords, just as you would at your own home.
- If using hotel day care, ask them the same questions you'd ask a day care center at home, and ask whether the employees are licensed to provide childcare.

- Understand that a locked hotel room safe may simply advertise to a thief that you have valuables to steal and that this is not a fail-safe way to protect your money, credit cards, or property.
- Consider using a "web"-type luggage protection system. These consist of a web of interlocking steel cables, resembling a chain link fence, that completely encircle your bag. A cable is then used to secure the bag to furniture or a radiator, sink pedestal, or other hard-to-move object. These systems will not stop a determined thief, but they will deter petty criminals and hotel staff from rifling or carrying away your bag. These systems are available at REI (www.rei.com), as well as other travel and outdoor stores.
- Consider leaving your television or radio on, with the volume low, similar to leaving lights on in your house to indicate that someone is home.
- Do not use "Maid, please clean this room" tags that advertise your absence from your room.
- Don't leave valuables in plain sight. While the maids may be honest, those who walk by your room when the door is propped open for cleaning may not be.
- When meeting with someone you don't know well, meet in the lobby, not in your room.
- Use the main hotel entrance, not a side door, when leaving or returning at night.

32

International Travel

Although international travel can require flexibility and patience and can sometimes require us to do without many of the comforts we expect at home, the rewards can be enormous. To experience firsthand the culture, heritage, customs, architecture, food, and natural wonders of a foreign country is to create memories that will last a lifetime. For youngsters, travel abroad allows them to see the world in a way that books, movies, and the Internet simply cannot recreate. Even the planning that goes into a trip can be exciting and educational in itself.

Having a safe and enjoyable vacation in most developed countries requires nothing more than a certain amount of advance planning and common sense. In other parts of the world, some extra security precautions may be in order. Even when traveling to countries that have experienced violent episodes in the past or that might not have the same level of law enforcement that we expect in the United States, you can reduce potential crime problems to a minimum by following some simple and basic guidelines.

In this final chapter, let's take a look at some ideas that can help keep your family safe while traveling outside the United States, as well as some information that may simply be helpful in planning your trip.

Insurance and Medical Needs

Find out if your personal property insurance covers you for loss or theft abroad. Your expensive laptop or camera gear may not be covered when you cross outside the U.S. border. Consider a supplemental policy for the duration of your trip.

Many medical insurance plans do not provide coverage when you are outside the United States. Check with your insurance provider and purchase short-term supplemental coverage if necessary. Note that Medicare and Medicaid do not provide payment for medical care outside the United States.

When traveling to countries or areas where medical help may not be available, where medical professional and equipment may be in short supply, where care may be of questionable quality, or where blood supplies may be contaminated with HIV and other pathogens, consider medical evacuation insurance. This insurance can cover the costs of your emergency transportation to a high-quality medical facility if you are seriously injured or become ill. These plans are generally purchased on an annual basis but may be available at a lower rate for short-term coverage during the duration of your trip.

Check to see if any inoculations are required for entry into the country you intend to visit. For example, proof of a yellow fever vaccine may be required in order to enter certain tropical countries. If you have not done so in advance, you may be required to be inoculated at the point of entry, and you will have no guarantee that the vaccine or syringe is completely safe. Keep your inoculation record with your passport. For information about required and recommended vaccinations, visit the Centers for Disease Control (CDC) Web site (www.cdc.gov/travel/content/vaccinations.aspx).

Additional Medical Tips

Be sure to complete the emergency information page of your passport. If you use medications, pack these in your carry-on bags. This is especially important on international trips since many prescription drugs that are commonly used in the United States are simply not available in other countries. Sometimes, these medications are available under different brand names. You may wish to research these alternate names before you leave.

To avoid problems when passing through customs, keep medicines in their original, labeled containers. If a medication is unusual or contains narcotics, carry a letter from your doctor attesting to your need to take the drug. If you have any doubt about the legality of carrying a certain drug into a country, consult the embassy or consulate of that country before you travel.

If you wear glasses or contact lenses, pack an extra pair in your carry-on luggage.

Passports and Visas

A passport is an internationally recognized travel document that verifies the identity and nationality of the bearer. For American citizens, passports are issued by the U.S. Department of State. While travel to some countries did not require a passport as recently as a couple of years ago, heightened security concerns now require passports for reentry into the United States from any foreign country, including Canada and Mexico.

A new, wallet-size "U.S. Passport Card" is now available that can be used to enter the United States from Canada, Mexico, the Caribbean, and Bermuda *at land border crossings or sea ports-of-entry only*. Although a passport card is easier to carry and less expensive than a passport book, it *cannot* be used for international air travel.

Some countries require that an American citizen's passport be valid for at least six months from the date of entry into the country.

All children, regardless of age, must have a valid passport for international travel. Children under sixteen years of age must apply in person, with both parents present.

If a visa is required for entry into a country you plan to visit, check with the country's embassy or consulate in the United States to see if you can obtain the visa in advance. In some countries, visas are issued quickly and routinely at points-of-entry, for a fee of a few dollars. However, in other countries, the process can be complex and take hours.

Acquiring your visa in advance can save you this unpleasantness. For more information about passport requirements or to obtain or renew a passport, visit the State Department Web site (http://travel.state.gov/passport/).

Please note also that, to combat international child abductions, many countries have instituted additional requirements for traveling with children. Contact the embassy or consulate of your foreign destination for more information. A listing of foreign consular offices in the United States is available at http://www.state.gov/s/cpr/rls/fco/.

In the event that your passport is lost or stolen, understand that security precautions may delay the issuance of a new, full-validity passport. We'll discuss lost and stolen passport procedures later in this chapter.

U.S. State Department Information

The U.S. Department of State administers a Consular Information System to provide information about travel to any country in the world. This "Country Specific Information" is best accessed through the State Department's Web site (http://travel.state.gov OR (http://travel.state.gov/travel/travel_1744.html) and includes the locations of U.S. embassies and consulates, health conditions, entry regulations, political disturbances, crime and security information, and more. Each country has its own Web page to describe conditions, and I strongly recommend that you consult these pages for the countries you intend to visit.

"Travel Warnings" and "Travel Alerts" are issued for countries in which Americans should be particularly vigilant. Travel Warnings are issued when long-term conditions make a country especially dangerous or unstable, or when the U.S. government has limited ability to assist citizens in that country due to an embassy closure. Travel Alerts describe short-term conditions that may pose special risks to U.S. citizens, including natural disasters, terrorist attacks, election-related violence, and so forth. If the State Department specifically advises Americans against travel to a particular country, that information will be provided as well.

While this State Department information can be invaluable to the traveler, keep in mind that no country is completely immune to violent and non-violent crime. To an inexperienced traveler, this information has the potential to sound quite ominous. Even some of the safest international destinations have their share of crime warning on the State Department's Web site, but this information will help you to gain a better understanding of any particular risks in the destinations you wish to visit.

Cash or Credit?

Determine in advance the best way to pay for your travels. Throughout most of Europe and in large cities around the world, credit cards will be almost as widely accepted as in the United States. However, in many countries, credit cards may be virtually useless. Traveler's checks, thanks to modern printing technology which makes them easier to forge, may not be as useful as they were in years past, with many establishments refusing to accept traveler's checks altogether and many banks requiring a waiting period of several days before you can collect the funds. When traveling to countries where the economy is based on cash, find out if ATMs are available in airports, hotels, or other locations, and as well as which ATM networks are supported (Cirrus, PLUS, etc.). By using ATMs, you can replenish your cash along the way and avoid carrying large sums, and ATM exchange rates are generally very competitive. Keep in mind that American dollars and Euros are highly prized in many countries and may be more appreciated for tips than the local currency.

You may also wish to let your credit card issuer know that you will be traveling abroad during a certain time period. Otherwise, your card issuer may suspect fraud when foreign charges begin appearing, and suspend the use of your card. At the same time, ask your credit card issuer how to report the loss of your card when you are abroad. Keep track also of the credit limit on each credit card that you bring. In rare instances, Americans abroad have been arrested for exceeding their credit limit.

To make it easier if you should have to report a lost or stolen wallet or purse, go through its contents before you leave and decide which credit cards or other items you can safely leave behind, To protect your purse or wallet, review the precautions we discussed at the beginning of this section of *Safe*.

Finally, don't change money with people on the street offering you a better rate. Not only could these exchanges potentially subject you to arrest, but you are far more likely to be scammed than to receive a better deal. Exchange bureaus, banks, and ATMs generally offer the best rates, although the fees may vary. Hotels and retail establishments are your next best bet for changing your dollars into the local currency.

Crime and Safety Abroad

If a particular pattern of crime against foreign tourists has come to the attention of the U.S. State Department—for example, if tourists are experiencing an unusual amount of crime on public transportation—that information will be posted to the U.S. State Department's Country Specific Information as noted above. For the most part, avoiding crime overseas is a matter of using the same common sense that you would at home, being aware of your surroundings, and avoiding areas that seem unsafe.

General Safety Tips

- Don't be flashy with expensive goods, money, or credit cards. Leave expensive jewelry at home. Even in desperately poor third-world countries, the vast majority of people are law-abiding, friendly, and caring individuals who would gladly give of themselves to help others in a time of critical need. But when the camera around your neck might represent an entire year's income for a family, the temptation may be too great for some to resist.
- Don't unnecessarily announce your travel intentions to others.
- Be aware that petty scammers, such as those who offer to exchange foreign currency at bargain rates, are extremely commonplace in many areas of the world. Smile and ignore them. Larger scams, such as money-laundering "opportunities" and so forth, can be avoided by following the same precautions we discussed in our chapters on identity theft and fraud.
- Avoid obvious public demonstrations and civil disturbances, and avoid taking photographs of police and other officials involved in a disturbance.
- Try not to look lost, even if you are. Preferably, ask directions from police, hotel clerks, store clerks, or others who appear to have responsible jobs.
- Know how to ask, in the local language, if someone speaks English.
- Know how to contact the U.S. embassy or other consular offices in the countries to which you will be traveling. Our embassy personnel can be extremely helpful in guiding you through a wide range of problems that can be experienced on foreign travel. Visit their Web site (http://travel.state.gov/travel/) for this information as well as other helpful travel advice for any foreign country.

Public Transportation

- Ask at your point of entry or hotel whether cabs are licensed and what markings a licensed cab should have. If cabs are unregulated, agree on the fare before getting into the vehicle. Otherwise, the driver can try to charge you any arbitrary amount he chooses.
- If in doubt, try to travel during daylight hours.
- For train travel, consider a "web"-type luggage protection system or cable lock discussed above under hotel and motel safety. In a train compartment, keep your door locked. Consider placing your luggage behind you in your sleeping compartment, or use it for a pillow.
- Use covered luggage tags to avoid casual observation of your identity or nationality.

Rental Cars

- Determine in advance whether your U.S. driver's license will be valid in the countries you intend to visit, and procure an International Driver's License if need be.
- Before leaving home, check with your auto insurance agent to determine whether your coverage extends to vehicles rented outside the United States. If not, make arrangements for extended coverage if possible. You should review car rental agreements to determine what your liability will be if the car is damaged or stolen.
- Ask your rental agent about any special problems or precautions you need to be aware of. All of the precautions we've discussed in this book about carjacking and theft apply to foreign travel as well.

Don't *Become* a Criminal

Just as foreign nationals entering the United States are subject to our laws, you are subject to the laws of the countries you visit. Some infractions that may be considered minor in the United States could constitute major crimes overseas. Familiarize yourself with local laws using the Country Specific Information on the State Department's Web site as well as the travel books you use in planning your trip. These books, as well as other information provided by travel agents and tour companies, can also be helping in learning more about local customs and manners. For example, some gestures that may seem perfectly polite in the United States would be considered offensive in other cultures around the world. Here are some of the more common problems to watch out for.

Photography

In many countries you can be detained or arrested, or have your camera gear confiscated, for photographing police and military installations, government buildings, transportation facilities, and so forth. In some cases, rules may seem quite arbitrary to Americans and something as simple as a snapshot of your family that includes a customs building could cause a problem. Be aware of local regulations.

Antiquities

If you are purchasing items that are old or that may have an important cultural significance to the country you're visiting, be aware of regulations regarding their export and secure the needed export requirements if needed. Certain items such as precious or semi-precious gems may require an export permit as well, or paperwork issued by the dealer from whom you purchase the items.

CITES Violations

The Convention on International Trade in Endangered Species of Wildlife Fauna and Flora (CITES) is an international treaty that governs trade, exportation, and importation of plant and animal products around the world. Roughly five thousand species of animals and twenty-eight thousand species of plants are regulated to some degree under CITES. Hunters need to pay particular attention to CITES regulations before attempting to transport hides, horns, or other animal parts from another country into the United States.

Species and products that are highly regulated under CITES include elephant and whale ivory, rhino horn, turtle shells and reptile skins, coral, orchids, cacti, and wood products made from rare or endangered trees. Be careful when purchasing products or souvenirs that are made (even in part) from local animals or plants and try to ensure that the products you buy are not made from animals or plants that are considered endangered under CITES or local law.

Assault

In some countries, you can be charged with the equivalent of assault and battery if you strike someone, even if they attacked you first and you acted only in self-defense. While you may eventually be cleared, the problem may take time to sort out, and you could be incarcerated in the meantime. Remember that possessions can be replaced.

Drug Violations

More than one-third of U.S. citizens incarcerated abroad are held on drug charges. Some countries do not distinguish between possession and trafficking, and drug laws abroad can be extremely harsh, even for possession of small amounts of illegal drugs including marijuana. Some countries do not provide jury trials, and pre-trial detention can drag on for months, often in appalling conditions. Sentences can include long jail terms, hard labor, and even the death penalty. Needless to say, do not travel with illegal drugs, and do not attempt to purchase illicit drugs while traveling.

In rarer cases, Americans have been arrested abroad for possessing prescription drugs, particularly tranquilizers and amphetamines, that were purchased legally elsewhere. Information about local drug laws is included on the Country Specific Information on the State Department's Web site. Travel only with the medications you need, and keep medications in their original packaging as they arrived from your pharmacy.

Terrorism, Hijacking, and Hostage Situations

Obviously, there is no way to completely protect yourself against terrorists and other criminals while traveling abroad, just as there is no way to completely protect yourself in the United States. Only in a relative handful of countries are Americans specifically targeted for crime because of their nationality.

In the extremely unlikely event that you are caught up in a hijacking or hostage situation, here are some very general guidelines:

- Understand that the U.S. government does not make concessions to terrorists. However, the government will make every effort, from the outset of a hostage-taking situation, to ensure your safe release.
- Remain as calm as possible. Be cooperative and speak in a normal tone of voice. If questioned, keep your answers short, and don't volunteer information that you haven't been asked for.
- Remember that you are a valuable commodity to your captors. It is important to them to keep you alive and well. Prepare yourself for the possibility of a long ordeal, and establish a daily program of mental and physical activity.

If You Become a Victim

If your possessions are lost or stolen, report the loss immediately to the local police, and keep a copy of any police report for insurance claims.

Next, report the loss or theft of credit cards or traveler's checks to the issuing company. Report missing airline tickets to the airline or to your travel agent, and report a lost or stolen passport to the nearest U.S. embassy or consulate.

If you become the victim of a major crime overseas, you should also contact the nearest U.S. embassy or other consular agency. Although U.S. government officials cannot directly intervene in the prosecution of criminals, they can provide you with information about local government agencies and the criminal justice process in the country you're visiting. Our embassies and consular offices can also help with services such as:

- Replacement of a lost or stolen passport
- Contacting family, friends, or employers in the United States
- Obtaining medical care
- Providing contact information for local attorneys who speak English
- Providing information about victim assistance and compensation programs abroad and in the United States
- Addressing other emergency needs that may arise as the result of a crime

Medical and Legal Emergencies Abroad

In a medical emergency requiring immediate treatment, follow the same procedures as you would in the United States. Seek emergency assistance and transport to a medical facility, and provide immediate First Aid to the best of your knowledge and experience.

Your next step, in medical or legal emergency, is to contact the U.S. embassy in the country you're visiting, or the nearest U.S. consular office. Generally, personnel will be on call at these offices twenty-four hours a day to assist you. For medical emergencies, U.S. consular officers overseas can provide you with:

- Listings of local physicians and medical facilities
- Notification to family or friends in the United States
- Transfer of funds from the United States

For legal emergencies, international treaties and customary international law give you a right to speak with U.S. consular officials. If you are denied this right, be polite but persistent. Try to have someone reach consular officials on your behalf if you are not allowed outside communication yourself. For legal emergencies, U.S. consular officers overseas can provide you with:

- Advice about your rights under local laws
- Listings of local attorneys who speak English and who may have had experience in representing U.S. citizens
- Notification to family or friends in the United States
- Transfer of funds from the United States
- Efforts to ensure that you are treated humanely as fairly under local laws
- Efforts to provide you with adequate food and clothing if needed
- Monitoring of your health and welfare and the conditions under which you are being held

Death of a U.S. Citizen Abroad

Each year, more than six thousand American civilians die abroad. Only a miniscule fraction of these deaths will be as a result of criminal or terrorist activity.

Some will result from accidents, especially motor vehicle accidents, but most will be from natural causes, especially in the case of Americans who have chosen to live or retire overseas.

In the event that a U.S. citizen dies outside our borders, the nearest embassy or consular office should be notified. State Department officials can provide a variety of assistance, including confirmation of the death, identity and U.S. citizenship of the deceased, notification of next-of-kin, advice about disposition of the remains as well as personal effects, and guidance on special estate matters that can arise when an American dies on foreign soil.

Have a Backup Plan

Before you travel abroad, there are some specific steps that you can take in order to diminish potential hassles, lost time, and costs of travel mishaps. Here are some steps you can take in the unlikely event of problems, or simply to have greater peace of mind when you are abroad:

- Leave copies of your itinerary, passport data page, airline tickets, driver's license, and credit card and traveler's check information with a family or friend. It will be far easier for them to contact your banks or credit card issuers if your wallet is lost or stolen. This Web site will be helpful to you: https://travelregistration.state.gov/ibrs/ui/.
- Pack an extra set of passport photos, along with a photocopy of your passport's information page, to make passport replacement easier abroad. In addition, make copies of your airline tickets, driver's license, and credit card and traveler's checks information. Pack this separately from the documents themselves for easier replacement if necessary.
- Carry a list of your traveler's checks numbers and cross them off the list as you use them.
- Keep in mind that your U.S. cell phone may not work outside the country. Often you can purchase a cheap phone in your destination country and reload it with minutes as needed. A local calling card may also be an efficient and easy way to make needed calls during your trip.
- Consider registering your travels with the State Department. If you have registered your travels, State Department officials will attempt to contact you in the event of a family emergency at home or if a political or

other problem develops in the area where you are traveling. Information supplied to the State Department is confidential and will not be released to others without your prior authorization. For more information, visit the State Department's travel registration Web site (https://travelregistration.state.gov).

In the event a family member needs to reach you, they can call 1-888-407-4747, and the State Department will relay the message to the local consular officers who will attempt to get in touch with you and, if you grant permission, report back to the person who tried to reach you.

Should you have difficulty accessing U.S. funds in an emergency, contact the local U.S. embassy or consulate. Special procedures are in place to help you contact your family, bank, or employer for emergency funds.

Should your passport be lost or stolen while travelling, report it immediately to the local police and to the nearest U.S. embassy or consular office. These officials can generally provide you with a replacement travel document quickly, although it may not carry the full validity of a regular passport.

One Final Tip

Don't let anything in this chapter deter you from exploring the world. The vast majority of international travelers experience virtually no problems while overseas. In fact, the unusual situations that sometimes occur during foreign travel often make the best stories for you to tell and retell in the years to come.

For the latest information as well as consumer ratings for products mentioned throughout this book, see www.SafeBookProducts.com. In addition, go to this Web site to sign up for a free monthly newsletter on new products to help keep your family safer.

AFTERWORD

Throughout this book, we have discussed literally hundreds of different dangers that exist in our world. And yes, all of us have a responsibility to protect ourselves and our families from hazards that we can control. But we must not spend our days or our lives worrying needlessly about things that are unlikely to occur, with the idea that "the world is a dangerous place" always in the back of our minds. To me, this is an extremely important distinction.

Compared to every other generation in human history, Americans now enjoy the greatest measure of safety and security that humans have ever known.

Our telephones give us instant access to police and fire departments. Our medical technologies enable us to save accident victims who, even a few years ago, might have had almost no hope. Our laws are, by and large, designed to give victims an unalienable right to defend themselves against criminal predators.

After the terrorist attacks of September 11, 2001, there was a great deal of debate in this country about the extent to which we should use homeland security measures, such as increased surveillance, to prevent future attacks. We faced then, and continue to face now, an enemy that hates our American traditions of individual rights and freedom. Clearly, we do not want to recklessly give up that freedom for the sake of a little extra security, handing over to the terrorists a portion of the victory they hope to achieve.

This great debate can also be applied to our own lives and families. If we wish, we can try endlessly to make ourselves safer and safer, and attempt to insulate our families from every possible danger. But if we spend our days worrying about the next hazard we might face, the criminal who might want to harm us, or the dangers that might lie around every corner, we risk losing the very thing we hope to preserve—giving up "the pursuit of happiness" and the opportunity to fully experience the extraordinary world that past generations have built for us.

That is not what this book is about. This book is about using your common sense and the practical lessons that others have learned so that your family will have more opportunities to enjoy life, rather than to fear it. So that you can feel more secure if the power goes out. So that you can enjoy your home with less fear of crime. So that you can take your family on a trip to one of our great national parks, or anywhere else in the world you want to go, *without undue fear*.

I firmly believe that it is better to accept some risk than to spend your days worrying about the next disaster, the next criminal, the next accident, mishap, or threat to come along.

I remember vividly, on January 28, 1986, President Ronald Reagan's televised message to the American people on the day that the space shuttle Challenger exploded shortly after liftoff, killing all seven astronauts aboard. Among those lost was classroom teacher Christa McAuliffe, whose students and millions of other schoolchildren were watching the launch on live television.

President Reagan's message was direct and solidly grounded in the American experience. Yes, our nation had suffered a great tragedy, but that would not stop us from the exploration of space. The astronauts who perished, Reagan told the nation, were pioneers. America's quest for exploration and discovery would continue, despite the tragedy. As the President reminded us all, "The future doesn't belong to the fainthearted; it belongs to the brave."

Centuries ago, our ancestors left everything they'd ever known in search of the next great dream beyond the horizon. They risked. They dared. That is still our American spirit, and nothing in this book should dampen that spirit. By providing you with the information in this book, I hope to give you more freedom to live your life with more confidence and more self-reliance, in the way you choose.

I wish you a safe and happy journey.

APPENDICES

Emergency Phone Numbers

ALL EMERGENCIES: 9-1-1

Hospital name: _____ Phone: _____

Doctor's name: _____ Phone: _____

Dentist's name: _____ Phone: _____

Pharmacy name: _____ Phone: _____

Veterinarian name: _____ Phone: _____

Out of state emergency contact:

Name: _____

Address: _____

City, State, Zip: _____

Home phone: _____

Cell phone: _____

Other family emergency numbers:

_____

_____

_____

_____

_____

American Association of Poison Control Centers: 1-800-222-1222

To register your whereabouts during a large scale disaster:
   Red Cross Safe and Well Hotline: 1-866-GET-INFO

To contact travelers abroad (if registered with the U.S. State Department):
   Department of State Overseas Citizens Services: 1-888-407-4747
   National Center for Missing and Exploited Children: 1-800-THE-LOST
   (843-5678)
   National Domestic Violence Hotline: 1-800-799-SAFE (7233)
   National Sexual Assault Hotline: 1-800-656-HOPE (4673)

To report identity theft:
   Federal Trade Commission: 1-877-ID-THEFT (438-4338)

Emergency Checklists

Emergency Supply Kit

To sustain your family in an emergency without outside help:

- ❑ Three-day supply of nonperishable food (store in a cool, dry location and replace food items as necessary)
- ❑ Three-day supply of water—one gallon of water per person, per day (store in cool, dry place and replace water every six months)
- ❑ Portable, battery-powered radio or television and extra batteries (Crank-type radios requiring no batteries are also available.)
- ❑ Flashlight and extra batteries
- ❑ First Aid kit and manual
- ❑ Sanitation and hygiene items, including moist towelettes and toilet paper
- ❑ Matches and waterproof container

- ❑ Whistle
- ❑ Change of clothing for each family member
- ❑ Kitchen accessories and cooking utensils, including a can opener
- ❑ Photocopies of credit and identification cards
- ❑ Cash and coins (in case ATMs do not work)
- ❑ Special needs items, such as prescription medications, eye glasses, contact lens solution, and hearing aid batteries
- ❑ Items for infants, such as formula, diapers, bottles, and pacifiers
- ❑ Waterproof container for above items that can be quickly packed in your vehicle

Additional Items to Consider

- ❏ Paper cups, plates, and plastic utensils
- ❏ Household liquid bleach to treat drinking water (do not use scented bleach)
- ❏ Sugar, salt, pepper
- ❏ Aluminum foil and plastic wrap
- ❏ Small cooking stove and fuel
- ❏ Duct tape
- ❏ Scissors
- ❏ Games, cards, toys, and books
- ❏ "Comfort" items for children including a stuffed animal, toys, and nonperishable candy
- ❏ Paper, pens, and pencils
- ❏ Work gloves
- ❏ Instant coffee and/or teabags
- ❏ Inventory of valuable household goods
- ❏ Heavy-duty "contractor" garbage bags
- ❏ Extra car keys
- ❏ Blankets and/or sleeping bags, especially if you live in a cold climate

For Infants

- ❏ Formula
- ❏ Powdered milk
- ❏ Bottles
- ❏ Diapers and wipes
- ❏ Medications
- ❏ Lotion and diaper rash ointment
- ❏ Baby food/juice

For the Elderly

- ❏ Medications
- ❏ Denture items
- ❏ Extra eyeglasses
- ❏ Hearing aid batteries

Household First Aid Kit

If you choose not to purchase a prepackaged kit:

- ❏ Adhesive bandages, various sizes
- ❏ 5" x 9" sterile dressings
- ❏ Conforming roller gauze bandage
- ❏ Triangular bandages
- ❏ 3" x 3" sterile gauze pads
- ❏ 4" x 4" sterile gauze pads
- ❏ Rolled 3" cohesive bandage
- ❏ Germicidal hand wipes or waterless, alcohol-based sanitizer
- ❏ Antiseptic wipes
- ❏ Several pairs large, medical-grade non-latex gloves
- ❏ Tongue depressor blades
- ❏ Adhesive tape, 2" width
- ❏ Antibacterial ointment
- ❏ Instant hot and cold packs
- ❏ Small scissors
- ❏ Tweezers
- ❏ Needle
- ❏ Safety pins in assorted sizes
- ❏ Cotton balls
- ❏ Thermometer
- ❏ Tube of petroleum jelly or other lubricant
- ❏ Sunscreen
- ❏ CPR breathing barrier, such as a face shield
- ❏ First Aid manual
- ❏ Aspirin and non-aspirin pain reliever
- ❏ Anti-diarrhea medication
- ❏ Antacid for upset stomach
- ❏ Laxative
- ❏ Syrup of Ipecac
- ❏ Activated charcoal
- ❏ Hydrogen peroxide
- ❏ Antihistamine
- ❏ Rubbing alcohol
- ❏ Cold and cough medicine

Vehicle Emergency Supply Kit:

If you are unable to return home in an emergency:

- ❏ Battery-operated radio and flashlight; extra batteries
- ❏ Blanket
- ❏ Jumper cables
- ❏ Five-pound ABC-type fire extinguisher
- ❏ Bottled water and nonperishable, high-energy food (granola, peanut butter, raisins, etc.)
- ❏ Maps

- ❏ Shovel
- ❏ Flares
- ❏ Tire repair kit
- ❏ First Aid kit and manual
- ❏ Change of clothes
- ❏ Climate-appropriate gear, including hat, gloves, hand warmers, waterproof poncho

Backcountry Vehicle Travel Kit

In addition to the Vehicle Emergency Supply Kit above:

- ❏ GPS unit and manual (or cell phone with GPS capability)
- ❏ Tire inflator (such as Fix-a-Flat)
- ❏ Extra quart of oil
- ❏ Extra gallon of antifreeze
- ❏ Basic tools, including an adjustable (crescent) wrench, Phillips and flathead screwdrivers, pliers, multi-tool
- ❏ Blankets and extra clothing, especially socks, gloves, and hats
- ❏ Flashlight and extra batteries
- ❏ Windproof, extreme condition butane lighter, and/or waterproof matches and fire starter or candle
- ❏ Small can to melt snow or for boiling drinking water
- ❏ Water purification tablets or iodine
- ❏ Roll of duct tape
- ❏ Granola, nuts, dried fruit or energy bars, beef jerky
- ❏ Bottled water
- ❏ Knife
- ❏ Heavy rope or strap for pulling vehicles from mud, sand, or snow
- ❏ 50 feet of light rope
- ❏ Small shovel
- ❏ Tire chains
- ❏ Sunscreen and sunglasses
- ❏ Whistle and/or other signaling devices, including a small mirror
- ❏ Handheld GPS with mapping capability
- ❏ Compass

Backcountry First Aid Kit

Lightweight items for travel on foot:

- ❏ Non-latex medical gloves
- ❏ Tweezers
- ❏ Small scissors
- ❏ Thermometer
- ❏ Mylar blanket
- ❏ Acetaminophen tablets
- ❏ Ibuprofen tablets
- ❏ Antihistamine tablets
- ❏ Antacid tablets
- ❏ Burn relief spray
- ❏ Antiseptic wipes
- ❏ Antibiotic ointment
- ❏ Epi-Pen (epinephrine for acute, life-threatening allergic reactions such as to bee stings)

- ❏ Eye wash
- ❏ Eye patches
- ❏ Butterfly bandages (used to close wounds)
- ❏ Adhesive bandages, various sizes
- ❏ 5" x 9" sterile dressings
- ❏ Conforming roller gauze bandage
- ❏ 3" x 3" sterile gauze pads
- ❏ Thermometer
- ❏ Duct tape or adhesive First Aid tape
- ❏ First Aid manual or emergency action cards

Index of Web sites

Below are the Web sites listed in *Safe*. For the latest information as well as consumer ratings for products mentioned throughout this book, www.SafeBook-Products.com. In addition, go to this Web site to sign up for a free monthly newsletter on new products to help keep your family safer.

Section I

Red Cross First Aid courses:
www.redcross.org

Red Cross Safe and Well Web site:
www.redcross.org

Prepackaged First Aid kits:
www.cabelas.com
www.bassproshops.com

FEMA Emergency Management Guide for Business & Industry:
www.fema.gov/business/guide/
index.shtm

Section II

U.S. Consumer Product Safety Commission (for recall information):
www.cpsc.gov

Drug Abuse Resistance Education (DARE):
www.dare.org

Neighborhood Watch manual:
www.usaonwatch.org/assets/
publications/0_NW_
Manual_0909.pdf

National Association of Insurance Commissioners (for resolution of insurance disputes):
www.naic.org

NRAe-Safe (for online storage and retrieval of important documents):
www.nraesafe.com

NRA Web sites (for information about firearm ownership and applicable laws):
www.NRA.org
www.NRAILA.org

Firearms storage:
www.ftknox.com
www.browning.com
www.libertysafe.com
www.cannonsafe.com
www.gunvault.com

NRA Basic Personal Protection instruction:
www.nrainstructors.org/search course.aspx

Section III

National Park Service (National Park information):
www.nps.gov/index.htm

National Oceanic and Atmospheric Administration (weather forecasts and information):
www.noaa.gov

U.S. Geological Survey (topographic maps):
www.usgs.gov

DeLorme (topographic and outdoor recreation atlases):
www.delorme.com

National Outdoor Leadership School (Wilderness Medical Institute First Aid training):
www.nols.edu

NRA Youth Hunter Education Challenge (YHEC):
www.NRAHQ.org

All-Terrain Vehicle Association (all-terrain vehicle safety and usage):
www.atvaonline.com

Section IV

For monitoring children's Internet usage:
www.cyberpatrol.com
www.pctattletale.com

To report cyberbullying:
www.wiredsafety.org

National Center for Missing and Exploited Children (to report criminal activity online involving minors):
www.missingkids.com

Federal Trade Commission's Bureau of Consumer Protection (for assistance in resolving credit card and credit bureau issues):
www.ftc.gov/bcp/

National Association of Boards of Pharmacy (to verify standing of online pharmacies):
www.nabp.net

For ratings of charitable organizations:
www.guidestar.org
www.charitynavigator.org

FBI New E-Scams and Warnings Webpage:
www.fbi.gov/cyberinvest/escams.htm

Section V

To receive your free annual credit reports:
www.annualcreditreport.com

Federal Trade Commission (to file an identity theft claim or affidavit):
http://www.ftc.gov/bcp/edu/micro sites/idtheft/

Companies offering identity theft protection services:
www.lifelock.com
www.trustedid.com
www.identityguard.com

To verify standing of credit counseling companies:
www.aiccca.org
www.nfcc.org

Section VI

National Rifle Association (firearm training for personal protection):
www.nrainstructors.org/search course.aspx

NRA Refuse to Be a Victim seminars:
www.nrahq.org/RTBAV

National Center for Missing and Exploited Children (NCMEC):
www.missingkids.com

Family Abduction Prevention and Response (NCMEC brochure):
www.missingkids.com/en_US/ publications/NC75.pdf

To receive AMBER alerts via text message:
www.wirelessamberalerts.org

Luggage protection systems:
www.rei.com

Centers for Disease Control (information about inoculations for foreign travel):
www.cdc.gov/travel/content/ vaccinations.aspx

U.S. Department of State foreign consular offices list:
www.state.gov/s/cpr/rls/fco

What Every Family Member Needs to Know

These key items should be memorized by every adult family member, and by every youngster in the family as soon as they are able to do so.

Emergency procedures:

- ❏ How to call 9-1-1.
- ❏ Locations of household fire extinguishers and procedures for their use.
- ❏ The best escape routes from your home in case of fire or other emergency. *Ideally, there should be two escape routes from each room.*
- ❏ The safest locations in your home for each type of disaster, including the location of your "safe room" if an intruder enters your home.
- ❏ Where to meet in the event of a disaster. *Choose two locations. The first should be right outside your home in the event of sudden emergency such as a fire. The other location should be outside your neighborhood in case a disaster prevents you from returning to your home.*
- ❏ Steps to be taken in the event of an emergency, including evacuation procedures and the care or transport of family pets.
- ❏ How to shut off water, gas, and electricity at the main switches, and when these steps might be necessary.
- ❏ The location of your emergency supply kit.
- ❏ Name, address, and telephone number of your out-of-state "family contact."
- ❏ How to register at the "Safe and Well" Web site maintained by the American Red Cross.

Before leaving your child at home, make sure he or she knows:

❑ *His or her full name, address, phone number, and the full names of both parents.*

❑ *Phone numbers for both parents, including work and cell numbers.*

❑ *When and how to call 9-1-1.*

❑ *How to contact another trusted adult if you cannot be reached.*

❑ How to react in a fire or other emergency.

When children are outside the home, make sure they know:

❑ How to contact (or instruct others to contact) family members. A child should know his or her full name, address, and phone number, as well as work and cell numbers for parents and the name of another trusted adult if parents cannot be reached.

❑ Where to rendezvous with parents if the family becomes separated at a theme park, sports arena, or mall.

❑ How to react if they get lost.

❑ How to react if someone attempts to grab him or her, or asks your child to get in a car or go with them for any reason.

❑ How to react is someone touches them inappropriately or says something that bothers them.

When children are online, make sure they follow these guidelines:

❑ Don't give out personal information on the Internet or when sending instant messages—including name, home address, school name, or telephone number—without parents' direct supervision and permission.

❑ Don't post pictures of themselves, or other identifying information such as a picture of your home, without parents' supervision and permission.

❑ Never meet face-to-face with someone they've met online without the direct supervision of parents.

❑ Understand that information posted on the Internet is not private and may be used against them.

❑ Understand that people online may not be who they say they are.

❑ Do show parents any suspicious or disturbing e-mails.

INDEX

Eloquent, winsome and charismatic, Barack Obama has emerged from almost total obscurity to quickly become the most powerful man in the world.

But most Americans know almost nothing about their 44th president.

Until now.

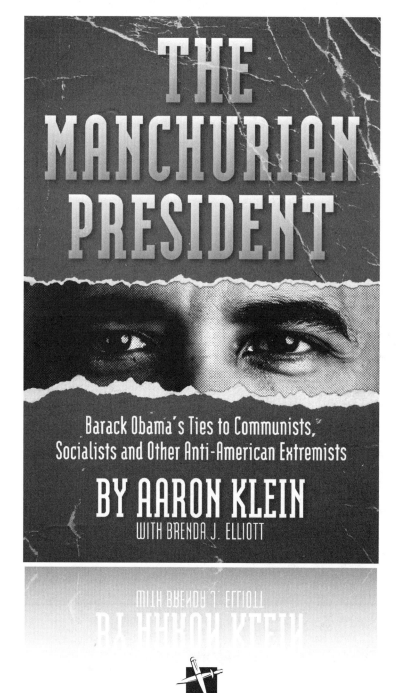

What does the tea party movement really stand for? And where does it go from here? Joseph Farah, founder, editor, and CEO of WorldNetDaily, was a tea partier before there was even a tea party movement. In his new book, Farah fleshes out the origins and evolution of the movement.

Defining the terms of the debate, the true meaning of independence, the danger in waiting for political messiahs, and the vital need for a spiritual core, Farah provides an inspired road map for this country's citizens to extricate themselves from the overreaching grip of government and reclaim the beliefs of the Founding Fathers.

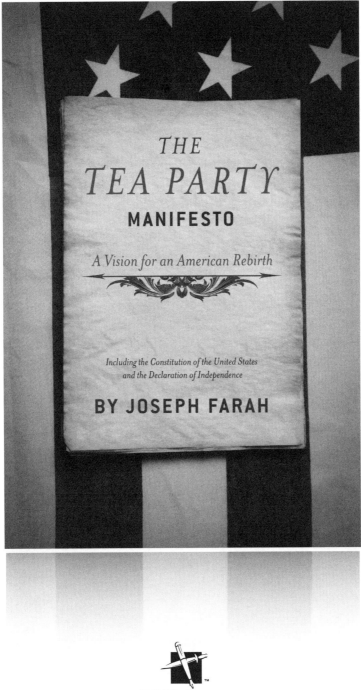

WND Books

WND Books   •   A WorldNetDaily Company   •   Washington, DC   •   www.wndbooks.com

Dangerous winds are blowing across America's culture today,
creating an atmosphere of extreme anxiety.

So why is the government making things worse?

Former TV meteorologist turned talk show host Brian Sussman wondered that for years,
and a decade's worth of investigation has yielded one of the most shocking stories of our time.

CLIMATEGATE

A VETERAN METEOROLOGIST
EXPOSES THE GLOBAL WARMING SCAM

BY BRIAN SUSSMAN

WND BOOKS

WND Books • A WorldNetDaily Company • Washington, DC • www.wndbooks.com

whistleblower

How I stay well-informed.

Every month, Whistleblower researches, reports and delivers to my door the kind of in-depth, groundbreaking reports on crucial topics that matter most to me; topics that impact directly on my well-being and freedom; topics that almost no one else in the media will even touch. Topics like Barack Obama's "Shadow Government," the epidemic of sex-predator school teachers, the proven link between firearms and freedom, and how to survive economic meltdown. Whistleblower is simply the best magazine I've ever read.

And how I intend to keep it that way.

Subscribing or renewing couldn't be simpler, and a full year of Whistleblower (12 issues) is only $49.95. Call our toll-free number today: 1-800-4WND-COM (1-800-496-3266) or go to WND.com and click on the Whistleblower cover image. Thank you!

In this tribute to that spirit of America, *Don't Tread on US!* offers a pictorial record
of the new tea parties and their participants: classic signs that communicate most effectively
with our brethren all across the land who oppose what's going on in Washington today
With a radical health-care agenda being marched across open territory,
those citizens — tens of millions of them — are rallying, and will make their voices heard.

The colonial heart still beats today, and the people have spoken: ***Don't Tread on US!***

WND Books

WND Books • A WorldNetDaily Company • Washington, DC • www.wndbooks.com